A DEFENSE OF THE BIBLE

AGAINST THE CHARGES

OF

MODERN INFIDELITY;

CONSISTING OF THE SPEECHES OF ELDER JONAS HARTZEL, MADE DURING A DEBATE CONDUCTED BY HIM AND MR. JOSEPH BARKER, IN JULY, 1853.

BY JONAS HARTZEL.

"WE HAVE NOT FOLLOWED CUNNINGLY DEVISED FABLES."

CINCINNATI:
COLUMBIAN PRINTING COMPANY PRINT.
1854.

SYNOPSIS.

The debate is on the proposition —

The Jewish and Christian Scriptures contain a series of communications, supernaturally revealed and miraculously attested; from the latter, man may acquire a perfect rule of life.

The Book contains —

I. Preliminary Correspondence.

II. A consecutive history of Mr. Barker's refusal to comply with the stipulations of agreement for bringing out the reported discussion in book form.

III. J. Hartzel's speeches, in which will be found copious extracts from Mr. Barker's writings in defense of the divine inspiration of the Bible, while a Methodist Minister. Also, that it does not sanction despotism and oppression, etc.

IV. Notes interspersed through the volume, which were intended as an appendix to the work as originally contemplated.

HOPEDALE, HARRISON COUNTY, OHIO, February 23, 1854.

CORRESPONDENCE.

LETTER I.

JONAS HARTZEL'S FIRST LETTER.

RESPECTED SIR: After a few weeks mature reflection upon what passed at the recent Bible (or, rather, anti-Bible Convention,) and the expressed wish of many of our mutual friends, and my position in society as an acknowledged advocate of the Gospel, I feel disposed to meet you in public discussion, upon a fair and equitable distribution of labor. I therefore submit the following propositions:

I. That the Creator has endowed man with the requisite mental capacity, to acquire from the developments of Nature, a perfect knowledge of his *relations*, *duties* and *destiny*.

You affirm, I deny.

II. That the Jewish and Christian Scriptures, contain a series of communications, supernaturally revealed and miraculously attested. From the latter, man may acquire a perfect understanding of his *relations*, *duties* and *destiny*.

I affirm, you deny.

Now, sir, if you can maintain the first, I shall have neither interest nor inclination to debate the second; for I believe there is much good sense in the old Heathen maxim, "Call for a God, when there is an occasion worthy of a God." The above propositions contain the *pro* and *con* of the seven resolutions read by yourself at the opening session of the aforesaid Convention, and will afford (according to my understanding) an opportunity to call out all that is debateable between disbelievers and believers of a supernaturally revealed religion. I would further propose, that, as the discussion may be somewhat protracted, I have the privilege of calling one to my assistance, and that you have the same.

Also, that the discussion shall be conducted according to parliamentary usages — time and place, with all necessary preliminaries, to be arranged by mutual agreement.

Yours, with respect,

JONAS HARTZEL.

Hopedale, Harrison Co., O., Jan. 18, 1853.

LETTER II.

JOSEPH BARKER'S FIRST LETTER.

A note we have received from Joseph Barker, informs us that he has never received the number of the *Bugle* containing Mr. Hartzel's proposition for a public discussion. He had, however, been informed of the questions proposed. Of these, under date of February 5th, he says:

As to Mr. Hartzel's propositions, I do not believe that God has endowed *every* man with the requisite mental capacity to acquire from *any* source, a perfect knowledge of his relations, duties and destiny. I question whether he has so endowed any man. It will certainly take eternity to gain a perfect knowledge of all our relations, &c. I cannot, therefore, take the affirmative of that proposition.

I have no objection to take the negative of the second proposition, though I had rather the proposition had been more comprehensive. However, I will take the affirmative of the following proposition:

That mankind are able to obtain the knowledge needful to their improvement and welfare, without supernatural revelations or infallible teachers.

Perhaps you will publish this in the *Bugle*. I have not yet seen the *Bugle* containing Mr. Hartzel's propositions.

Where must the discussion be, and when? And what the particular arrangements?

For the information of both Messrs. Hartzel and Barker, we append their respective Post Offices: Jonas Hartzel, Hopedale, Harrison County, Ohio. Joseph Barker, Millwood, Knox County, Ohio.

LETTER III.

JONAS HARTZEL'S SECOND LETTER.

HOPEDALE, O., *Feb.* 28, 1853.

MR. ROBINSON — *Respected Sir:* Joseph Barker's note to you, Feb. 5th, is now before me, in which he says: "I have not yet seen the *Bugle* containing Mr. Hartzel's propositions." He does not say, he has not seen my letter to him, Jan. 18th, but, that he has been informed of the questions proposed by myself for discussion. The questions are all that is important in my letter to him. Why did he not address me, as I did him? Did he intend to put a stop to a direct correspondence? I preferred the press, as the medium of communication between us. I knew Mr. Barker's address, and he obtained mine, before we took the parting hand at your house.

My proposition for a discussion with Mr. Barker on the Bible question, grew out of a challenge uttered by himself, before the Bible Convention of last November, and a personal interview at your house and in your presence. From these circumstances, a report went abroad, that Mr. Barker had respectfully invited me to a discussion, and that I had declined. This, I could not deny. Having acquired a little celebrity as a disputant, my decline has been prejudicial, creating a suspicion that there were doubts in my own breast, with reference to a rational defense of the claims of the Bible. This suspicion was soon confirmed by an article in the *Plain Dealer*, by one who says he was in the Convention as spectator and reporter. Speaking of me, he says: "He offered no argument which led me to think that he believed the Bible a work of divine inspiration." These things were not done in a corner, and my negotiation with Mr. Barker should, therefore, be conducted through the medium of the public press.

I will now come to Mr. Barker's objections to the proposed issue, and 1st, The questions (the first of which he will not debate,) were legitimate deductions from the seven resolutions read before and accepted by the Convention, but not debated. These resolutions were in the order of climax; the last two being the concentration of the preceding ones. They declare, that man has an infallible rule of life, and in what that unerring rule consists. I will here insert them:

VI. *Resolved*, That man has an infallible rule of life, on the knowledge of which depend the progress, perfection and happiness of his nature, in all states of his existence.

VII. *Resolved*, That the rule is found, not in the Bible, the Koran, the Shastres, nor in any supposed arbitrary revelation, but is engraven on the nature of each human being, by the hand of his Creator.

Where, then, will man find an infallible rule of life? Not in the Bible, &c., but "engraven on the nature of each human being, by the hand of his Creator."

Mr. Barker has here given us an unequivocal confession of his faith, or what it was *two months ago;* he has stated affirmatively where man's infallible rule is, and negatively, where it is not. But what is his present position?—let us see. *Anti-Slavery Bugle*, Feb. 19: "As to Mr. Hartzel's propositions, I do not believe that God has endowed every man with the requisite mental capacity to acquire, from any source, a perfect knowledge of his relations, duties and destiny; I question whether he has so endowed any man. It will certainly take Eternity to gain a perfect knowledge of all our relations, &c. I cannot, therefore, take the affirmative of that proposition." *This is progressive, indeed it is.* In November, 1852, every man had an infallible rule of life; that is, a rule incapable of mistake, and this he received from the hand of his Creator; but on the 5th of February, 1853, he says: "I do not believe that God has endowed every or any man with the requisite mental capacity to acquire from any source, a perfect knowledge of his relations, duty and destiny," and think it will require "Eternity," &c. Why, sir, man's relations and duties in Eternity are not the subjects of discussion. What then? Why, this: Mr. Barker said in Convention, that man had an infallible rule without the Bible; and to this, he challenged investigation; can any thing be a rule of life, that does not reveal to man his relations, duties and destiny? Relations must be understood, before duty can be defined, and their destiny, whether present or future, or both, to give value to relation, and inspire with motive, to the discharge of duty. Surely there can be no misunderstanding in regard to a rule of life.

Mr. Barker will, however, take the affirmative of the following proposition: "That mankind are able to obtain the knowledge needful to their improvement and welfare, without supernatural revelation or infallible teachers." This is a very different thing from an infallible rule of life. How gloriously indefinite. "Knowledge needful." This much might be affirmed of a horse.

But Mr. Barker's proposition contains an affirmative and a negative. First, "That mankind are able to obtain the knowledge needful to their improvement and welfare." Second, "Without supernatural revelation or infallible teachers." He will then take the affirmative of a negative. Mr. Barker being a logician, I can but regard his proposition as an artful piece of management to get up a false issue; and, further, a refusal on his part to defend, in orderly discussion, the doctrine contained in those offensive resolutions, of which he will not deny the *paternity*, for he was first in committee, first in report, and first in defense."

He has, then, in seven resolves, and in his other publications, preferred many and grievous charges against that Book, which has been for ages, and yet is, revered by millions of the better portion of mankind. These accusations he ought to prove, for he certainly does know, that *the more weighty the calumny, the clearer should be the proof of it*, and then, as the Apostle of rationalism, he should show to us superstitious devotees of that Book, ("whose origin is wrapt in darkness," "which carries on its very face the marks of human imperfection and error," whose authority is not decisive as to the truth or falsehood of any principle, or the goodness or badness of any practice," "and that the belief that the Bible is a perfect rule of faith and practice, is not only altogether erroneous, but exceedingly mischievous,") that we have a more sure word of prophecy, to which we shall do well to take heed.

Mr. Barker cannot get up a false issue with us, neither can he hide himself from the public gaze in responsibilities he has incurred, in offering himself as a worthy guide to the ignorant and erring of his race.

In view of the whole premises, I must again urge upon his consideration the propositions submitted in my former letter.

First — "That the Creator has endowed man with the requisite mental capacity to acquire from the developments of nature, a perfect knowledge of his relations, duties and destiny. You affirm, I deny." Or, if he prefer this, given over his own signature, (as we might say,) "That man has an infallible rule of life, engraven on the nature of each human being by the hand of his Creator, on the knowledge of which depend the progress, perfection and happiness of his nature, in every state of his existence."

Second—"That the Jewish and Christian Scriptures contain a series of communications, supernaturally revealed and miraculously attested—from the latter, man may acquire a perfect rule of life. I affirm, you deny."

So matters present themselves to my mind at present; but if I have not understood the original resolutions, I ask to be corrected, for I do not ask Mr. Barker to defend any doctrine he has not avowed. If his mind has changed with reference to the infallible source of knowledge since the Convention, we only ask him to use his influence in blotting from the public records those resolutions.

If Mr. Barker can show good reason why he should not be required to defend either of the propositions contained in this article, the second of which is couched in the precise language found in the 6th and 7th resolutions, we shall then proceed to discuss my affirmative, the negative of which he has accepted.

Debate to be held at some point on the Western Reserve, and to commence the 25th of May next. Other preliminaries to be settled by mutual agreement. Hoping to hear from Mr. Barker soon,

I remain, yours, for the Truth's sake,

JONAS HARTZEL.

LETTER IV.

JOSEPH BARKER'S SECOND LETTER.

EDITOR OF THE BUGLE — *Dear Sir:* In answer to Mr. Hartzel's letter, I would observe,

1st. That I have never received a letter from him, or I certainly should have answered it, for I have no objection to a direct communication with him.

2d. Mr. Hartzel is quite mistaken in supposing that in the sixth and seventh resolutions laid before the Convention, I have given a confession of my faith. I had nothing to do with those resolutions, except to express my dissent from them. The first five resolutions were the only ones I acknowledged or advocated. It is a mistake to suppose that in November last I believed that every man has an infallible rule of life, with which he was capable of becoming perfectly acquainted. It is a mistake to suppose that I said anything in the Convention about man having an infallible rule.

3d. That I have preferred many and grievous charges against the Bible, or rather that I have brought forward many arguments to prove that the Bible is not the word of God, I admit; but I think myself able to make good what I have said.

4th. Mr. Hartzel need be under no fear that I shall shrink from any responsibilities that I have taken upon myself, or that I shall try to hide myself from public gaze. But he must not expect me to acknowledge any charge he prefers against me to be true, when I believe it to be false.

5th. Though I do not like Mr. Hartzel's second proposition as well as I like the five resolutions offered to the Convention, yet, if he will not discuss those resolutions with me, I will discuss his second proposition with him, at such time and place as may be considered best. The 18th or 25th of May will suit me, I think, and as to *place*, I should as soon have the discussion at Salem as anywhere else.

I ought, however, to state, that some weeks ago, I wrote to Alexander Campbell, requesting him to send me a copy of *his* challenge, and offering to discuss the merits of the Bible with him, and have not yet had an answer from him; but should he agree to a discussion with me, I shall feel bound to give him the preference.

Yours affectionately,
JOSEPH BARKER.

P. S. I am obliged to you, sir, for the statement of facts with which you have accompanied the publication of Mr. Hartzel's letter. It would be just as reasonable for me to try to make Mr. Hartzel answerable for the first five resolutions, as for Mr. Hartzel to try to make me responsible for the last two. He said as much in favor of the one, as I did in favor of the other.

I repeat my offer to meet any acknowledged minister of any influential church, and to discuss the whole question as to the origin, the character, and the tendency of the Bible. I wish Mr. Hartzel would discuss the whole question. J. B.

LETTER V.

JONAS HARTZEL'S THIRD LETTER.

1st. Mr. Barker will not defend the 6th and 7th resolutions, says he had nothing to do with them, "except to express his dissent from them." How then came the President and Secretaries of the Convention to make such a blunder — on whose report I fixed the responsibility of defense — on J. Barker. My apology for them, and myself, is, that we never heard his dissent till now.

2d. But he does acknowledge the paternity of the first five, and these he is willing to discuss. He will then lead in the discussion, with five negative propositions, and have the respondent to take the place of the affirmant. *Strange mode of warfare.*

3d. In the fifth resolution there is an implied affirmation:

"*Resolved*, That the prevailing notion or belief, that the Bible is a book of divine authority, and that we need no other guide to truth and duty, is not only altogether erroneous, but exceedingly mischievous."

Here are points of agreement between Mr. Barker and myself: 1st. That man needs a guide to truth and duty. 2d. That man has a guide, etc. 3d. That this guide consists in a revelation of God's will. The point of disagreement is simply this: Where is this guide to be found? He, as the assailant, says not in the Bible. I, as respondent, say yes, in the Bible God has given us a perfect guide to truth and duty, as in Mr. Barker's own words, see report of the Bible Convention, page 33: "For myself, I believe there is a God, and that he has given a revelation of his will to mankind." We understood Mr. Barker to concur with Mr. Wright, that this revelation of God's will consisted in the divine engravings on the nature of each human being, &c. But as we now stand corrected on that point, we only ask Mr. Barker not to be so cautiously *non committal*, but, for the enlightenment of all, to embody in an affirmative proposition, where this revelation of God's will is to be found? If not in the Bible, where then? This now becomes the painfully interesting and perplexing question. I appeal to Mr. Barker's magnanimity and philanthropy, for an unequivocal answer. When I heard him in Convention, I supposed we had in the person of J. Barker, a candid and honorable skeptic, who would not ask to rob the Christian of his rejoicings in Christ, without offering him something as an equivalent. If his rock is as our rock, let him show it. If there is a "guide to truth and duty," let him affirm it, define, defend it, and let the merits of the rival system be brought into a fair comparison. But if there is no guide to truth and duty, I hope he will cease to trouble this community with his notions about the wrongfulness of slavery, war, priestcraft, &c.

4th. As the books now stand, Mr. Campbell has the preference, if he will accept. As it relates to myself, I shall wait for future information, specifying only that if Mr. Barker will debate with my humble self, the proposition upon which we have agreed, that he will fix the time, giving me at least eight weeks for arranging my appointments and other matters.

I hope Mr. Barker will answer soon and let us have done with these preliminaries.

Yours, as ever,

JONAS HARTZEL.

LETTER VI.

JOSEPH BARKER'S THIRD LETTER.

To the Editor of the Anti-Slavery Bugle— *My Dear Friend:* The impression left on my mind after reading Mr. Hartzel's long rambling letter, is anything but favorable. Why not come at once to the point, and keep to it? In his first letter, Mr. Hartzel offered to meet me in discussion on the following proposition:—"That the Jewish and Christian scriptures contain a series of communications supernaturally revealed, and miraculously attested — from the latter man may acquire a perfect rule of life." I accepted this offer. He named the 18th or 25th of May, for the discussion. I agreed. Why attempt to mystify so plain a matter, by a multitude of words about other subjects?

But I gave Mr. Campbell the preference. I did. But Mr. A. Campbell has not answered my letter, so I give him up.

Mr. Hartzel says: "If Mr. Barker will debate with me the proposition upon which we have agreed, he has only to fix the time, giving me at least eight weeks for arranging appointments and other matters." Very well. I *will* debate with him the above proposition, and I will give him eight weeks for preparation. I fix the first Monday in July, for the commencement of the debate, and I name James Barnaby and Jacob Heaton, as my committee to make the necessary arrangements.

Yours, respectfully,
JOSEPH BARKER.

LETTER VII.

JONAS HARTZEL'S FOURTH LETTER.

RESPECTED EDITOR: Mr. Barker says my last letter is "long," "rambling," "unfavorable;" and asks, "Why not come to the point at once, and keep to it."

It would be a reflection upon the intelligence of your readers, to say one word by way of defense, but as this will probably close the correspondence on preliminaries, it is important that Mr. Barker should be corrected in the following statement: "In his first letter Mr. Hartzel offered to meet me on the following proposition — 'That the Jewish and Christian Scriptures,'" &c. If Mr. Barker has forgotten, you have not — your readers have not — that I proposed to meet Mr. Barker on condition he would defend the 6th and 7th resolutions offered in the Convention, namely: "that man has an infallible rule of life," &c. This he refused, and gave his reasons, but he would discuss with me the first five; to this I consented, if he would put them in a debateable form. This part of my letter he calls "mystification," "a multitude of words about other subjects." Let me give an extract from my letter: "If there is a guide to truth and duty, let him (Barker) affirm it, define it, defend it, and let the merits of the rival systems be brought into a fair comparison." In view of the position Mr. Barker took in the Convention, against the Bible as a guide to truth and duty, standing at the head of this aggressive movement, challenging investigation to this only practicable point, (guide to truth and duty,) permit me to say, that Mr. Barker has evaded, what all had reason to expect from him, which is, to affirm something as a rule of life, as the measure of human responsiblity. We cannot relinquish our claim upon him in this respect *for he says:*

"God has made a revelation of his will to mankind;" we ask again, where is it? Bring out your light from under the bushel. Let it shine.

> "He that has a truth and keeps it,
> Keeps what not to him belongs,
> But performs a selfish action
> And his fellow-mortal wrongs."

Finally, as Christians are not afraid to come to the light, I shall, the Lord willing, be ready to maintain the proposition, on the first Monday of July, "That the Jewish and Christian Scriptures contain a series of communications, supernaturally revealed and miraculously attested—from the latter man may acquire a perfect rule of life."

Mr. George Pow will act as my committee.

Let the committee act promptly, that early notice may be given through the columns of the *Bugle*.

Yours, respectfully,

JONAS HARTZEL.

PROPOSITION:

The undersigned having been chosen to make the preliminary arrangement respecting the management of a debate between JONAS HARTZEL, of Hopedale, Harrison County, and JOSEPH BARKER, of Salem, Columbiana County, on the following proposition:

"The Jewish and Christian Scriptures contain a series of communications, supernaturally revealed and miraculously attested; from the latter, man may acquire a perfect rule of life."

AFFIRMATIVE,	NEGATIVE,
MR. HARTZEL.	MR. BARKER.

Notice is hereby given, that the discussion will commence in the Town Hall of Salem, on the FOURTH OF JULY, at 2 o'clock, P. M., and continue four days, unless the parties shall otherwise determine.

GEORGE POW,
JAMES BARNABY,
JACOB HEATON.

A Consecutive History of this Report of Mr. Hartzel's Speeches, and Mr. Barker's Refusal to have his part of the Discussion Published.

This being the time and place agreed upon for the commencement of a discussion between Jonas Hartzel, of Hopedale, Harrison County, and Joseph Barker, of Salem, Columbiana County; Cyrus McNeely, selected by Mr. Hartzel, as Moderator. Charles Griffin, selected by Mr. Barker. These two selected Wilson Thorn, of Youngstown, Mahoning County, Presiding Moderator. The congregation was called to order, and the rules for governing the discussion read.

RULES:

I. Mr. Hartzel shall open and close the discussion.

II. The disputants shall each speak one-half hour alternately, save the opening speeches, and Mr. Barker's final negative, which shall be one hour.

III. The debate shall continue four days *only*, unless by mutual consent of the disputants.

IV. The discussion shall be conducted with that candor and fairness, necessary to the eliciting of truth.

The reader will enquire, how came this debate to be published, there being nothing said about a report in the correspondence? The following conversation, which occurred at the close of the first session, will answer the question:

Mr. Hartzel.—I perceive that Mr. Barker has employed two

stenographers to report this discussion. He has done this without my consent or knowledge. Had Mr. Barker informed me in person, or by our committee of arrangements, I would have acquiesced. I know nothing of the competency of his reporters, or their probable impartiality. This makes my position extremely embarrassing. My preparation has been with a view to oral discussion only; but, now that it is to appear in book form, makes it quite another matter. Had I been apprised of that fact in due time, my mind would have profited by such a stimulant. And now I must say, Mr. Barker has departed from all the rules of courtesy and fair dealing between honorable disputants.

Mr. Barker. — I never engaged in a public discussion that was not reported. Mr. Hartzel may have an appendix if he wish, and I will have one of equal length. As to the reporters, James Barnaby and Caroline Stanton, I believe them well qualified; they have reported some speeches for me, to my entire satisfaction.

Mr. Hartzel. — I shall consent to a report, (as a matter of *safety*) and such are my conditions:

1st. I shall require from the reporters some evidence of competency — say that they write out a part of my first speech, and give me a specimen of what they can do.

2d. That I correct and revise my speeches, and read the proof.

3d. That we sell the copy-right to some publishing-house.

4th. That all that shall accrue from the sale, over and above paying us for our time and expense, shall be devoted to two benevolent institutions, as we may severally prefer.

Mr. Barker. — I agree to Mr. Hartzel's conditions. I shall give mine to the anti-slavery cause; or, he may pay the stenographers, publish the work himself, and have the profits, or I will do so.

But the reader will again enquire, why this one-sided report? To answer this question, we call attention to the following:

On the 27th day of August propositions were submitted to me to purchase the copy-right. I immediately informed Mr. Barker that the manuscripts must be delivered to the publishers by the 18th day of October, corrected and ready for publishing — gave him an invitation to come to Hopedale — and for him to get proposals, that we might have a choice, and to fix upon a price, &c.

To this I received in answer:

SALEM, Ohio, Sept. 21, 1853.

DEAR SIR: — I cannot come to Hopedale, but I shall be glad if you can come to Salem. I shall be at home on the 4th of October. As I have not yet received the manuscript of my speeches, of course I have not corrected any of them. I am going to Salem to-day, and, if my speeches are written out, I will correct them as soon as possible. But I shall be busy for two or three weeks. I have no proposals from any publishing house; but I will agree to any reasonable propositions which may have been made to you. I should like to have from fifty to one hundred copies of the work for my trouble and time, allowing you the same number. If anything more can be got for the copy-right, let my share go to the Western Anti-slavery Society, and your share to any cause you are most desirous to promote.

I should have written sooner, but I have but just returned from Knox County.

We shall be glad to see you at our house, when you come to Salem. We will not compel you to talk about theology, you shall enjoy yourself in your own way. Though we differ so widely with you in opinion, we think you a good and worthy man; and we are not so anxious to bring others to our views as we are to see all seeking diligently for truth, and working zealously for the general good. Devotion to the interests of humanity (which in this country seems to mean devotion to the cause of anti-slavery) pleases me more than agreement with me in opinion. Indeed, I cannot doubt, but that all honest and benevolent men are ever moving near to truth, on all subjects of importance.

With kind regards to your wife and family, and to your excellent friends and neighbors, Mr. and Mrs. McNeely,

I am, yours, respectfully,

JOSEPH BARKER.

I now informed D. S. Burnett, of Cincinnati, that on account of Mr. Barker's delinquency, the manuscript could not be handed over for "examination" at the time specified — "will you still entertain your propositions to me?" — and received in reply:

CINCINNATI, Oct. 25, 1853.

Send your manuscripts — say definitely what will be the cost of the manuscript in our hands? Can we pay that cost in books at wholesale price? Yours, in haste,

D. S. BURNETT.

I again wrote Mr. Barker, in substance:

"DEAR SIR:—It is important that the book should appear as soon as possible; public expectation will soon die away, and the value of the manuscript is daily depreciating."

I received in reply some apologies, and the following promise: "Put off as long as you can and let me know, and I will be ready for you." I said to Mr. Barker, by return mail — "I will give until the 18th of November to prepare your speeches, when I shall call for them on my way to Cincinnati," etc.

The following letter came to hand after I had left for Salem:

SALEM, Ohio, Nov. 14, 1853.

DEAR SIR: — I am sorry to inform you, that in consequence of having been called twice away from home, I have not yet been able to do anything at the report of my speeches. I could begin now, but on Thursday I have to leave for Philadelphia and other places east: and, after I return, I have to visit Indiana. If I had had the report earlier I could have made the corrections, but I did not receive it till about three weeks ago, and I have been from home almost ever since. Could you not take my speeches as they are, and let me correct them as they are wanted for the press? If not, I will have to keep them some time longer.

Yours, very respectfully,

JOSEPH BARKER.

Had I received the foregoing letter before leaving home for Salem I should not have gone; for it was an indefinite postponement of the publication. "*I would begin now, but on Thursday I must leave for Philadelphia, and other places East, and, after my return, I have to visit Indiana.*" Was Mr. Barker under obligation, by previous engagement, to visit the east and the west at this time? Was the period between the 4th of August and the 14th of November too short to make the corrections? If so, why did he pledge himself to his opponent, and the public, to be forthcoming in the joint publication of his speeches with those of his opponent, and thus foolishly lay the foundation for his future regret, "I am sorry to inform you," etc.

The apology offered for having violated his promises I could have but understood as an act of treachery, and that further effort to publish the discussion, as originally contemplated, *would be in vain*. Mr. Barker says—"If I had had the report earlier I could have made the corrections." Why did he not have it "*earlier?*" His residence is only about one mile from Salem, which is the residence of the reporters. Is it not presumable that Mr. Barker was frequently in town during this period of some three months? But let us have the testimony of Mr. James Barnaby, one of the reporters. He says in a letter to me, dated August 4th, 1853—"We write out Mr. Barker's speeches as we do your own, and ***hand them over to him*** as he wants them." Mine were all received, corrected and ready for the publishers before the 12th day of September. Now, the facts are, Mr. Barker did receive his speeches as I did or he did not want them. So matters stood on the 14th day of November, viz: That I must take his speeches to the publishers, uncorrected, "or they must remain in my hands sometime longer." How much longer? till he would "go to Philadelphia, other places east, and to Indiana." Now, I ask, do not these facts clearly show that Mr. Barker intended to withold his speeches from the publishers?

But to proceed: I went to Salem, at the time specified, and, in the presence of James Barnaby and Jacob Heaton, we entered into the following article of agreement, written by Mr. Barker himself:

AGREEMENT, RESPECTING THE REPORT OF THE DEBATE BETWEEN JOSEPH BARKER AND JONAS HARTZEL:

Mr. Jonas Hartzel offers to transfer his right in the report to me, and to hand me his corrected speeches, on condition that I publish it as soon as I well can, and pay the expense of reporting, leaving it to my sense of right to give him thirty or forty copies of the work or not.

I accept this offer, and engage to begin the printing of the work within eight weeks from Nov. 18th, 1853. I do, at the same time, leave Mr. Jonas Hartzel at liberty to sell the report to any publisher, if he can sell it to better advantage, on condition that he give me seventy-five copies of the report, bound in muslin and boards, for my labor in correcting the report of my speeches, and he pay the expense of reporting. In case *I* publish the report, Mr. Jonas Hartzel engages to certify to the correctness of the report, supposing I publish his speeches as he hands them to me; while, in case *he* takes the work, to sell or publish it, *I* agree to give the same certificate, on condition my speeches are published as handed by me to him. Whichever publishes the report, the certificate of the reporters to the correctness of the report to be appended.

The speeches of each disputant to be published in the same type.

Each disputant to have the liberty to add an appendix; the appendixes to be of equal length.

Mr. Hartzel to let me have the work by the 12th of December, 1853, if he does not sell it before that time.

In case Mr. Hartzel takes the work, I engage to give him my speeches, corrected, within two months from the date of this. A portion of them shall be handed to him corrected in four weeks and the rest as soon as possible. Each to correct his own proof sheets.

JOSEPH BARKER,
JONAS HARTZEL,

I then went to Cincinnati, presented the report to the publishers, and, after due examination, the following agreement was entered into:

Agreement between the American Christian Publication Society and Jonas Hartzel, Nov. 28th, 1853.

The American Christian Publication Society agrees to take the financial responsibility of the publication, by Jonas Hartzel, of his debate with Mr. Barker, and to superintend the execution of the same, and will give to Jonas Hartzel (who hereby relinquishes the entire interest in the copy-right and sale of the work for himself and Mr. Barker) seventy-five copies of the work, when published, for Mr. Barker, and the amount of one hundred and twenty-five dollars, also in copies of the work at the cost price. The Publication Society not to be liable for the expense of reporting.

THOMAS J. MELISH,
GEORGE LENT,
A. M. LESLIE. } Publication Committee.

JONAS HARTZEL.

On the 3d day of December I requested Mr. Jacob Heaton, of Salem, to act as my agent, in handing over Mr. Barker's speeches, and to see that they were duly mailed, &c. On the 13th of December Mr. Heaton wrote me:

DEAR SIR: — Mr. Barker came home on Saturday, and, at the earliest opportunity, I called on him to hand him his speeches, and ask him to correct forthwith. He said: "I won't hand him over any of my speeches, until he pays the reporters, and give me security that he will publish my speeches according to contract. From what I have learned since, Mr. Hartzel designs to publish an appendix, which he does not design me to see. *This I will never consent to.* I must see his appendix, and shall write a reply of the same length, and he must give me security that he will do it." I became satisfied that he either did not comprehend a business obligation, or that he was unwilling to do what was right.

So, you see, another difficulty has sprung up. But, so far as security is concerned, your friends here will vouch for that. Write immediately. Truly, &c.,

JACOB HEATON.

To which I replied:

As to Mr. Barker's troubles, they are all provided for in the article of agreement: I am under no obligations to pay the reporters in advance, but, if they are not willing to trust me, you may give them security; on condition, that as soon as the last of Mr. Barker's speeches are mailed by you, and received in Cincinnati, "we, or either of us, will pay," &c. The publishing of his speeches according to contract is in his own hands, as he will correct them himself, and read his own proof sheet. The article says: "Each disputant shall have the liberty to add an appendix, the appendixes to be of equal length." "What is written, is written."

I requested Mr. Heaton to take the copy of the agreement, and ask the reporters to accompany him, and have an interview with Mr. Barker, etc. To this I received as follows:

SALEM, December 21st, 1853.

Your letter came to hand, in reply to mine, and I went, with Mr. Barnaby and Miss Stanton, (sent Mr. Pow word, but he did not come) to see Mr. Barker, but he is inexorable, and I fear you will have some difficulty, if the book is ever published. He takes the stand that he must see your appendix, and write a reply, and that you must pay him, for the appendix, one hundred copies of the work. In the last request, we unanimously concurred that it was not right, and I told him so. Mr. Barnaby desired that I should not write to you for a few days, hoping that Mr. Barker would reconsider it, but he has not done so, therefore, we write you the result of our interview. Mr. Barker has corrected most of his speeches for the press, but says he would, rather than submit to the wrong and insult you offer, by attempting to write an appendix, which he shall not see, pay the reporters himself, and burn the speeches. He alleges that you might fill your appendix with personal or new matter, which it would be unfair for him not to see.

I am satisfied that the work will not be published, unless you agree to publish without appendix, or else you agree that he shall see yours and write a reply. Probably, under the circumstances, the least trouble would be to publish without appendix, then his speeches would be forthcoming immediately.

As ever, your friend,

JACOB HEATON.

P. S The copy of the article of agreement is in my possession, and it does look as though he had not intended to sell his appendix, still it would be fairly inferable that he should not be paid for what was merely granted as a privilege. J. H.

Reply to the foregoing: (I have quoted all my letters from memory, as I kept no copies.) " Mr. Barker then has given up two of his difficulties, and, as to the remaining one, why did he not say, (when charged by myself with unfairness, in having made arrangements to have the discussion reported, without informing me,) Mr. Hartzel may have an appendix, and I will have one of equal length, *and reply to his.*" Then I might have thanked his *clemency* for his generous offer. Or, why did he not so specify in the article of agreement — "Mr. Barker intends to have a written discussion appended to an oral one, and then call the written controversy appendix," and thus send forth the book with a lie in its mouth."

Some days after the date of this, I went to Salem in person, but

Mr. Barker had left for Philadelphia, and, after consultation with Messrs. Barnaby, Heaton and Pow, (our committee of arrangements) I said to Mr. Heaton, "I will publish without an appendix, on condition that Mr. Barker's corrected speeches are delivered into my hands immediately. To which Mr. Heaton replied: "Mr. Barker left his corrected speeches, with the understanding that, if you came, and would comply with that condition, or an appendix of three or four pages only, his speeches should be given up; do you go and ask Mr. Barnaby to go to Mr. Barker's house and get the speeches." To this Mr. Barnaby cheerfully consented, but returned without them. The three gentlemen before named, were now in attendance, and, after some deliberation, we agreed to write to Mr. Barker.

As I received no word for some time, I wrote Mr. Heaton: "If Mr. Barker does not give up the speeches before his return, or soon after, please write me, and I will come to Salem immediately and make another effort," and received in answer:

SALEM, January 19th, 1854.

Your letter of enquiry, in regard to the speeches of Mr. Barker, came duly to hand, and, in reply, will say, that as soon as I heard that his family had received a letter from him, I immediately went down to their house to see whether he had not ordered his corrected speeches to be given up, because I felt it was due from me to see that he complied with his promise to me, but the letter was merely giving an account of the debate with Dr. Berge. The next day, however, he wrote again, in reply to Mr. Barnaby, and his own sons, and regrets that it is now, for the present, out of his power to comply. He alleges that the "*two* speeches" which he did correct he wants to review, and that with his present excitement, he cannot spare *mind* enough to think about, much less to correct his Ohio speeches. And says, "Mr. Hartzel has himself to blame for this, I was at home for weeks, and could and would have corrected all my speeches, if he had not been so unjust in his demands, and now he must wait until I get back—then I will attend to them.

Thus, you see, the cause of the delay, which I know must annoying. Still, I hope that it will not militate against your sale in Cincinnati. He will surely attend to it when he comes back.

All well, with best wishes for your wife and family, believe me, as ever, yours, for the ultimate triumph of truth,

JACOB HEATON.

A few days after this I received the following:

CINCINNATI, January 26th, 1854.

BRO. HARTZEL: — Your letter of 24th of last month, was placed in my hands. Debates are somewhat like hot cakes, (to use a common expression) commanding a rapid sale only while the public mind is eager and excited on the subject of the discussion. So much time has elapsed since the debate came off — so much delay in furnishing the manuscripts — so much doubt about ever getting Mr. Barker's speeches at all, and so late a period would arrive before the book could be presented to the public, that we have thought best for the Society not to attempt the issuing of the work.

Wishing you much success in the cause of the Lord, and much individual happiness, we remain yours, in the good hope.

J. A. DEARBORN,

On behalf of Pub. Com. of the A C. P. Society.

Such is the history of my ill-fated effort to bring out the report of the discussion, according to stipulation. I am sure no one can censure me for not having made sufficient effort, unless so be that I erred in not consenting to recall my appendix from Cincinnati — for it was not until after it was deposited with the Publishers that Mr. Barker raised the question of right to reply. But on what did Mr. Barker base his right of reply? Not upon any stipulation, verbal or written; but upon this, viz: "That I might fill my appendix with personal or new matter." In this I subjected myself to the same liability, for I never asked to reply to his; neither had I any fears on that score. Had he filled his with irrelevent matter, rather than relevant after-thought, it would only have been the better for my argument, and public sentiment would have chastised him for such misdemeanor.

But I did consent to publish without appendix — not because it was right I should — but to facilitate the business; for, if his benevolent efforts to convince the world that the Bible must be abjured, in order to elevate mankind, required so much of his time that he could not find sufficient leisure to correct his speeches for the press from August 4th to November 14th, *though tending to promote the object of his great mission*, how much would he have required to revise his argument, and write out some forty pages of new matter? No wonder that he should now ask as compensation one hundred books for that which he merely claimed as a privilege, in the article of agreement. Having been informed by Mr. Heaton, a man of acknowledged veracity, that Mr. Barker had corrected most of his speeches ready for the press, I felt disposed to give up my rights, but when I was informed, by a subsequent letter, that the two corrected speeches had to be revised before they could be given up, the last, lingering hope was disappointed, and "patience was no longer a virtue."

MR. HARTZEL'S FIRST ADDRESS.

Books have prefaces, some have exodiums, and important controversies should be entitled, at least, to a brief introduction. With the consent of the Chair, I wish to spend a little time in miscellaneous remarks and readings.

First: Christian Friends and fellow-citizens, you will ask of me an apology for bringing into public discussion the evidences of the Christian Religion. Christians are required to be always ready to give a reason for their "hope." This demand is now being made, and, if there were but one individual making such inquiry we would feel ourselves bound to bring forward the evidence of our faith and hope. If the Gospel be true, we have a reason to give; if it be a "cunningly devised fable," we can have no reason to offer. In that case, we must say, with the Apostle, "our preaching is vain, and our faith is also vain," and, as a matter of course, our hope will never be realized.

Christians are required to "contend for the faith once delivered to the saints." This pre-supposes opposition. We do not labor to promote opposition.

We do not invite opposition. But, when it presents itself, we cannot, in view of our responsibilities as Christians, refuse to meet it. To meet promptly the opposition that has, from time to time, been arrayed against the Bible, has been, on the part of Bible believers, one great means of spreading and propagating the Gospel and increasing the number of its faithful followers.

Second: A brief explanation is due myself and that part of the audience who sympathise with me in the present controversy.

This controversy has grown out of a Convention which was held in this place in November of last year. That Convention was called together, if I am not mistaken, by individuals on the other side of the question. The call of that Convention was to the "Friends of free discussion," to discuss the "origin, authority and influence of the Jewish and Christian Scriptures:" So far as I was acquainted with the names signed to that call, they were persons who supposed that "the origin of the Bible was wrapped in darkness;" that the authority of the Bible "is not decisive as to the truth or falsehood of any principle, or to the goodness or badness of any practice." "That the influence of the Bible is most prejudicial and unfavorable to human happiness." There were some seven resolutions offered during that Convention. It was my desire, if a discussion was had at all, that these seven resolutions should be brought under investigation. We accordingly made an effort to concentrate these resolutions and bring them into fair discussion. In this we have been baffled; Mr. Barker declining the defense of those resolutions so derogatory to Bible, and offensive to Christians. The present discussion is not that, which in the first place, we wished to engage in. Suffice me to say, then, on this point, we are not the aggressors. We have been called out, and compelled to meet a responsibility which we, as Christians, could not throw off.

We had a right to expect that those on the other side would appear before the public, taking an affirmative position. It was expected they would declare their creed and give us a synopsis of their principles. In this we have been disappointed, as the published correspondence between Mr. Barker and myself will sufficiently show.

Third: The divine origin of the Christian religion has always been under discussion. There have never been wanting friends to advocate its claims and enemies to oppose them. We are sorry there have been those who were so unfriendly to their own interests, and the interests of their race, as to wish to oppose it, (I speak, of course, for myself and the friends of the Bible,) but we must take the world as it is. We must act with reference to things as they are, and will be, and not as they should be. Our Lord said, "because iniquity shall abound, the love of many shall wax cold." This was speaking of things as they would be and not as they should be, for the superabounding of iniquity should have caused the love of the many to wax warmer.

Fourth: Christians have nothing to fear from the issue of a thorough investigation. Though the controversy has been going on from the earliest ages of Christianity to the present day, we believe that it has invariably resulted in good. I wish here to read an article from "Christianity Triumphant," (a happy title,) by Joseph Barker. Perhaps he could not have selected one more descriptive of the subject matter of the work. The title-page is as follows: "Christianity Triumphant; or, an enlarged view of the character and tendency of the religion of Christ; showing that it is every way calculated to remedy the evils of a disordered and miserable world, and make mankind truly good and happy." I have read the work carefully, and wish to say, without flattery, that it is a work of great merit. The masses of the people need instruction upon the very points noticed in the title page. It is a beautiful comparison between Christianity and Paganism, Heathen Philosophers and the teachings of Jesus Christ and the Apostles, and their comparative influence upon mankind. We are so far removed from Paganism, both as to time and location, that the masses of our countrymen seem not to have any proper estimate of the merits and benefits of Christianity. If we could but have a true idea of Paganism, I am sure the great majority of mankind would prize Christianity more highly than they do. It is to throw light upon this matter that I read from the work before me.

Before I enter on the great question which I am called upon to discuss, I am wishful to make a few observations. And in the first place, let me advise the friends of Christianity not to be afraid of the attacks which are made upon the Gospel. We cannot but be sorry that any should be so ill-informed, or so ill-disposed, as to assail the Gospel, but we have no need to be afraid of the result. It is no new thing for the religion of Christ to be opposed. It has had its enemies in every age, from that day that it was first revealed to the world to the present time, but it was all in vain. The Jews opposed it, but it still spread; the Pagan Philosophers opposed it, but it still rolled on; the Magistrates and Rulers opposed it, and shed the blood of its teachers and disciples like water, but nothing could stay its progress. The Priest and the Magician, the Prince and the Philosopher, were all borne down before it. The patience of its martyrs, affection and courage of its converts, subdued the hearts of its enemies and brought them with tears to implore the blessings of its Salvation. The voices of fishermen were mightier than the fleets and armies of the whole earth, and the persecuted Gospel put to silence the boasted Philosophy of Greece and Rome. The corrupt interests and passions and customs of a dark and degenerate world gave way before it, and through blood and fires, and many hideous forms of death, it still went forward, in meekness and in majesty, uninjured and undismayed, "from conquering to conquer."

The Gospel was opposed at the time of the Reformation; the power of the Popedom was against it, and the powers of many nations were against it; but it still pursued its course, and multiplied its conquests on every hand. Since the time of the Reformation it has been opposed by a new kind of enemies. A number of men appeared in England, in France, and in America, some years ago, professing to be the children of reason, and claiming for themselves alone, of all the people upon earth, the honors of rationality. They also united their counsels and joined their energies for the overthrow of the Gospel, and made great efforts to destroy Christianity from the face of the earth; but they passed away. Their boasting was turned into silence, their pride and their pretensions all perished; but the Gospel still lives, and goes forth with quicker step and with greater glory to illumine and to bless the world.

At length another foe has entered the field against the religion of Christ, which boldly threatens to sweep it, in a few years from the face of the earth. But we cannot be afraid. The Gospel will triumph again, and the system of infidel socialism will go down to the grave of its fathers, and know no resurrection. The men who at present are fighting against the Gospel are loud in their boasting, and fierce and headlong in their attacks; but they are strangers to the system with which they are warring, and to the powers which are joined together in its behalf. A few more struggles will reveal to them their folly, and extinguish their mad hopes for ever. All that is in Heaven is against them, and all that is good and true and strong upon earth is against them. They fight against the light of the whole world; they fight against the strongest feelings of every uncorrupted human being; they war against the rights, the joys, and the hopes of the whole intelligent creation. And as soon will they blot out the sun and the stars, as extinguish the light of the Gospel, or tear from the hearts of men their belief in God, and their hopes of a blessed immortality. O yes, the Gospel will triumph again; and the efforts of its enemies, instead of checking its progress, shall only make it roll on the faster, and win to itself new fame and glory.

Truly, this discussion has not been in vain. If this is true, then all that is conservative in matters pertaining to religion or civil government, will be found in the fact, that no important controversy will retrograde. It will continue to be agitated; it will be discussed and re-discussed, until the question will be amicably adjusted by the parties, or the discomfiture of the one and the triumph of the other, of which we have the clearest proof in Luther's advocacy of Protestantism, Locke's defense of religious toleration, the abolition of English slavery, by Wilberforce, and Christians with unbelievers in their defense of the inspiration of the Bible.

The discussion of the great proposition: Is the Gospel true, or is it false? Is it of divine or human origin? Is it from Heaven or from Hell? is still an interesting question, and another proof that no important principle will suffer by investigation.

As Mr. Barker has said, "as soon will they blot out the sun and stars as extinguish the light of the Gospel, or tear from men their belief in God, and the hopes of a blessed immortality." But it may be said, the question of the divine origin of the Bible is not yet settled. True; but all the forms of infidelity belonging to former generations *are settled.* Where now the old theory of diabolical agency and magic, and the more modern theories of Lord Herbert and Thomas Paine, to account for the miracles of the New Testament upon the principle of fraud?

I shall here read a few passages from "The Christian," by Joseph Barker. We shall depend much upon the testimony of others in this controversy. "For if I (alone) testify of myself my testimony is not to be regarded." The point in the extract which I am about to read, is this: that Christianity has gained something; that the old arguments are abandoned by those who are now in the field:

It is a fact that the unbelievers of the present age, lay no stress on the objections brought forward against Christianity by the unbelievers of the first ages of Christianity. Unbelievers of the present day regard the objections of the unbelievers of the first ages of Christianity, whether Pagan or Jews, as altogether powerless. The objections of each preceding age have been abandoned by the unbelievers of each succeeding age. Is there not reason to believe, that as the objections of all preceding ages have lost their power, and gone out of date, so the objections of unbelievers of the present age will lose their power, and go out of date in like manner?

The arguments in favor of the truth and divinity of Christianity are more numerous and powerful at present, than they were in ages past; and they are becoming more numerous and powerful still.

Even unbelievers themselves are obliged to acknowledge now, that many of those doctrines which were objected to, during the last two or three generations, as irrational and incredible, are in truth, no parts of the religion of Christ, and therefore no proof that Christianity is irrational and incredible.

Is there not reason to believe that those doctrines which are brought forward by unbelievers of the present day as incredible, irrational, or inconsistent, will also prove, when properly examined, to be no part of the religion of Christ?

First: That we may discriminate clearly, I wish first to show the points of agreement. So far as known to me, all Philosophers, of every school agree in this: that man, as he is, needs instruction. All Philosophers have put forth some effort in this direction, atheists not excepted. Who has traveled farther, delivered more lectures, and published more books for the purpose of benefiting and enlightening mankind than Robert Owen? and so of others of this class. They are as indefatigable in their labors, in publishing books and pamphlets, in delivering speeches and reading lectures, as though the salvation of the world depended on their efforts.

Second: That man is capable of receiving instruction.

Third: That man is greatly profited by receiving instruction, provided it be of the right kind.

Fourth: That the Creator has, in some way made provision for man's enlightenment in all important matters pertaining both to time and eternity. In relation to this point, also, there is agreement, however we may differ in other respects. Without some common ground it would be impossible for us to meet together upon any settled issue whatever.

The different philosophers may, perhaps, be classified under a few general headings, as, Rationalists, Spiritualists, and believers in a supernaturally revealed religion, as found in the Jewish and Christian Scriptures.

With the first, *Nature* is man's instruction book, and reason is both the pedagogue and the pupil. Some of our Conventionists belong to this school, as may be seen from the report of the Bible Convention, page seven. Our friend, Mr. Barker, does not belong to this school.

Spritualists have not much confidence in this philosophy. Nature, with them, is not a trustworthy guide, and reason is a dull scholar. They have a peculiar kind of parlance who belong to this party. "The still small voice;" "Spiritual intuitions;" "Turn your eyes inwardly;" "Look into the depths of thine own soul." The above phrases are highly descriptive of the leading elements of their creed. If I understand my opponent, he is not of this school. The following will define his position: "For myself I believe there is a God, and that God has given a revelation of his will to mankind." (See Report of the Bible Convention, page 33.)

From this confession of his faith we see his entire concurrence with all other philosophers. 1st: That man *needs* instruction. 2d: That man is capable of receiving instruction. 3d: That man is greatly profited by receiving instruction, provided it be of the right kind. 4th: That the Creator has, in some way, made provision for man's enlightenment. The following quotation from Hebrews, 1: 1-2, "God, who at sundry times, and in divers manners, spake in time past unto the fathers by the prophets, hath in these last days spoken unto us by his Son, whom he hath appointed heir of all things, by whom also he made the worlds;" is our theological basis on which our religion rests. Our friend does not belong to this school, but he agrees with us, that God has, in some way, made provision for man's instruction.

The point in debate, then, is simply this: Where is this revelation to be found? What are God's means for enlightening mankind in the great questions of human duty and happiness? I hope the audience will not lose sight of this. The question is not whether man *needs* instruction — whether he is capable of *receiving* instruction. But the question is, where is the *source* of instruction? To what *department* of the natural or spiritual universe should man look for the needful information? There are then points of agreement. The great question between Atheists, Deists, and Christians is, what is the reliable source of knowledge? Every man who proposes to teach this, proposes to himself something as the object of his toil. I do the same in the present discussion. I do not expect to convince all who listen to this controversy of the truth of my position — perhaps I shall convince none. Many believe in reason alone; these do not see the need of a verbal or historic revelation, but, to show the *utter helplessness* of man without such revelation, I will read an article from the "Edinburg Review," October, 1849, pages 298, 299, 300:

But perhaps the most striking example of the helplessness to which man is soon reduced if he relies upon his reason alone, is the spectacle of the issue of his investigations into that which one would imagine he must know most intimately, if he knows anything, and that is, his own nature—his own mind. There is something to one who reflects long enough upon it, inexpressibly whimsical in the questions which the mind is for ever putting to itself respecting itself; and to which the said mind returns from its dark caverns only an echo. We are apt, when we speculate about the mind, to forget for the moment, that it is at once the querist and the oracle; and to regard it as something OUT of itself, like a mineral in the hands of the analytic chemist. We cannot fully enter into the absurdities of its condition, except by remembering that it is our wise selves who so grotesquely bewilder us. The mind, on such occasions, takes itself (if we may so speak). into its own hands, turns itself about as a savage would a watch, or a monkey a letter; interrogates itself, listens to the echo of its own voice, and is obliged, after all, to lay itself down again with a very puzzled expression—and acknowledge that of its very self, itself knows little or nothing! "I am material," exclaims one of those whimsical beings, to whom the heaven-descended "Know thyself" would seem to be ironically addressed. "No!—immaterial," says another. "I am both material and immaterial," exclaims, perhaps the very same mind at different times. "Thought itself may be matter modified," says one. "Rather," says another of the same perplexed species, "matter is thought modified; for what you call matter is but a phenomenon." "Both are independent and totally distinct substances, mysteriously, inexplicably conjoined," says a third. "How they are conjoined we know no more than the dead. Not so much, perhaps." "Do I ever cease to think," says the mind to itself, "even in sleep? Is not my essence thought?" "You ought to know your own essence best," all creation will reply. "I am confident," says one, "that I never do cease to think—not even in the soundest sleep." "You do, for a long time, every night of your life," exclaims another, equally confident and ignorant. "Where do I exist?" it goes on. "Am I in the brain? Am I in the whole body? Am I anywhere? Am I nowhere?" "I cannot have any local existence, for I know I am immaterial," says one. "I have a local existence, because I am material," says another. "I have a local existence, though I am not material," says a third. "Are my habitual actions voluntary," it exclaims, "however rapid they become; though I am unconscious of these volitions when they have attained certain rapidity; or do I become a mere automaton as respects such actions? and therefore an automaton nine times out of ten, when I act all? To this query two opposite answers are given by different minds; and by others, perhaps wiser, none at all; while, often, opposite answers are given by the same mind at different times. In like manner has every action, every operation, every emotion of the mind been made the subject of endless doubt and disputation. Surely if, as Soame Jenyns imagined, the infirmities of man, and even graver evils, were permitted in order to afford amusement to superior intelligences, and make the angels laugh, few things could afford them better sport than the perplexities of this child of clay engaged in the study of himself. "Alas!" exclaims at last the baffled spirit of this babe in intellect, as he surveys his shattered toys—his broken theories of metaphysics, "I know that I am; but what I am—where I am—even how I act—not only what is my essence, but what even my mode of operation,—of all this I know nothing; and boast of reason as I may, all that I think on these points is matter of opinion—or is matter of faith!" He resembles, in fact, nothing so much as a kitten first introduced to its own image in a mirror; she runs to the back of it, she leaps over it, she turns and twists, and jumps and frisks, in all directions, in the vain attempt to reach the fair illusion; and, at length, turns away in weariness from that incomprehensible enigma—the image of herself!

One would imagine—perhaps not untruly—that the Divine Creator had subjected us to these difficulties—and especially that incomprehensible TRILEMMA,—there is an union and interaction of two totally distinct substances, or that matter is but thought, or that thought is but matter,—one of which must be true, and all of which approach as near to mutual contradictions as can well be conceived,—for the very purpose of rebuking the presumption of man, and of teaching him humility; that He had left these obscurities at the very threshold—nay within the very mansion of the mind itself,—for the express purpose of deterring man from playing the dogmatising fool when he looked abroad. Yet, in spite of his raggedness and poverty at home, no sooner does man look out of his dusky dwelling, than, like Goldsmith's little Beau, who, in his garret up five pair of stairs, boasts of his friendship with lords, he is apt to assume airs of magnificence, and, glancing at the Infinite through his little eye-glass, to affect an intimate acquaintance with the most respectable secrets of the universe!

It is undeniable, then, that the perplexities which uniformly puzzle man in the physical world, and even in the little world of his own mind, when he passes a certain limit, are just as unmanageble as those found in the moral constitution and government of the universe, or in the disclosures of the volume of Revelation. In both we find abundance of inexplicable difficulties; sometimes arising from our absolute ignorance, and perhaps quite as often from our partial knowledge. These difficulties are probably left on the pages of both volumes for some of the same reasons; many of them, it may be, because even the commentary of the Creator himself could not render them plain to a finite understanding, though a necessary and salutary exercise of our humility may be involved in their reception; others, if not purely (which seems not probable) yet partly for the sake of exercising and training that humility, as an essential part of the education of a child; others, surmountable, indeed, in the progress of knowledge and by prolonged effort of the human intellect, may be designed to stimulate that intellect to strenuous action and healthy effort — as well as to supply, in their solution, as time rolls on, an ever-accumulating mass of proofs of the profundity of the wisdom which has so far anticipated all the wisdom of man; and of the divine origin of both the great books which he is privileged to study as a pupil, and even to illustrate as a commentator — but the text of which he cannot alter.

Our present situation, then, is a state of discipline, a state of trial, and, therefore, a state of perplexities, and in such a state, it is an easy matter to raise objections and start difficulties with reference to anything, however true or good.

Men may raise objections against Christianity, or the testimony upon which it is based. Much depends upon the state of the mind in approaching testimony, and in the investigation of testimony. If an individual is under a certain mental bias, it is impossible for any amount of evidence to produce conviction. In another state of mind men will acquiesce too readily. The mind, in one case, becomes too credulous, in the other it is too stubborn — too incredulous, so that reasonable evidence will not produce the desired result, which is a conviction of the truth of my proposition.

But on this point, I beg leave to call attention to my worthy friend. He has *spoken words* so important that I cannot, in justice to myself and the audience, pass them by without attention.

See "Christianity Triumphant," pages 384–5, in

answering the infidel objection, "If man were supplied with a sufficiency of evidence, belief would follow as a matter of course."

Mr. Barker says:

You are in error, I imagine. A man's belief does not depend altogether on the amount of evidence with which he is supplied; it depends in a great measure on a person's state of mind, and on the attention and regard which he chooses to pay to that evidence. The evidence which convinces one man, does not convince another. Offer the fullest evidence in the world to a man who is wallowing in sensuality and drunkenness, and it will produce no conviction at all; but offer the same evidence to a man that is acting as becomes a rational and accountable being, and who is truly desirous to know and obey the truth, and he will be convinced at once. There has always been sufficient evidence afforded of the truth of the Gospel, wherever it has been promulgated; and when men have attended to that evidence with rightly disposed minds, they have become sincere believers. But no evidence can cure the unbelief of a man that is bent on living in sin, and disables and perverts his mental powers by lewdness and intemperance. Evidence is to the mind what light is to the eye. All the light in the world will not make a man see that shuts his eyes, or that puts them out. If a man is to see, he must make a proper use of his eyes, as well as have a good supply of light. At the moment that I am now writing, it is near mid-day, and the sun is shining brightly in the heavens, shedding down light in abundance; and yet there are numbers that see nothing of the surrounding scenery. Some are asleep; some have shut themselves up in dark rooms; and others refuse to place themselves in a proper situation for beholding the objects that surround them. And it is much the same with respect to the light of revelation and the minds of men. The doctrines of the Gospel are unfolded, and evidence of their truth is supplied in abundance, from every quarter. The Gospel carries along with it evidences of its divinity in its own doctrines; and evidences of its divinity are furnished by the whole current of history. Proofs of the truth of the Gospel doctrine are scattered through the whole universe, and not a day or night passes by, but what lifts up its voice in attestation of its divine original. Still some do not believe. And if the evidence was thousand times stronger, it is possible that some might be unbelievers still. Evidence has no power to such as will not regard it. Man has it in his power to close his eyes, and ears, and heart, to every sight, and sound, and gracious influence in the universe. If a person should say—"Give the man sufficient light, and he cannot help but see," when he knew at the same time that the man had put out his eyes, you would take the man to be quibbling, or else set him down as wanting in intellect. And it is the same with the man who speaks as if a person's belief depended solely on the amount of evidence with which he is supplied. No arguments can have any effect on dogs and swine, because they have not capacity to take in arguments; and it is possible for men to so far imitate the dog and the swine in their conduct, as to reduce themselves to a level with them in point of capacity. Men may so far corrupt and pervert their faculties by sin, that they shall put darkness for light, and light for darkness; call evil good, and good evil. There were such characters in the days of the Savior, and he appears to have had reference to such characters in his sermon on the mount, when he said, "Give not that which is holy to the dogs, neither cast ye your pearls before swine, lest they trample them under their feet, and turn again and rend you. Matt. vii., 6. If our opponents follow the advice of their leader, Robert Owen, with respect to the unrestrained indulgence of their appetites, they have no need to seek for the cause of their unbelief in the want of evidence; they may find it nearer home.

It is then true, that much depends upon the state of mind in forming a favorable or unfavorable opinion with regard to religious truth, or with reference to matters of any kind, whether ordinary or extraordinary.

In conclusion, let me say, "there is light enough for those whose sincere wish it is to see, and darkness enough to perplex and confound those of an opposite disposition." It is the former class only we expect to profit in the present discussion.

MR. HARTZEL'S SECOND ADDRESS.

You have heard the prefaces, both mine and Mr. Barker's. From these you can judge somewhat correctly of what is to follow. There are but a few things in the address of Mr. Barker that require a word of reply.

I am sure there was matter enough in my opening remarks upon which to have formed an issue and an opposite one, if he had desired it. To do this he admits is his province.

Mr. Barker claims, that, like Paul, he has become wiser than he once was. Paul did become wiser in abandoning *infidelity* and becoming a *Christian*, and Mr. Barker in forsaking *Christianity* and turning *Infidel*. It is said to be a good rule when it works both ways. The extracts read from Mr. Barker's writings are matters of history. Is it not a matter of history that Christianity was opposed from its very birth? Is it not true that the "Jewish Rulers and Pagan Philosophers were all directly against it?" Is it not a fact that it triumphed over all opposition, and went forth from conquering to conquer?"

If I had met my friend in discussion upon some scholastic dogmas, I ought not to hold him responsible for his sentiments, now disclaimed by him. But in matters of history, I have a perfect right to hold him responsible for what he stated when a Methodist preacher. A change from positive belief to disbelief does not change historic truths into falsehoods.

Calvinism and Arminianism are points of speculative theology, adopted without evidence and may be abandoned without reason. It would be unreasonable to hold a man responsible for his opinions, while every man should be held responsible for his faith.

On the same ground on which my friend disclaims what I have read, or may hereafter read from his writings, a man might claim to be exonerated from the payment of a debt. He might, with equal propriety, say, I was a Christian when I contracted that debt; I am an infidel now, and ought to be discharged from the obligation. I ask, is it not true that the unbelievers of "each succeeding age" have changed their mode of opposition to Christianity? Mr. Barker says: "The objections of each preceding age have been abandoned by the unbelievers of each succeeding age." Was my friend ignorant of the history of infidelity in 1844? or did he act the part of a "lying priest?" Surely not. I will not charge him with doing so, though he did belong to that priesthood, of which he has given a terrible picture.

But, Mr. Barker said, "that the Jewish priesthood were the children of the Devil, and that Christ called them so." This is foreign to the question. If God had communicated to us through the Scribes and Pharisees, then this remark would have some point. Did Jesus Christ call Moses and the Prophets children of the Devil? Did he thus designate those whom God had appointed as the mediums of divine communications? And even suppose there were some among them who were not good men, for we claim that God could appoint fallible men as instruments, by which he could impart infallible instruction, otherwise, he could not have spoken by man to man for the benefit of man. This point has no bearing in the present controversy.

The Bible has a positive existence. Portions of it have existed for *three thousand three hundred and forty-four years*; the whole of it, in its present form, has existed for *seventeen hundred and fifty-seven years.* Now, the question arises, how came it into existence? We have not come to the question of its transmission. The source from which it was derived is one thing, the medium of communication another. But, Mr. Barker says, "all we have to sustain our position, is other's people's word — hear-say — and this is not reliable." Is human testimony unworthy of rational belief in any case? I will ask the audience whether they believe there were such men as the Cæsras, Alexander or Napoleon? I ask, what is the strength of your belief in history, as to the existence of these persons? Is it but a weak and faltering faith? have you any mental dubiety as to this belief? For myself, I have none. I know of nothing that could strengthen my conviction; even *sight* could not. I can no more doubt that such men lived than I can doubt that I stand before you. I have the same mental and moral assurance of the one as of the other.

But, Mr. Barker says, "the early Christians were liars." Were the early Christians liars? Did their enemies so regard them? We will hear Mr. Barker to this point: "Christianity Triumphant," page 165.

The early Christians were celebrated for their sacred regard to truth; and Pliny, in his letter to Trojan, mentioned it as one of the peculiarities by which the Christians were distinguished, that they bound themselves not to deceive any one, nor to deny any thing entrusted to them, when called to restore it to its owner. The Christians of old, says Cave, looked upon honesty and an upright carriage as a considerable part of their religion, and to speak the truth, and to keep their words, to perform their promises, and to act sincerely in all their dealings, were as sacred and dear to them as their lives. They even used the greatest candor and simplicity in expressing their minds to one another, not pretending what was false, nor concealing what was true. Yea, yea and nay, nay was the usuual measure of their transactions.

His last discourse would not have been a very good preface for the book from which we have just now read. Either the author or disputant is under some misapprehension. The disputant, upon the authority of Joseph Barker alone, says, "that the early Christians were liars;" but the author says, upon the testimony of Pliny, one of the early enemies and persecutors, "that they were not liars." Is he sure that those lying professors, to whom he referred, were Christians? If he will refer us to the chapter and verse where either Jesus or the Apostles have approved of, or justified lying, then his argument will be to the purpose. He ought to be more careful how he charges men with being liars: and if he proves them such, and calls them Christians, then we demand of him the *proof*, that *they are* Christians. If he can prove this he has made an argument, and we will honestly confess the fact, that a man may be both a Christian and a liar. We have received our religion from

Jesus and the Apostles. Were they liars? We will hear Mr. Barker again to this point. "Christian," Vol. 1, page 19.

(Infidels) "cannot prove that the men who wrote the Gospels, the Acts, and the Epistles were not good men,—men of truth and integrity,—men of purity and charity."

I am sure Mr. Barker was not a Methodist preacher when he wrote this book. Can he prove that Christ and the Apostles were liars, now? He shall have the opportunity; and as soon as he shall have done this, I shall give up the controversy.

I will now speak a few words in the way of defining my proposition. The proposition is, "That the Jewish and Christian Scriptures contain a series of communications, supernaturally revealed and miraculously attested, from the latter, man may acquire a perfect rule of life." 1st, It is not at all necessary that I should go into all these explanations called for by my friend. When I use language, I wish it understood that I suppose those who hear me have common sense. I use language in its common acceptation. When I use the word "*supernatural*" or the phrase "*supernaturally revealed*," I wish to be understood as Bible believers have generally understood and applied those words. I use the word "*miraculous*" in its current meaning, according to the standards of our language.

2d. With reference to the second part of the proposition (for it contains two affirmatives,) my friend ought to award me some credit for being willing to take two affirmatives, when he refused taking one. The second member of the proposition reads thus: "from the latter, man may acquire a perfect rule of life." The word *acquire*, I put into the proposition for the purpose of meeting the issue raised in the Bible Convention, otherwise I should have written it, "*In the latter, man has a perfect rule of life.*"

Perhaps Mr. Barker will ask whether every man has this perfect rule of life in the New Testament.

I answer: every man, who is a proper subject of moral government, just as far as he has a capacity to understand the will of God, and to do it, has a perfect rule of life in the Christian Scriptures.

By a perfect rule of life, I understand that which reveals to man his relations, duties and destiny, for nothing less than this would constitute such a rule as would convey to man the needful instruction. I think this sufficient at present, by way of defining a perfect rule of life. Many other things in my friend's address may come up at another time; such as his dash at Abraham, and the character of some of the Old Testament Saints.

I am not required to defend the character of Abraham, or the absolute morality of the Law of Moses. The proposition does not make any such demand upon me. I heard my friend in the Bible Convention in November last, and I saw the many false issues he was raising in relation to this question. I saw it then, and I wish it understood now, that I am under no obligation to show the absolute perfection of the

Old Testament Scriptures, in order to sustain my proposition, "that the Scriptures contain a series of communications supernaturally revealed, and that in the New Testament we have a perfect rule of life."

I am willing to defend the Old Testament Scriptures, or the Old Testament writers, when we shall have come to the right place—when we enter upon the second feature of the proposition, namely: that in the New Testament man has a perfect rule of life.

We will now proceed to offer an argument in defense of the proposition, that the Jewish and Christian Scriptures contain a series of communications supernaturally revealed and miraculously attested.

Argument 1st: On the authenticity of the Old Testament Scriptures.

The word *authenticity* as defined by Walker and Webster, means *authority: genuineness: the quantity of being authentic: of established authority for truth and correctness.*

This, however, will only apply to the people who receive it as such, for many books are regarded as authentic, and yet not entitled to credit in all their pretensions.

Take for example the Book of Mormon, or the Koran. No one questions the truthfulness of these documents. They are every way reliable as to the origin of the religious systems they contain. Neither can we account for the rise and spread of Mormonism in America and Europe, and Mahometanism in the East, without acknowledging them to be truthful documents as to the origion of these frauds. It is true that in thus admitting the authenticity of the Koran we do not admit that Mahomet made several trips to Heaven and back again, borne upon his steed Borak. "Volney's Ruins," page 96.

"The supreme bounty had itself written the pages of the Koran: then explaining the particular dogmas of Islamism, the Imam unfolded how the Koran, partaking of the divine nature, was increate and eternal, like its author: how it had been sent leaf by leaf in twenty-four thousand nocturnal apparitions of the angel Gabriel: how the angel announced himself by a gentle knocking, which threw the prophet into a cold sweat; how, in the vision of one night, he had traveled over ninety Heavens, riding on the animal Borak, half a horse and half a woman."

It is true that these pretensions were made; but it is not true that these things transpired; therefore we say that the Koran is an authentic record with reference to that embodiment of religious faith, yet in many of its statements not entitled to credit. But did not the people who received it acknowledge its authority? Do they not regard it as genuine? This is true with regard to many other books.

How are we to account for the spread of Mormonism in the United States and in Europe, without acknowledging the authenticity of the book of Mormon? I cannot account for its prevalence, or even for its existence without this; perhaps Mr. Barker can. I can neither account for the existence of Mormonism nor Mahometanism without acknowledging the authenticity of both these books; that they are true and faithful reports of two systems of religous imposition, and yet unworthy of credit.

Why say unworthy of credit? you ask. We reply,

because they are wanting in the necessary *credentials* to prove them of divine or supernatural origin. Do you ask what these *credentials* are? We answer; They are, 1st, Prophecy; 2d, Miracles; with certain corresponding results. "Faber's Difficulties of Infidelity," page 170.

"They say; We will by no means believe on thee, until thou cause a spring of water to gush forth for us out of the earth; or thou have a garden of palm-trees and vines, and thou cause rivers to spring forth from the midst thereof in abundance; or thou cause the Heavens to fall down upon us, as thou hast given out, in pieces; or thou bring down God and the angels to vouch for thee; neither will we believe thy ascending thither, alone, until thou cause a book to descend unto us, bearing witness of thee, which we may read. Answer: My Lord be praised! Am I other than a man, sent as an apostle? And nothing hindereth man from believing, when a direction is come unto them, except, that they say: Hath God sent a man for his apostle? Say: God is a sufficient witness between me and you; for he knoweth and regardeth his servants. [Koran, chap. 17.] They have sworn by God, by the most solemn oath, that if a sign come unto them they would certainly believe therein. Say: Verily signs are in the power of God alone; and he permitteth you not to understand, that, when they come, they will not believe. [Koran, chap. 6.]

Neither the Jewish nor the Christian religion stand wholly upon Prophecy—neither wholly upon Miracle. They stand upon both these, and upon more than these. They, also, rest with ponderous weight upon the internal evidence,—the fruits they produce.

It is a fact that Mahometanism, in its moral and practical tendencies, is unworthy of God. Its results are mischievous. It is the patron of ignorance, superstition and crime, of which its entire history is ample proof. ["Volney's Ruins," page 86.]

"And this religion (Mahomet's,) has not ceased to deluge the earth in blood. Read the history of Islamism, by its own writers, and you will be convinced that one of the principle causes of the wars which has desolated Asia and Africa, since the days of Mahomet, has been the apostolical fanaticism of its doctrine."

Miracles, however, were never designed to make men Christians. Theobject of miracles was to secure for the truth a hearing. They have no power to make men Christians. But more of this at another time.

We say, then, that Judaism had a positive and authoritative existence for a period of *fifteen hundred years*, from Moses to Jesus Christ. It had certain public religious observances, as the Pentecost, Passover, Feast of Tabernacles, &c. These imply:

First: That there is a cause and reason to which they owe their origin.

Second: That there was a time when they commenced.

Third: That there is a place where they began to be observed.

Fourth: That there is a person, or, that there are persons who are mainly instrumental in establishing this system of Religion, with all its forms of worship.

These things enter into the very existence of every Religion, whether true or false, no matter when or whence they originate. This is true of all organizations and associations. It is true of civil government; it is true of our own government. There was a time when Judaism had no visible existence; a time when it began. There is, also, a reason,—a cause for its existence. It was brought into existence by some person or persons. The same is true of the Temperance organization. There is a reason for its formation and existence. There was a time when it began. It owes its existence to six reformed drunkards.

[Half hour up, but by agreement of both the Chairman and Mr. Barker, Mr. Hartzel continued for twenty minutes longer.]

I will not, then, enlarge upon the argument as I intended, but will hasten, though leisurely. The things named, we say, enter into every religion, true or false. These are vital points.

The authenticity of any historical religion is a simple question of *fact*, to be submitted to testimony, the only question being as to who are competent witnesses.

We offer then, in defense of the authenticity of the Jewish Scriptures—

1st. Their own sacred Historians, Poets, and Prophets as competent witnesses.

2d. We offer the writings of Josephus in defense of the authenticity of the sacred Books found in the Bible.

3d. We offer "Letters of certain Jews to Monsieur Voltaire, containing an apology for their own people and for the Old Testament;" a respectable volume, not only for its truthfulness, but, also, for its literary character. It was written in answer to Voltaire.

4th. We offer all the New Testament writers, eight in number. All these concur in the most explicit statements and base their historic facts upon the following admissions:

First. That their religion was derived from a supernatural source—that God himself was the cause and reason of it—that by a series of miracles wrought by the hand of his servant Moses, he brought about their emancipation from slavery, and destroyed their oppressors—that they were sustained by constant miracle for the space of forty years.

Second: That their religion began when God took them by the hand to lead them out of the land of Egypt, in the days of the Egyptian Pharoahs.

Third: That the law was given during their sojourn in the wilderness. Deuteronomy being a recapitulation of it.

Fourth: That Moses was the man chosen of God to be their deliverer and law-giver. That he confirmed his mission and authority by signs and wonders, in the presence of their fathers, Pharoah and his court.

So far as I know, all these witnesses agree. If there are any dissenters among them, my opponent will, of course, bring them forward.

We say, then, briefly, that the Passover was appointed in Egypt. That the children of Israel first observed this feast on the night of their exodus. That God on that night slew the first born of Egypt. Then we have the dividing of the Red Sea, the deliverance of Israel, the destruction of the Egyptians, the pillar of cloud by day, and of fire by night, the giving of the law upon Sinai, their idolatry. Here let me mention a singular fact. Josephus, in his account, passes over one case of idolatry; it is that of their making the molten calf. Josephus, it seems, was not fire-proof, and shrank from recording this most scandalous procedure. Poor, weak human nature! Nothing seems to be so onerous as to be compelled to testify to the disgrace of our fathers. Family pride, and a thousand other elements of man's nature operate against it. But the sacred writers tell the whole story. Moses records it in all its disgraceful particulars, and does not seem disposed to hide any of its deformed features. We must admit that in one particular Josephus failed to record the whole truth, but in the main, he agrees exactly with the other witnesses to which we have referred.

But, to proceed with our summary, we may name the frequent apostacies of the Israelites, God's judgments, fiery serpents, brazen serpents, dividing of the Jordan, the falling of the walls of Jericho, the division of the land—giving none to the tribe of Levi.

This is but a summary, while they agree in a thousand other particulars. There is one point in this argument that must not be overlooked, namely: That the New Testament writers and the unbelieving Jews were much engaged in controversies about things contained in the Law, the Prophets and the Psalms. Both parties appealed to these documents, and claimed them as authentic records. It would have been impossible to have submitted the Old Testament to a more severe test. Jesus Christ made some humiliating applications to the Jews of their own Scriptures. Speaking to the Jewish nation, he says: "Do not think that I will accuse you to the Father, there is one that accuseth you, even Moses, in whom you trust; for had you believed Moses you would have believed me, for he wrote of me." Again: "Did not Moses give you the Law? and not one of you keepeth the law. Why do you go about to kill me?"

As Jesus did, so did the Apostles. They turned the Old Testament Scriptures directly against their adversaries, the Jews; maintained the Gospel, and that Jesus of Nazereth, whom they had crucified, was the Messiah, by an appeal to their own sacred Books. Now if these had ever been contested documents, why appeal to them? Would I be likely to appeal to a contested document, between by friend and myself—one which we both admit to be of doubtful authority? It would be vain for me to hope to sustain myself by such an appeal. But when the Savior made an appeal to the Jewish Scriptures, if the authenticity of these had been disputed in that nation, would they not have thrown off that humiliating application? "Moses gave you the Law, and not one of you keepeth the Law; why then do you go about to kill me?" And so in many other cases, might not a Jew have said: "Your animadversions have fallen upon a contested point. We, as a nation, are not satisfied that Moses was the author of our Law. This question has never been settled. We have always been in doubt as to whether Moses was the author of the Pentateuch."

Now, if my friend will bring testimony bearing upon this point, in opposition to the view we have taken, we will give him credit for it. Our object is to prove that the Jewish nation acknowledged the authenticity of their own sacred Books. The Jews are the Christians' librarians, the keepers of the documents by which the divine character of the Christian Religion is established.

Our conclusions from the argument we have offered, are:

1st. That all religious usages are public monuments of facts.

2d. That they are, therefore, standing proofs through all successive time, that the persons whose memory they thus embalm, and the events they thus record, did once actually exist, and therefore are entitled to credit.

Can the origin of Judaism be accounted for without acknowledging the authenticity of their sacred Books? Can its continued existence for *fifteen hundred* years be accounted for without acknowledging the authenticity of their Scriptures? This is a matter that admits of great amplification. For if the Old Testament is authentic, which we think is proved, then it follows that their religion was communicated to them by God himself. The religion is either from God, or it is the most stupendous falsehood. If it is not divine, the authors have written the basest lies. To fabricate such a story as the destruction of the first-born in Egypt, or the passage of the Red Sea, with the destruction of Pharoah and his hosts, would, at least, be to invent most extraordinary falsehoods: for these are events in relation to which there could be no possibility of mistake. No trickster—no magician could have made the people believe that *they* had passed the Red Sea, while, at the same time, they were remaining in Egyptian slavery; nor that they saw Pharoah and his hosts overwhelmed in the waters of the Red Sea, when, in fact, nothing of the kind had taken place, I *ask*, could the people be thus deceived? We admit that men can be deceived in many things, but not in matters of that character. *Could the people think they looked upon Sinai when in fact they did not?* The account is either true, or it is a *prodigious lie.* So with reference to a hundred other things. The facts must have occurred, or the statements of the writers must have been wilful falsehoods. But I will close my remarks for the present, by offering the testimony of an infidel writer and traveler, with regard to the authenticity of the Pentateuch. The work from which I read, is, "Volney's Ruins," page 33.

"This stream of water without an issue is the river Jordan, and these naked rocks were once the theatre of events which have resounded through the world. Behold that desert of Horeb, and that Mount Sinai, where, by means unknown to the vulgar, a profound and adventurous leader created institutions whose influence extended to the whole human race."

How has it reached the whole human family? We answer, first, by the knowledge of God, imparted through these institutions; they being disseminated, to some extent, throughout the human family.

Second: "Influences have extended to all mankind" in the consummation of that religion; for the Jewish religion was never consummated till the Gospel, in all its glory and majesty, went forth to bear the message of joy and salvation to the world. What is Christianity? It is Judaism perfected—it is prophecy fulfilled—it is the type fulfilled by its corresponding antitype—it is Moses removed and Jesus filling his place. "The Lord thy God will raise up unto thee, a Prophet from the midst of thee, of thy brethren, like unto me; unto him ye shall hearken." "The voice crying in the wilderness, prepare ye the way of the Lord." When the Gospel came in all its fulness and glory, Judaism waned.

It is then, the testimony of Volney, this most learned infidel, that the institutions, created by Moses, "extended to the whole human race." How were they created? He says, "by means unknown to the vulgar." Now what does he mean by the vulgar? He meant, of course, the Jewish people. Volney was a full-blooded infidel, and, like other infidels, would deny everything and affirm nothing; make certain things doubtful, and nothing clear. "By means unknown to the vulgar." This language is characteristic of infidelity. Does he say who the vulgar were? Were they Jews or Gentiles? Was he one of them? He is guarded; all is implication and insinuation. Oh shame! Where is your candor? Where is your compassion for the ignorant and erring, with all your boasted infidelity? The world is deceived; you have the means of undeceiving them, and you will not do it. He knew thousands were as vulgar as I am, who did believe these stories; yet his benevolent soul would not impart the necessary information; for if Volney did not know the means by which Moses accomplished his purposes, how does he know that the means by which he created these institutions were unknown to the vulgar?

MR. HARTZEL'S THIRD ADDRESS.

The point in the address to which we have listened, if there be a point, was quite similar to his last speech of yesterday. The speaker seems to aim at this—to destroy all confidence in human testimony, and thus deprive man of one of the two great guiding principles with which his Creator has endowed him, namely: *faith* and *reason*. Faith and reason are sisters—they are twin sisters, only *faith* is the first-born. We believe before we reason. I do not say we believe before we *have* reason; for the fact is, that belief upon testimony pre-supposes that we have reason. But we believe before we can reason, from premises to conclusions, for it is by the exercise of faith, that reason is enlightened and matured. If the child could not believe that fire would burn—that deep water would drown—that poison would destroy its life, it would be difficult to save infancy from premature death. In that case reason would have to be enlightened by experience, and experience would be fatal.

It is true that he that believeth not shall be destroyed. (It is true with reference to the present life,) and in the Gospel, "he that believeth not shall be damned." Neither can man be educated without faith. Suppose the abecedarian could not believe the first letter in the alphabet was A. The reason why it was A could not be explained upon philosophical principles. He has not reason enough to be convinced of this—to be shown why the first letter is A, and the second B. He must receive this with implicit faith, in the confidence he has in his preceptor.

There are three different states of mind, described by the three following terms: Knowlege, faith and opinion. These are the result of different degrees of evidence. The *first*, is the testimony of our own senses; the *second*, the indubitable testimony of others, verbal or written; the *third*, is the result of testimony not quite reliable. To make myself understood, let me give a few examples.

First. I know there is a material universe—I know I am in this hall, that there is an audience before me. composed of men and women. These are matters of perception, of observation, and, therefore, belong to individual experience.

Second. I believe that Julius Cæsar was emperor of Rome; that Napoleon died in exile; that Cyrus, the Mede, conquered Babylon; that Victoria is now Queen of England; that which was once the experience of some—the present observation of others—is now my faith.

We do not *know* that there was such a man as Julius Cæsar, that there was such a man as Napoleon Bonaparte; or such cities as Babylon, Thebes, Rome, or Ninevah. These belong to the domain of faith. We rest upon the conviction as true and certain, and we feel the same amount of moral certainty, with regard to these persons and places, as we can feel with reference to our being within these walls.

I do not say that every item in history is reliable. We take no such position. But because there are a few inaccuracies in history, and historians differ a little in details, shall we, therefore, say that history is always untrustworthy, and thus destroy all confidence in that portion of history which is susceptible of satisfactory proof? It is not a matter of knowledge that Jesus Christ rose from the dead, (it was to some of the first Christians.) That belongs to faith.

Third. *Opinion*—doubtful testimony—amounting only to probability. There are many theologians who suppose that Melchisedec, King of Salem, was one of the sons of Noah. Others, that he was no other that Noah himself. This is but opinion, and will forever remain opinion until we have certain evidence,—then it will be faith. Again: there are many things in nature concerning which we can only form an opinion. It is the opinion of some that the *moon* is a world similar to that which we inhabit. That it is the abode of living beings; that there are lakes, and rivers, and mountains on it; but this is opinion, not faith, supported by analogy only. Men can reason beautifully from analogy; but analogy proves nothing, and can only produce that state of mind designated by the word *opinion.* In matters purely secular we are often compelled to act upon opinion, or on the stronger probability. I wish here to read Mr. Barker's distinction between faith and opinion. He says: [" Christian," Vol. 1, page 24.]

"My opinions are always undergoing some change; so that if I were to take to myself a name from my opinions, I must be frequently changing my name. But while my opinions undergo changes, my faith, my hope, my love remain the same; and the NAME CHRISTIAN serves me to the last. Again; if I take to myself a name from any of my opinions, I identify myself with all who hold that opinion; and cut myself off from all who do not hold it. I know no opinion which may not be held by BAD men; and I do not consider it proper to identify myself with bad men. And I know no opinion which may not be rejected by good men,—by Godly believers in Christ; and I consider it not right to cut myself off from the fellowship of any that are truly Christians. Besides, if I give myself a name derived from any particular opinion, and so identify myself with all who hold it, I am quickly made answerable for all the other opinions, which are held by such men, as well as for all their vices."

With reference to opinions, therefore, in matters purely religious, we have little to do. There are such things in the Bible. With regard to these we will say " let every man be fully persuaded in his own mind." But all the items of Christian faith and practice are so clearly defined, that he that " runs may read."

We are compelled to rest upon testimony, which

is but another word for faith, in many of the *impor-that*, affairs of the present life. We act more frequently upon faith than upon knowledge, and the reason of this is, *that we believe more than we know.* This must always be the case in the present world. Mr. Barker himself is compelled to act upon faith in his efforts to benefit human kind; for, some how or other, little confidence as he has in human testimony, little as he seems to have in human integrity, he has wrought himself up to the belief that by his repeated thrusts at religion, he will become the *savior* of the world and of his race; redeem us from superstition, and remove that mighty weight which crushes humanity; namely, a superstitious belief in the Bible. I cannot but admire my friend's zeal; it is worthy of imitation, and, in my humble opinion, a better *cause.*

If, then, faith is of such transcendant importance, as we have already shown, in all that pertains to human conduct in the affairs of the present life, even the most important, is it, therefore, marvelous, that God should have pitched our salvation upon this principle? It is a beautiful axiom of the New Testament, that Chrtstians "walk by faith, not by sight." *Our reason examines the testimony, and our credulity receives the truth upon the recommendation of reason.* Now the man believes; now he feels; now he acts, if the testimony is that kind which calls for action. I said we *believed* more than we *know.* Our knowledge is our own experience. It is what has passed under our own observation. "By faith we understand that the worlds were made by the word of God;" what others heard and saw from the beginning of the world is our faith, so far as history has transmitted their experience. Deprive me of faith and you deprive me of all the experience and observation of others, and the best means of improvement. This cannot be done:—*yes it can be done.* Our friend is a living example of its truth. Those who were present yesterday and heard his discourse, want no further proof that it can be done; and, for the benefit of those who were not in yesterday, we shall simply say, that he has no confidence in the testimony of Christians—none in the Bible—none in ecclesiastical history—none in his own; for, if I mistake not, he did concede, that, while he was an itinerating Methodist preacher, he did lie.

Mr. Barker. I certainly did not concede anything of the kind.

Mr. Hartzel. He disclaims it; but if my ears deceived me, mine were not the only ears that were deceived. Mr. Barker has, at least, very little confidence in his own testimony, or that of others. We ask him to be consistent, and shake out of his mind all that yet remains of historic information, as a man would shake the dust out of his garments. This done, then let him make a net estimate of the capital stock on hand. I judge his head would be as an emptied vessel, *comparatively.*

We thank Heaven that this wayward skepticism is wholly impracticable. We do receive the testimony of men; we could neither live in, nor enjoy society without giving credence to human testimony.*

Mr. Barker says that, "owing to man's propensity to falsifiy, we cannot place confidence in what men have spoken or written." *Well*, then, there *may have been* such a man as Napoleon, or there *may* not. He may have been a great general, and emperor, or he *may* not; he *may have died* in exile or he may not. So of all men, great and small, whose names have been handed down to posterity. Why these universal sweeping calumnies? It is true he did say this morning that there were *some* good men among Chris-

---

*Bible, or "the Book," so called by way of eminence. We do not here enquire whence came it, but what is it? what is it to me? In a certain sense it is history, all history to me. Its truths, facts, doctrines, statutes, ordinances, precepts, promises, threatenings, together with all the personalities — however awful in name — divinely glorious in character, or those of more humble title and character inferior, all come to me in the form of history.

History may be simple or complex. The history of Dr. Johnson, by Boswell, is the history of an individual, and, therefore, simple. But the history of the Decline and Fall of the Roman Empire, by Edward Gibbon, Esq., is the history of Empires, Governments, Subjects, Revolutions, etc., hence its complexity. The Bible, like the latter, is not the history of an individual in his DRAMATIC EXISTENCE; but the history of God and man, in their relations and doings. This would be the impression made upon the unsophisticated mind from the opening of the book. In the first chapter, God has but the one title, God, and is represented as Creator only. In the second, we find Lord as a prefix. "Lord, a master, a person possessing supreme power and authority, a ruler, a governor." "And the Lord God commanded the man, saying, of every tree of the Garden thou mayest freely eat." Gen. 2, 16.

The word LORD, in its introduction, is significant of a new relation. We have, then, in the literal use of these divine titles, the parties in the history, and their relative position to each other. God, Creator; Man, the Creature. "And the Lord God commanded," possessing supreme authority, Man, the humble subject.

What would we expect a faithtul history to be, when such are the parties? If, in its details, we should find nothing but what is perfect, divine, Godlike, we should be led to suspect that we had not understood the title-page, or the work was a fraud, or as PER CONTRA, if we should find nothing in the book but the weakness, imperfections, follies, wickedness, incident to humanity, (or humanity in its best developements) we would say the e is some misunderstanding, or deception, for the book does not fil. the terms of the prospectus.

A few words, then, in regard to the contents of this history. (Our space forbids even a summary.) God, as Creator, is Proprietor; as Lord, he is moral Governor; has the right to act legislatively, judicially, executively; also, as the instructor, (not of his brute offspring, governed by instinct,) but his rational offspring — the creature of education, capable of intellectual and moral improvement. Now, let the reader look at man in all these implied relations, dependencies, liabilities, etc. In all equitable governments, human and divine, are first, the capability of humble acquiescing obedience, and second, the fearful liability of revolt and rebellion — "FOR HE THAT CANNOT FALL CANNOT STAND," and vice versa. This is true in all governmental relations.

In the historical details of the Bible are brought together the infinite and the finite, the perfect and the imperfect in their widest range, with all their inequalities and disproportions, We would expect few parallels and many contrasts The writers, in

tians. I listened yesterday for something of the kind; but he made no exceptions. The direction of these eccentric views in relation to history, both sacred and profane, is quite obvious. If human testimony is reliable in human affairs, why not in things religious and divine? It is necessary to invalidate it in order to deprive the Bible of the benefit of that source of evidence. So infidels begin by doubting first the truth of human testimony, when it bears upon unwelcome truth; and secondly they doubt its credibility in the common occurrences of life, for the sake of self defense. These are but the different

---

passing from the one to the other, would introduce the extremes that exist between the parties; now a display of the divine, then of the human, with all their differential and characteristic peculiarities.

This view accounts for many things supposed to be objectionable in the subject matter of the volume. The perfect and the imperfect, the sublime and the ridiculous, the glorious and the in-glorious are found upon the same page of necessity.

God's effort to instruct man, and man's waywardness to receive instruction. God's laws and man's violations. God's judicial proceedings, both for the benefit of the offender and the vindication of his own government. Here we see God and man in loving peace and amity, and there in awful conflict; now enjoying the smiles of his beneficent countenance, and then feeling his chastening rod for diciplinary purposes and admonitory examples to others. Here we see man under different dispensations, different degrees of light and moral training.

To close these hints to the reader, let me briefly state, that, on account of the great antiquity of the book, the great brevity of its early portions, the variety of design, the different personalities appearing upon the stage, each casting his own shadow upon the canvas, and its wide expanse stretching over the world's entire history, to the morning of creation, when time, like a diverging ray of light, sprang from the bosom of eternity, then forward to the world's evening, when her last sun shall set and time shall be no more, the Bible has a complexity not found in any other book.

These things taken into the account, (and the candid will consider them) many of the supposed contradictions vanish, and others are easily reconciled. Much that appears to us gross in the conduct of the ancients, and uncouth in conversation, is palliated, and in many instances justified, without license or detriment to those living under a dispensation of clearer light and a more full revelation of duty; "where much is given, much will be required."

God, occupying a place so conspicuous in the Bible, reconciles the contradiction of all contradictions, namely: the concessions that all leading infidels make in favor of the Bible. As I have one before me I will transcribe it: "The Bible is pervaded by a sentiment which is implied everywhere, namely: THE SYMPATHY OF THE PURE AND PERFECT GOD WITH THE HEART OF EACH FAITHFUL WORSHIPER. This is that which is wanting in the Greek Philosophers, English Deists, German Pantheists, and all formalists. This is that which so often edifies me in Christian writers and speakers, when I ever so much DISBELIEVE THE LETTER OF THEIR SENTENCES." This concession in favor of the Bible, Christian writers and speakers, and condemnation of English Deism, Greek Philosophy, &c., is from the pen of Mr. Newman, one of the German Neologists. See Phases, page 188.

Similar concessions are found in all popular infidel books. Such admissions, coming from such a source are honorable to the Bible, and would be ineplicable upon any other principle than, that the infidel himself HEARS GOD, SEES GOD, FEELS GOD to be revealed in the Bible, as he is nowhere else.

stages on the road that leads to *sheer* atheism, until the madman says in his heart "there is no God."

We have an illustration of this in our friend Barker. He has told us how he passed on from one step to another in unbelief, until he has reached his present position. And, I fear, his rapid progress will carry him still farther. I do not know where he will stop, but I am sure our friend is a locomotive of more than ordinary speed.

But Christians "receive the witness of men: the witness of God is still greater." Christians have the benefit of the experience and observation of the whole world for their text-book, and all they can acquire by their own efforts. And yet they are not the most credulous people in the world. I think infidels are, in many cases, as credulous as Christians, and can believe on as weak evidence; indeed, I think many of them are more credulous. I ask, who have been the foremost, for the last ten or fifteen years, to go into the most extravagant delusions, receiving them as true? Have they not, upon the weakest testimony, been the first to run after the various forms of modern necromancy, and *spirit rappings?* Are they not more credulous in matters of that kind than Christians?

"The Bible," he says, "stands in the way of human improvement." We call for the proof. If our friend had not anticipated on this point, we should have called him out upon this subject in the second feature of our proposition, namely, "that in the

Christian Scriptures man has a perfect rule of life." He says that his father regarded every word in the Bible as true and divine; as the word of God, and he was taught to believe so. Well, I cannot be held responsible for his blunders, or what his father taught him. I do not know one intelligent Christian, who believes that the Bible is unqualifiedly the word of God. I may say of McIlvaine, Horne, Campbell, and all the defenders of the truth of the Bible, who are entitled to respect, do not hold to this view which Mr. Barker says has been generally taught; and the same is true of all Bible defenders of any credit.

A word as to translations, and the manner in which the Bible has been translated. I must say to my friend that he has anticipated a little too far. The *origin* of the Bible is the question at present. When the other shall come up in logical order we shall be ready to meet it. I will, however, notice a remark on different readings. He says there are one hundred and fifty thousand different readings of the Bible. This is a great number. I ask, do these different readings—mere verbal differences in the translations of certain portions of the Bible, necessarily effect its authenticity? I acknowledge there are different readings, but I *deny* the number given. The authorities do not give so many. Some of them say twenty thousand—some of them twenty-four thousand. But what then? Does it follow that the Book is not entitled to credit? I ask in the first place, whether the same things may not be told in different words? Different words may be selected to tell the same story, yet both forms be strictly true. We have many different ways in writing the same thing in our own language. We have many words that convey the same idea, and many others, with only shades of difference which, when placed in certain connections, have the same meaning. Once we spelled *favour*, now *favor; Saviour* now *Savior; labour* now *labor*. Once we spelled *antient*, now *ancient*. There have been great changes in the orthography of our language, but I ask whether these have effected any important change in the grammer of our language? So there are these different readings, we admit; but we deny the legitimacy of Mr. Barker's reasonings. Mr. Barker says there are a great many different versions of the Bible. I grant it. I have two on the stand. Let my friend take two or three approved versions, such as have been approved by Protestant Christendom, and compare their different readings for our enlightenment, and let the audience judge of the merits of these verbal differences in the present issue.

MR. HARTZEL'S FOURTH ADDRESS.

I claim I have the right to introduce any individual as a witness. If I can employ my opponent as a witness to establish my position, I will do so. I said yesterday that I did not hold him responsible on any scholastic question; or any question of speculative theology; but that I would hold him responsible on questions of historic fact, or references made in his own writings to history, for the purpose of establishing and sustaining the position which he occupied while he was a minister. I say so still. Mr. Barker says the sacred historians are not "competent witnesses." In this, however, he has only followed in the track of his predecessors, for they have always labored to discredit sacred history. Suppose we were discussing some question involving English institutions; what historians would we rely upon? Would we rely upon German historians only, in things appertaining to the early existence of English institutions, or would we go to the French writers to decide upon English customs and usages? Certainly not. We could not reject all English writers—those who lived at the very time the events transpired, or those of the next subsequent period—and seek in the writings of other nations the true history of English institutions, and how they were brought into existence. But, in some instances, we would prize English history more than French or German, supposing that all were relating facts highly disreputable to the nation. I ask, whether we would not have more confidence in the English historians than either the French or the German, though all related the same things? The latter would have no sacrifices to make.

The writers, both of the Old and New Testament, have detailed matters disreputable to their own people. I ask, whether this should not be received as additional testimony of their integrity?

The Papacy, our friend says, has an existence. We agree in this. But how can we account for that existence without acknowledging history to be authentic and reliable?

We did not say that the religion of the Jews, as a whole, began in a day; we only say that it had a beginning, and that it dated its commencement in Egypt; that the Law was given during their forty years sojourn in the wilderness.

With regard to the magicians, referred to by my opponent, I did not expect to hear that old infidel hobby from him. We had a right to expect something new and original from him, after his declaration "that infidels had abandoned all the arguments of their predecessors." He must have been either ignorant or dishonest when he declared that fact to the world. I am not disposed to charge him with either the one or the other, yet his recurrence to these old objections looks a little suspicious. I believe that infidels, generally, have looked upon their predecessors as having failed to answer fully the arguments that have been offered in favor of the claims of the Bible. His objection, drawn from the affair of the magicians, is an old objection. It is not in the premises that the magicians were equal to Moses or to God; not in the premises that there was any doubt as to the result of the contest. "Then came the magicians with their enchantments."

It is not admitted at all by the writer that these magicians were equal to Moses or to Aaron. They brought up frogs, covering the entire surface. Now, could the magicians do this to the same extent, when the surface was already covered by the frogs, brought up by Moses? All they could do was to clear off a little spot which the frogs of Moses and Aaron had pre-occupied. They could only operate on a small scale. But divine interposition was required to do what was done by the hand of Moses and Aaron. But enough of this.

[Here followed a recapitulation, for the benefit of those not present on the preceding day, which is omitted.]

[*Some new matter added to the Recapitulation.*]

If all these witnesses, sacred and profane, are to be thrown aside as worthless, then there is an end to all credit due to historic testimony. If they all concur in their statements, when they had so many inducements to contradict them, is not this proof that the matter was well established? If there had been any question as to the facts recorded by Nehemiah, and pressed home upon the Jews by Christ and his Apostles, would they not have said? "show that we have departed from the Law of the Lord. Prove your charges to be true." If the question had not been settled—if the law had not been regarded as authentic, these individuals would have said: "Stop, sirs; these are contested points. First prove that Moses gave us that Law, before you charge us with departing from it."

Nehemiah charged the Jews with disregarding the law of marriage, and he contended with them and rebuked them for their transgression. If there had been any question among them, with reference to the authenticity of the Pentateuch, would they not have said, "Nehemiah you are a little too fast, sir. This is a disputed matter. Our Scribes and Elders are not agreed among themselves upon this question. We are not sure that our Law has not been corrupted by interpolations. The genuineness of our Law, in its present form, is with many a matter of doubt."

Nothing of this kind is developed in the way of self-defense, but all, both accuser and accused, appealed to the supremacy of the Law. And the Apostles never found so much as one unbelieving Jew, who did not acknowledge the Old Testament Scriptures to be reliable, but differed with them only in the application of Prophecy to New Testament times and circumstances. I believe no documentary evidence could be stronger than that we have given. Certainly nothing can be more clear than this, that the Jews received their sacred books as authentic, and if authentic, true; because *fully*-sustained by Prophecy and Miracle.

We now proceed with the argument, in proof of our proposition "that the Jewish and Christian

Scriptures contain a series of communications supernaturally revealed and miraculously attested."

We shall read from Genesis, chap. 12: 1—3.

1. Now the Lord had said unto Abraham, get thee out of thy country, and from thy kindred, and from thy father's house, unto a land that I will show thee.

2. And I will make of thee a great nation, and I will bless thee, and make thy name great, and thou shalt be a blessing.

3. And I will bless them that bless thee, and curse him that curseth thee, and in thee shall all families of the earth be blessed.

The first of these promises will be the beginning of a series of supernatural communications, that is, communications which could not have been discovered by man's perceptive powers. These promises form the basis of the Christian Religion.

Here are three promises. We propose to base an argument on each of them. By the word *promise* in this place, we mean a declaration of a benefit intended, or the bestowment of some future good. Promises are like Prophesies, in the future tense.

"And I will make of thee a great nation."

Argument second: This promise was made to Abraham while, as yet, he had no child. We must refer to the subsequent history of Abraham and his descendants, for the fulfillment of this promise. First: The Jews, the descendants of Abraham, yet are. This gives them a high antiquity, an essential element to national greatness. What nation can now claim the same? and by its own history trace its origin back for four thousand years, to one *man* and one *woman*, and say, "here is the flesh and blood of Abraham and Sarah." Is there a parralel in the history of mankind? The descendants of a man who existed four thousand years ago can yet lift up their arms and say, "here is the *flesh* and *blood* and *sinew* of Abraham." We have no list of the number of the Jews, but it is supposed by many to be as great as at any former period. The Jewish nation is a family nation. It is not made up of many nations, as the American nation, which is a nation of nations. But here we have a nation derived from one single family. We have no statistical account by which we can determine the whole number from the birth of Isaac to the present day. We can only say that, in point of numbers, they are the greatest nation that ever existed.

Second: Great men are also essential to national greatness. The Jews had Kings, Prophets, Judges, Artists, Musicians, Orators, Historians and Poets.

"Who shall ascend into the hill of the Lord? and who shall stand in his holy place? He that hath clean hands and a pure heart. Who hath not lifted up his soul unto vanity or sworn deceitfully." Is there a Poet to be found in antiquity that gives such exalted views of God and moral worth as David? They had also very distinguished female Poets; such as Miriam, the Prophetess, who, with timbrel in hand, breaks forth: "Sing ye to the Lord, for he hath triumphed gloriously; the horse and the rider he hath thrown into the sea." There was also John the Baptist, the greatest of all Prophets, and Jesus Christ, the son of Abraham, according to the flesh, and all the holy Apostles and Evangelists of Jesus Christ our Lord, who were, under God, the redeemers, the benefactors, the saviors of mankind.

Third: This nation was great, on account of its varied fortunes. First, they were *captives*, then *captors;* great in war, mighty in battle, when executing their mission against the Canaanites. "*One* chased a thousand, and *two* put ten thousand to flight." Again they became captives — their Capitol and Temple were destroyed, and the nation held in captivity for seventy long years. Again emancipated, they return to their own land — rebuild their metropolis, and their Temple — which was the wonder of the world, on account of its magnificence — restore their religion, and become once more an independent nation, for some five hundred years; then became tributary to Roman despotism — and finally, besieged by their enemies for three years, and after a most terrible and unparalleled resistance, were destroyed by those who had long oppressed them. When compared with others, they were great in privileges, in goodness, in crime, in sufferings, in honors and sins; and God's judgments upon them were always proportionate, and yet they existed under circumstances most *peculiar*.

MR. HARTZEL'S FIFTH ADDRESS.

It is always embarrassing when a great mass of irrevelant matter has been introduced into a speech. This is my present embarrassment. To select from this mass that which is worthy of a passing remark, and omit the balance, is not the most easy task.

"Dr. Nelson" is a man of no authority with us; and, so far as I am informed with his celebrity as an ecclesiastical writer, he was never *famous* for his defense of the authenticity of the Scriptures. Whatever importance Christians have attached to his work, has been from other considerations than his defense of the Old and New Testament Scriptures against the assaults of infidelity.

So many witnesses, all concurring in so many facts, are sufficient to establish the authority of any book. It was for this purpose, we offered the Old and New Testament writers—Josephus and "Letters of Jews to Voltaire." We did not introduce witnesses to prove that the Old Testament was true. The point of our whole argument, was simply as to the *authenticity* of the Scriptures, more especially of the Old Testament. Now, I say again—if so many concurring witnesses in any one fact, or series of connected facts, do not prove one point, then there is an end to credulity in testimony. "In the mouth of two or three witnesses every word shall be established," is an old law maxim. My opponent says, it was a long time before the Jews had any authentic history. I beg leave to differ from him. Are not the books of Kings, Samuel, Judges, witnesses? They had these historical writings long before Chronicles, etc., Josephus or the New Testament. My friend said, the Jews never originated a book.* He admitted, that he was not quite certain that they had not. Why then bring matters of that kind into controversy? Is it merely to perplex and confuse? I thought all extraneous matters should be left out. I propose, then, to show by reference to my friend's own writings that, that matter is not quite so doubtful as he seemed

* The Christian Religion has had a positive existence for, at least, eighteen hundred years. Its facts, commandments, promises, with all that enters into its constituency are found in the New Testament. That the Book is, is not a debateable question, but how came it to be, is one of the many points upon which the Christian and infidel take issue. The way Christians account for the origin of this Book is known to all, and their faith in this respect has been uniform ; namely, that the several parts of the Book were written by those to whom they are accredited. Infidels take issue, and say, not so. Still this does not reach the main question, for the BOOK did not produce the RELIGION, but the RELIGION produced the BOOK. The religion was, and many were its adherents before it assumed its historic book form. What, then, are the infidel theories upon the simple question of origin? No man on earth can tell. They have been numerous and varied. But Mr. Barker has now abandoned the old theory, that Christianity originated in fraud, and has adopted a modern discovery ; namely, that Christianity never had a beginning. Well, then, it is eternal. "No, why don't you understand us? it began by degrees." I think I get your meaning now ; as a volcano or a river forms its alluvial, deposits a little at a time, not of earth to be sure, but a deposit of tradition, say on this wise, some good men discovered a good idea involving an important moral duty ; perhaps he added another, that made two ; (well, that was a beginning,) he revealed it to another; he enlarged upon it; he to a third; he made some advance, and now it became a growing tradition ; in this way all the moral precepts were brought into existence, and no inspiration in the question. Tell me, now, how of miracles? Pshaw, there is no trouble about them. "I have raised the dead myself ;" that is, I gave a man some medicine, who was supposed to be dead ; he soon revived ; the people who saw this said I had "raised the dead ;" so the story went, and you, a good honest man, let it go at that ! Why not? You know a story never loses anything ; no, no, and so the story obtained currency and credit until every body believed it. In this way all the miracles in the Bible were invented. We can acconnt for all these tales about miracles upon the principle of man's credulity, his love of the marvelous, and his known propensity to exaggerate, without the exercise of any supernatural power, or the charge of deliberate falsehood. Then, this religion in its primordial state was clearly not an origination, but a growth, the production of many minds, acting together for ages, contributing to the general stock of traditionary information.

1st. How, then, came these floating gossiping traditions to be worked up into a book? Was it the work of an individual? How did it get into his head to collate and embody them? If he took all the traditions as he found them it must have been a traditionary religion *par excellence.* I judge, however, he rejected some. On that supposition he must have been a man of fine taste, and no ordinary genius in classification and arrangement.

to insinuate. Mr. Barker handed me the pamphlet I now hold in my hand, in November last, and accompanied the gift with this remark—"This contains my views of the Bible."

Mr. Barker. Mr. Hartzel's statement is incorrect. I could not have used the words he attributed to me, as the views expressed in that book have not been held by me for a number of years.

Mr. Hartzel. Mr. Barker, you did positively say so. Farther, this "Review" was published in '48.

Mr. Barker. '46.

Mr. Hartzel. No, sir, 1848 is the time on the

As we have substituted dogmatism for testimony in this investigation, I incline to this opinion; that the eight writers of the New Testament met together in convention, for the purpose of embodying these invaluable traditions, that they might not be lost by the "moulderings" of time, nor yet corrupted by the wicked; and, as they could not agree upon the whole among themselves — what should be admitted and what rejected — they each recorded what he thought worthy of presentation and transmission. Will not this account for their agreement and disagreement? *If it does infidelity has gotten out of one trouble.*

2nd. How did it happen that this vast deposit of tradition originated wholly among the Jews, who had done so before, transplanting a few traditions, (out of whose garden I don't know, neither do I care just now,) got them growing, and from these grew a religion, and from that religion grew a huge folio.

3rd. This last book of Jewish tradition, imperfect as it now is, is yet much admired, and by many it is supposed to be the best book in the world. What must it have been in its *more perfect state*? It is said by some that it has been greatly marred by "transcribers, translators," by "interpolations," additions," "through mistake and policy." We know that structures in the process of time, will "moulder" down to "ruin," and when we shall see palaces moulder into existence, then may we bestow more thought upon this way of accounting for the origin of the Christian religion.

4th. The Christian religion like the United States government, had its incipient stages. These were the times of their origination; not by the gathering up of vaporus traditions, but by the discovery of and right appreciation of religions and political truth, and the development of a series of connected facts.

The one gave rise in the short period of three years to *a new religion*, the other in the space of some seven years called into existence a *new form of civil government*. The time, the facts, the instrumentalities employed in the originating of our Republic are matters of historic credibility. Before George the III, King of England, I find nothing in the history of the world with reference to our "Constitution," "laws," and national independence. Since then our body politic has been a prominent portion of the civil history of the world. So in regard to the origin of the Christian church. Before the reign of Tiberius Cæsar, we never find the words "Jesus Christ," "Christianity," "Christian," "church of Christ," in any history Since then these terms are as familiar history as household words in the domestic circle.

There are no facts in the history of human kind that have more, and more credible vouchers than, that the Christianity of the New Testament assumed a positive existence in A. D. 34: that it was called into being by the supernatural agencies to which its inspired history refers the readers for an account of its origin; and, we can only say, we pity the man who has so far lost his balance as to adopt the vague conjectures and strongly asserted dogmatisms of skeptical doubters.

title-page. I proceed to read from Mr. Barker's Review of the Bible, pages 4 and 7.

4. "The Mosaic account of creation is, in general, true: but in many of its particulars it is, in my judgment, doubtful, or plainly fabulous." 7. "In substance, the account of Moses in reference to these matters may be perfectly true: but as to the particular form of the story, I believe it to be fabulous."

This is good testimony for me: for he must regard the matters which he has written out as true. He must have received this from a reliable source or he could have regarded the subject matter of "Genesis as true." Can my friend, after what he has written, still say that there are some doubts whether the Jews ever originated a book? If he can prove this, I must fail in my effort to maintain the proposition. But I will read farther on this point, from Mr. Barker's "Review of the Bible," page 10:

"Who originated those accounts is unknown. It would be foolish to suppose that any single individual originated them. They were probably the production of a multitude of minds operating for ages. The person who first wrote them, only collected them perhaps, and reduced them to something like form and order. The person who first put them in the form in which they stand in the book of Genesis, very probably, took them from records or books that had been written previously. No doubt he regarded them himself as true. He probably selected them from other accounts or traditions, less worthy of regard."

From these we infer, that Moses was the author of the Pentateuch. Certainly we may hold our friend responsible for this matter of historic knowledge in his recent writings. Surely, my learned friend had the means of knowing at the time he published that pamphlet, whether Moses or somebody else was the author of Genesis. The account of creation was called in question. With reference to the supposed discrepancy between Geology and Genesis, we may simply say that all his remarks on that subject have fallen upon a contested point. There are authors on both sides; some of them we will name: Brewster, Pye, Smith, Hitchcock, Horsely, Harris, Smucker, Dr. Bedford, &c. These all claim a perfect harmony between Geology and the cosmogony of Moses. The inquisitive, we refer to these works. I have not read all of them, but have examined some, and have referred to others. This investigation is not legitimate in a question of this kind. My proposition does not require me to reply to these cavils. The question is not, is the Mosaic account of creation in harmony with physical science? Permit me to say, however, that when Geologists shall have harmonized their conflicting views with reference to this science, many of the present difficulties may be obviated. As the science of Geology advances they will vanish. This has already been the result to some extent; and, I doubt not, will be more so as the science shall be better understood. I admit there are apparent difficulties; but I do not admit that they effect the question. Geology is a young science, and should be modest.

As Mr. Barker has not met me, I shall proceed with the series of arguments I introduced in this morning's session: To prove that the Bible contains a consecutive series of communications, which man could never have discovered by the exercise of his perceptive faculties, or by his own meditations. I was broken off, in my last, before I had reached the conclusion of my argument. I was saying that notwithstanding all the varied fortunes of the Jews, they still exist as a nation under circumstances most peculiar.

If the Jews possessed *originality* enough to invent a system that has stood for four thousand years, through all the vicissitudes of fortune to which they were subjected, they must have been in advance of all the nations that have ever lived, in originality and inventiveness. Has not God, then, fully sustained his pledge to Abraham? "And I will make of thee a great nation."

Argument 3d: "And I will make thy name great."

Many of the reasons of Abraham's great name were given in the preceding argument; to which we may add, that perhaps his chief personal excellence consisted in believing what God said to him, and in doing what He commanded him. None of the great names of antiquity will compare with his. They are all wanting in the right kind of association. The greatest nation on earth has said for *four thousand* years, "Abraham is our father." The seers and prophets of olden time pronounced his name with filial respect. So did Paul and Peter, and all the Apostles and first Evangelists of the kingdom of Heaven. And even John the Baptist the "greatest" of all the Prophets, and Jesus the son of Mary, in whom dwelt all the treasures of wisdom and knowledge, claim Abraham to be their father according to the flesh; and, with delight, did honor to his venerable name. He has other children by the law of Gospel adoption. See Galatians, chap. 3: 26, 27, 28, 29: "For ye are all the children of God by faith in Christ Jesus. For as many of you as have been baptised into Christ, have put on Christ. There is neither Jew nor Greek, there is neither bond nor free, there is neither male nor female: for ye are all one in Christ Jesus. And if ye be Christ's, then ye are Abraham's seed, and heirs according to the promise."

There will be an innumerable host which no man can number. The excellent ones of all the earth—the benefactors of their race—the redeemers of mankind from ignorance, idolatry, slavery, intemperance—all these associate with this name the whole scheme of human redemption—and this name is still increasing in greatness in the exact ratio to the spread of the Gospel, both at home and in distant heathen lands. The Gospel bears it upon its wings, and every edition of the Bible gives it a wider circulation and more enduring fame; and it will increase in greatness while sun and moon endure.

Here, we ask, has God been a defaulter in relation to this promise? "And I will make thy name great."

Argument 4th: "And in thee shall all families of the earth be blessed."

But Mr. Barker quarrels with this promise. We

cannot do better than to refer him and the audience to his own testimony given in former times. See "Christianity Triumphant," page 186:

"But turn to the religion of Christ, and the scene is all changed. Here charity is inculcated in all its glory: here we find ourselves living and breathing in a new element: here we walk up and down in a universe of love. The religion of Heaven is a religion of love from first to last. Even in its earliest dispensations it breathed the spirit of its benevolent Author, and taught men to look forward to the regeneration of the world as the end of all his plans. In the revelations which were given to Abraham, God declared it to be his purpose, that through him and his seed, "all families of the earth should be blest." All succeeding intimations of the purposes of God are of the same description: all bear the stamp of unbounded and impartial goodness."

To bless, is to make "happy; to prosper." Men are blessed when the means of happiness are afforded them. For example, the people of Ohio are greatly blessed by their public improvements. The people of our State are greatly blessed in their means of traveling and transportation. We go by railroad speed. We are, also, blessed by our means of telegraphic communication, by our various internal improvements. We say, in our village, we are greatly blessed with facilties for the education of our children; a benevolent individual having made an appropriation of some ten thousand dollars in the erection of a beautiful structure, with philosophical apparatus, library, etc., and now tenders the occupancy to our community.

This promise imports "that in Abraham and his seed should all families of the world be blessed" with the means of happiness. This is all God or man can do to promote the happiness of our fallen race; fo happiness implies man's own free agency, and the voluntary use of the means of improvement and salvation.

As this language is promissory, it is, therefore, in the future tense. Shortly before, and about the time the Messiah made his appearance, there was a general expectation all over the East, that some illustrious personage would soon make his appearance both among Jews and Gentiles. Orators spoke of him, and poets sang of him. This expectation was created by prophetic announcements, to which we shall pay some attention in due time. In the mean time we shall open to the New Testament, and read the first verse of the first chapter of Matthew.

"The Book of the generation of Jesus Christ, the son of David, the son of Abraham."

This is the commencement of the genealogy of Jesus Christ, or rather Matthew's preface to it.

Jesus Christ is, then, the son of Abraham, through David. Abraham is the progenitor of the Messiah by oft repeated promises. Matthew wrote to the Jews of Judea, who were in possession of both the promises and prophecies. It was, therefore, all important that he should convince them that Jesus Christ had descended from Abraham through King David. Upon this would depend his success with the Jews. He could not reasonably expect that any of his countrymen would receive him as their long promised Messiah without being fully satisfied on this point. Many Jews were satisfied. The Apostles themselves were satisfied, otherwise they would not have received Jesus of Nazareth as their Messiah. He might have been a son of Abraham, by another branch of his family; but the Prophets had named David, and as he could not be a son of David without descending from Abraham, therefore in proving the *latter* you establish the *former*. We, therefore, affirm that Jesus of Nazareth is a son of Abraham after the flesh.

I now call attention to the second feature of this promise, namely; that Jesus Christ was a blessing to all families of the earth. We would infer this from the angelic announcement of his birth. "Fear not; for, behold I bring you good tidings of great joy, which shall be to all people." Mark the reading. These words are rich with blessings "*unto all people*." These give to the blessings a universal application "*unto all people*." This was a grand conception. Something new and original in the history of our world. Hitherto there was no religion that embraced all nations. Judaism was the religion of a single family. It was not adapted to all people.

The different forms of Paganism were nothing but State instruments, used by State agents, for State purposes. They rose with the State and perished with the State, hence there were State Gods and Provincial Gods. But not so with the Christian Religion. Its very announcement shows that it was intended for the benefit of all nations — a religion in which " all families of the earth should be blessed" — a religion, such as the human mind could not have originated — such as the human family, during their existence of four thousand years, with all their wisdom and intelligence had never conceived of.

When this personage, of whose nativity we have been speaking, was about to finish his earthly mission, we hear him say, in the language of authority, to eleven men, "Go ye, therefore and teach all nations. Go preach the Gospel to every creature — he that believeth, and is baptised, shall be saved, and he that believeth not shall be damned." Make the tender of salvation to all nations!

What a coincidence between the promise, in its expressed designs, through Abraham's promised seed, and the birth of Christ! The anthem sung by the angels at the nativity, was: "Fear not, for behold, I bring you glad tidings of great joy, which shall be to all people. Glory to God in the highest. Peace on earth, good will to men." The promise to Abraham was: "In thee and thy seed shall all the families of earth be blessed." In the anthem, not the literal descendants of Abraham alone, but all the world is invited to partake of the blessing. "Behold I bring you glad tidings of great joy, which is unto all people. For unto you is born this day, in the city of David, a Savior, who is Christ the Lord." Now, the commission which Christ gave to the Apostles, was: " Ye shall be witnesses unto me, both in Jerusalem and in Samaria and unto the uttermost parts of the earth. "

Though this commission was not immediately carried out, it must have been in the original design. There is such a perfect coincidence between the commission to the Apostles and the promise to Abraham — the long lapse of time between them, and the leading ideas — blessings to man, universal man — that fraud is out of the question.

That the Jews should here invent a religion with special reference to a union between themselves and the Gentiles, is so contrary to their prejudices, their history, that we can see no motive unless it were a benevolent one, and that forbids the idea of falsehood and deception.

Was this commission executed? We say, yes. And here I offer as authority my learned friend, so well acquainted with history, who has read almost all the writings in the world! I appeal to him, therefore, with the greatest assurance. I quote from "The Christian," vol. 1, page 18:

"Unbelievers can never prove that the religion of Christ did not originate about eighteen hundred years ago. They cannot prove that the religion of Christ did not first make its appearance in Judea. They cannot prove that the religion of Christ was not first preached and established by Jesus of Nazareth. They cannot prove that Jesus of Nazareth was not a true Prophet—a Teacher sent from God. They can never prove that Jesus of Nazareth did not prove himself the Messiah, by many miraculous works and mighty signs. They cannot prove, that the religion of Christ was not first preached in Europe, Asia and Africa by Paul and Peter, and other Apostles, their companions and fellow-laborers. They cannot prove the account given in the Acts of the Apostles, and other ecclesiastical records, respecting the first spread and triumphs of Christianity, to be untrue. They can never prove, that the Gospels, the Acts, and the Epistles, were not written by the persons whose names they bear. They cannot prove that they were written by any other men."

We claim then, that this commission was executed. Mr. Barker says, "the Gospel was preached in many parts of the world," and this agrees with the New Testament. Christ said, his Disciples should be his witnesses unto the uttermost parts of the earth; and Paul declares, (Colossians chap. 1: 23,) that "the Gospel was preached to every creature under Heaven." This testimony is sufficient for our present purpose.

It remains now to be considered whether the Gospel has been a blessing to mankind? We say it has. I will give one quotation which, for the present, must suffice, though many others might be given. Peter in preaching Christ to his own nation says, (Acts 3: 25, 26,) "Ye are the children of the Prophets and of the covenant which God made with our fathers, saying unto Abraham: And in thy seed shall all families of the earth be blessed." "26. Unto you first, God having raised up his son Jesus, sent him to bless you, in turning away every one of you from his iniquities."

MR. HARTZEL'S SIXTH ADDRESS.

There are but few things in Mr. Barker's last speech of sufficient importance to merit a word of reply. If he thinks that I shall follow him through his long list of objections, he will be disappointed. We would pass them entirely, only that there are children in the audience, who may require something to enable them to see the character of his criticisms. It would not be needed for men and women.

If my friend had understood this most important truth, a truth which is canonised in the literary world, "that *man*, constituted as he is, can only *know* things by things already *known*," I am sure he would not have raised a quarrel with Hitchcock.

It *is a truism* not to be questioned, that man must know one thing in order to know another, and that one item of information only becomes a stepping-stone to another. This principle will account for most of the difficulties he has attempted to raise, in his march through the Bible, from the beginning of Genesis to the end of the book—for he has given us one course.

Mr. Barker says, that the Jews exist in contradiction of prophecy—that God said, that those who would not receive the Prophet, like unto Moses, that should be sent to them, should be cut off from his people; that they did not receive him, and were not cut off. Were they not cut off from the people of God? To the testimony: "Then Paul and Barnabas waxed bold and said: It was necessary that the word of God should first have been spoken to you; but seeing ye put it from you, and judge yourselves unworthy of everlasting life, lo! we turn to the Gentiles." Acts 13: 46. "Well; because of unbelief they were broken off, and thou standest by faith. Be not highminded, but fear: for if God spared not the natural branches, take *heed* lest he also spare not thee. Behold therefore the goodness and severity of God: on them which fell, severity; but towards thee, goodness, if thou continue in his goodness: otherwise thou also shalt be cut off." Romans 11: 20, 21, 22. Mr. Barker says, "Jesus sent his Disciples only to the Jewish nation." This is not true. He gave to his Apostles *two* commissions. One reads thus: "Go not into the way of the Gentiles, and into any city of the Samaritans enter ye not: but go rather to the lost sheep of the house of Israel." Matthew 10: 5, 6. On the same night in which he was betrayed, his own earthly mission to the Jewish nation expired, so did that of the Apostles, and in a most orderly manner he took it back, that he might give them another. This he did shortly before his ascension. In the second, we have the most sublime plan ever contemplated by the human mind — a plan for gathering together, into one happy and loving brotherhood, all the nations of the earth, both Jews and Gentiles. It is a fact in New Testament history that a multitude of people of different religions were brought together, and made of one heart and one soul, as the result of Christ's commission, "Go ye into all the world, and preach the Gospel to every creature."

"But Christ did not go to the Gentiles." True. Jesus says he was sent to the lost sheep of the house of Israel; does that necessarily confine his mission to the salvation of the Jews? Did he not set on foot a system of teaching—a vast missionary scheme—when he commanded the Apostles to go and preach the Gospel to every creature? Is it true that because Mark's wording of the commission differs from that of Matthew, therefore, it was written by another hand than his? In this, the Evangelist did as in recording other incidents, one records what was omitted by another; so, in this case, all that Matthew has recorded of Christ's commission to the *eleven* is implied by Mark, and *vice versa*. But the words of Matthew are another proof that Christ did not confine the blessings of his salvation to the Jews. "Go ye, therefore, and teach all nations." We have the same sentiment in Luke, conveyed in the most emphatic terms: "Thus it is written and thus it behooved Christ to suffer and to rise from the dead the third day; and that repentance and remission of sins should be preached in his name among all nations, beginning at Jerusalem. Luke 24: 46—47. And again, Luke, in his second treatise—the Acts of the Apostles—alluding to this commission, says: "And ye shall be witnesses of me, both in Jerusalem and in all Judea, and in Samaria, and unto the uttermost parts of the earth."

Mr. Barker said that "Peter would not go to the Gentiles until a miracle had been shown him." I am glad my friend mentioned this, as it brings out an important fact. The fact I refer to, is this: When God employs Prophets or Apostles, as messengers of his will, we do not find that this fact implies that these individuals are thereby deprived of all their human weaknesses — that, in other words, God employs, for the accomplishment of his purposes, men, and nothing but men. If the Apostles had ever claimed to be anything else than men, then they might have been thus reproached. Paul says: "We have this treasure in earthen vessels, that the excellency of the power may be of God, and not of us." It seems that the Apostles did not understand that the Gospel was to go to the ends of the earth. I am not compromising any truth by this admission, for it appears upon the face of the whole book. The Apostle Peter says, that the Prophets did not understand, when they predicted the sufferings of Christ and the glory that should follow, and that even angels did not understand the plan of redemption, but desired to look into it. 1st Peter, 1: 10, 11, 12. It was not necessary that Peter should understand that the Gospel was to be preached to every creature, until the time had come, in the arrangements of Providence, for him to go forth and teach the Gentiles, and when that time came he was more fully instructed in that part of his mission. It is true, as Mr. Barker says, "a miracle was required to do this." But this only proves that these men were the messengers of Heaven, appointed to convert the Gentiles. The fact is fully established that they did go, and preach to the Gentiles the unsearchable riches of Christ. Notwithstanding their natural aversion, their inveterate prejudices against the Gentiles, they went among them, and made them a tender of the Gospel. We can account for the fact upon no other principle than divine interposition. But I fear we are taking up too much time with matters not directly involved in the controversy.

In the next place, we wish to say a few things in regard to these "fabulous" accounts in the Bible. Our friend says "fabulous." I did hope he would give us the definition of the word *fable*. According to Webster it has two meanings; the first is, "a fictitious narration, intended to enforce some useful truth or precept." The other meaning is, "a falsehood, a lie." What does he say in his own writings, after he had well studied the fabulous book? I read from Mr. Barker's "Review of the Bible," pages 5 and 7:

> "I regard the Mosaic account of Creation, I mean its PARTICULAR STATEMENTS, as fabulous. 7. I believe that God made man, and that he made woman; that he made woman to be a help-meet for man, and that he provided man food at his creation, and that man and woman were intended to live together in marriage, in a devoted and lasting union. I believe, too, that man was tempted and sinned."

Here, let me ask, on what testimony he believes that woman was made to be a help-meet for man, if he regards this account as a fable? Does he use the word in its first or second meaning?

Again, on page 9, of the same work, Mr. Barker says:

> "I may state, that, though I regard the early portions of Scripture as fabulous, I still consider them, in many cases, as truthful and useful fables. Though they are fables, they are still, to some extent, in harmony with the great principles of religion."

Now, I shall read you fifteen principles from Mr.

Barker, which I regard as honorable to God and the Bible:

"For instance, they are based in general upon the great principles that there is a God—that God created the Heavens and the earth—that God made man—that man is an accountable creature, a moral agent, the subject of divine Government—that there is a distinction betwen good and evil—that there are some things which man is bound to do, and other things that he is bound to leave undone—that man's happiness depends on his obedience to the law of God—that if man does evil he will be punished, and that if he does good, or lives aright, he will be rewarded—that the man who obeys God is safe, but that the man who disobeys God is in danger—that obedience to God and happiness are inseparable, and that disobedience to God and wretchedness are equally so—that the whole universe is under God's control, and that He does what He pleases, both in heaven and in earth—that He can make all nature an instrument of chastisement to offending man, or a means of joy and blessedness to obedient man."

I repeat, that I consider these principles alike honorable to God and the Bible.

Obedience to law, implies a law-giver. Obeying a command, pre-supposes a commander. I wish Mr. Barker would not be so non-committal as he has been hitherto. If God has given us a law, and that law is not in the Bible, *where* is it to be found? I do wish the same benevolent feelings that have prompted him to be thus secretive would make him a little more communicative on this point.

I have yet one more extract to read from this "Bible Review." The author will separate the chaff from the wheat. He is going to separate the false and fabulous from the true and the good. What a benevolent work! He will doubtless favor the world with a new edition, improved and corrected, by Joseph Barker. "The Bible Review," page 89:

"The course which I am pursuing will not diminish the good influence of the Bible, but only destroy that evil influence which has counteracted the good. The course which I am pursuing will still leave the Bible the friend of all truth, and the opponent of all error; the patron of all virtue, and the opponent of all vice."

Now, can this much be said of any other book under heaven, Mr. Barker himself being judge? I will submit to him a proposition: If Mr. Barker will bring forward a book, written I care not *when*, *where*, or by *whom*, though it be by *himself*, of which a disinterested committee (to be appointed by mutual agreement) will say that it is "the friend of all truth and virtue, and the enemy of all error and vice," I pledge myself to pay the sum of one thousand dollars, on the presentation of that book. I have but little — I need it all — yet I will cheerfully pay the sum named for another such book. Or, if he can produce a book in which the elements of the fifteen principles, which I have read to you, are embodied, upon which to base our obligation to God and man; and, secondly, a book that is "the friend of all truth and virtue, an enemy of all error and vice," I will pay for that book one thousand dollars, and consider myself a happy man. I submit this overture to my opponent. If I cannot advance the money on the presentation of the book, I pledge my honor to give him my obligation, with good security, payable in sixty days.

But, Mr. Barker says, "the Bible is full of contradictions." It is an easy matter for a talkative man to raise objections and start difficulties, and especially to a document which is so very brief in its details. A few chapters spread over a period of sixteen hundred years before the flood, and a few more passing over a period of two thousand years. Can you conceive of a document, such as this, in which a person with the mental bias of Mr. Barker could not point out at least an equal number of seeming contradictions? And, upon the whole, how do these contradictions, as he is pleased to call them, effect the whole amount of evidence? Discrepancies between witnesses are never considered as disparaging their testimony; it is supposed rather against the credibility of witnesses if there is an exact verbal agreement between them.

Upon the real or supposed contradictions in the Bible, infidel writers have taken opposite ground. Thomas Paine assumes that the Biographers of Jesus Christ were independent writers, and, *therefore*, the want of harmony in their narrations destroys their credibility.

Robert Taylor, an apostate from the Episcopal church assumes that the first three Evangelists wrote in concert, *hence* the verbal agreement. He has arranged in parallel columns some of Christ's prophecies concerning the destruction of Jerusalem, and because of the verbal sameness, he concludes that one might have furnished the original, and the others were copyists; at any rate, they all drew from a common source, and that their absolute independence was given up by the learned as no longer tenable.

(I quote from memory.) From a verbal sameness he proves concert, and from concert, fraud. So, the Doctors disagree. The one says the Apostles *disagree, therefore, they are liars;* the other says they *do agree, therefore, they are liars.*

Upon the ground that the writers of the Books of the Bible contradict each other, Mr. Barker says: "The Bible represents God as hating some persons and loving others." A little disposition to do justice to the record would have saved Mr. Barker some trouble and me some time. What is the meaning of the word "hate?" We will refer to Webster. "Hate"—second definition—"In Scripture, to love less." He gives the following example: "If any come to me and *hate* not father and mother." Give Christ the preference. "Jacob" have I preferred to "Esau" would be, and truly is, the meaning.

In view of the meaning of the word "hate," Christ has not contradicted himself. It is further true, that, according to the Hebrew idiom, when there are two things in comparison and one is considered vastly more important than the other, the less important is spoken of in the language of *negation*, and the more important is expressed *affirmatively*. (This we say upon the highest literary authority.)

With regard to sacrifices it is true, as Mr. Barker says—for we will agree with him whenever we can, and join issue with him only when an important principle is involved. It is true, we may say, that God, by the Prophets, often spake to the Jews as though he took no delight in sacrifices. "I am full of the burnt offerings of rams, and the fat of fed beasts, and I delight not in the blood of bullocks, or of lambs, or of he-goats."

But why does God say this? Because they had paid more attention to the positive part of the Law than to the moral. The moral was always more valuable than the positive. There never was any real intrinsic virtue in the latter. They were ordained by heaven for other purposes, hence, God reproves them in view of their blind observance of mere outward forms. There is nothing incongruous, or in contradiction with His commandments, in condemning them for attaching so much consequence to sacrifices and offerings, while they neglected justice, mercy and love of God. All the Books of the Bible harmonise in relation to these, as well as all the other facts of the Scriptures. But, if I were going to build an argument on these sacrifices, I would take this ground: that the universality of the practice of sacrificing among all nations of the earth proves that it is of divine origin; at least there are arguments to be produced in favor of this position. As I have a few minutes of time left me, I will proceed with my argument, based upon the promises to Abraham.

It remains yet to be considered whether the Gospel is a blessing to mankind. Acts 3: 25, 26:

"Ye are the children of the Prophets and of the covenant, which God made with our fathers, saying unto Abraham: and in thy seed shall all the kindreds of the earth be blessed.

"Unto you first, God having raised up his Son Jesus, sent him to bless you, in turning away every one of you from his iniquities."

To comply with this condition is itself a blessing, and proposes the way for still greater and more extended blessings, both in this life and that which is to come.

The coming of the Messiah was promised unconditionally, but personal blessings through him are only to be enjoyed on certain covenanted stipulations. The Gospel must be heard before it can be believed; believed before it can be obeyed; and it must be obeyed before its proffered blessings can be enjoyed in their divine and glorious fullness. The blessing that came upon the nations by the original promulgation of the Gospel was the free tender of the means of moral illumination and salvation, through Jesus Christ, the promised seed. "For the Gospel was preached among all nations, for the obedience of faith."

I will now speak of the benefits enjoyed by those who are only under the reflex influence of Christianity — the record God has given of his Son. But, it will suffice to say, they are all that civilization is worth to man. Mr. Barker has set this forth in terms most happy. You shall hear him to this point. "The Christian," Vol. 1st, pages 5 and 6: In a tract entitled "Mercy Triumphant:"

"Writing is one of the principle means of spreading religion, and of doing good to the souls of men. It was by means of writing that Jehovah taught his laws to the Israelites, and instructed them in the history of creation, and in all his dealings with their fathers. The Almighty commanded the Israelites to teach his laws to their children, not only by talking of them, but by writing them on their door-posts, and on the gates of their houses; (Deut. 6: 11.) and he directed all his laws and judgments to be written in plaster, on large monuments, for the benefit of all the people. (Deut. 27.) By means of writing, the Almighty has communicated to us the whole system of Revelation. Writing is the means which God has chosen for imparting the knowledge of religion to the universe, and diffusing through the human family the holiness and joy of heaven. God has honored writing above every other acquirement, and taught mankind to regard it as one of their first and highest blessings.

God has employed the same art under the New Testament Dispensation as well as under the old. He would not allow the instructions and labors of our Redeemer and his Disciples to be committed in trust to the memories of men; but gave to his chosen servants his choicest inspirations, that they might commit them to writing, and thus secure their transmission, unimpaired, to future generations, and to the remotest parts of the earth. Had the revelations of the Mosaic and Christian Dispensations been left unwritten, their excellency would have lasted but an age or two. The great truths of religion would have been supplanted by error—the precepts of God would have been made to give way to the will of man, and a corrupt priesthood would have enslaved and held in chains the whole race of men. Tradition would have been the creed and the law of the world, and in the hands of an interested and ruling priesthood, it would have been converted into an engine of insupportable cruelty. The multitudes of men would have been at the mercy of a few savage tyrants, and we must have groaned our weary way to the grave beneath the double yoke of superstition and tyranny, without consolation and without hope. We have heard what darkness covered the nations, and what crimes and cruelties wasted the earth, when a corrupt priesthood succeeded in concealing the writings of heaven from the people. But what could have checked the extravagance of their impositions and cruelties, if they could have entirely blotted out the handwriting of heaven, and employed their spurious traditions without all fear? Blood and rapine would have raged without restraint; freedom, and peace, and hope must have expired; and ruin would have sat and mocked the agonies of a despairing world. But, thanks be to God, he employed the heavenly art of writing, and, by this means, baffled the enemies of mankind, and secured to us the perfect system of his truth and laws to latest times."

MR. HARTZEL'S SEVENTH ADDRESS.

Mr. Barker says, "the Jews were commanded to go into the territory of other nations, kill the inhabitants, and take their property and lands."*

I wish to call attention to an important misrepresentation. Mr. Barker continues to represent me as holding that the whole Bible is the word of God. I disclaim such belief. He referred to "Nelson" to show that that was the current orthodoxy of the age. However that may be, I know not; but I know that among those authors who are the acknowledged defenders and expounders of the Bible, that have come under my observation, not one of them has taken such a position.

That I may not be further misrepresented to the

---

* I will let Mr. Barker meet his own objection, and *let him* justifiy the ways of God in this particular. See Christianity Triumphant, by Joseph Barker, pages 427, 8.

Obj. 147. "The Old Testament teaches us that God commanded the ancient Jews to kill the people of Canaan, and take possession of their land."

Ans. It is true, but I see in this no argument against the beneficial influence of Christianity. 1. At the time when the Jews were directed to drive out the nations of Canaan, and take possession of their land, Christianity was not in existence. The religion then in force was Judaism, a religion which, though glorious, when compared with the idolatrous and unclean systems of Paganism, had yet no glory when compared with the religion of Christ. Many things were allowed under the Jewish dispensation, and were properly allowed, which are not allowed under the Christian dispensation.

2. Nor can I see any thing in the command given to the Jews in reference to the expulsion of the Canaanites, which was at variance with the justice and benevolence of God. 1. The land was God's, and he had a right to give it to what people he saw best. 2. The Canaanites were expelled for their sins. If they had obeyed God, they would never have been expelled; and if they rebelled, who, that acknowledges a God at all, shall call in question his right to punish transgressors? 3. The Canaanites were not cast out till their iniquities were full. Their sins were of the most loathsome and revolting character; they prevailed among all classes, and infected the whole people; and God had borne with them for many generations. They had sinned beyond measure, and beyond all hopes of reformation. 4. Though expulsion from their land, or extermination, was a terrible punishment to the transgressors, it was calculated to prove a mercy to others, by admonishing them of their danger in sinning against God, and bringing them to repentance. 5. They had already rendered their lives a misery to themselves, by their licentious and unnatural vices. They had filled their bodies with loathsome and horrible diseases, so that the land was "eating them up," "and spewing them out:" they were neither in a state to be happy themselves, nor capable of pro-creating their species,

audience, I would say that the Bible contains the words of men, and yet it is not the *word* of man—that it contains the words of angels, and yet it is not the *word* of angels—that it contains the words of demons, and yet it is not the *word* of demons—that it contains the words of God, and yet it is not *unqualifiedly* the *Word* of God to speak in chosen language. But it is the *Word* of God in a sense that it is not the *word* of men, or of angels. To illustrate farther: here is a book, the words of Joseph Barker. But in this volume, claimed and acknowledged by Joseph Barker, I find the *words* of Wilberforce, Home, Clarkson, Ryan, Robertson, Seneca, Cicero, &c., and yet it is the *word* of Joseph Barker in a sense that it is not the *word* of any of these, and yet, strictly speaking, it is not the *word* of Joseph Barker. But if it were not for the *word* of Joseph Barker, we should not have the words of these individuals in such an

---

without perpetuating and spreading disease and wretchedness in their worst forms. In mercy to their posterity, and to the interests of humanity at large, their expulsion or extermination was necessary. 6. Why God employed the Israelites in punishing and destroying them, I cannot tell; but I have no doubt he had good reasons for so doing. It might, for one thing, fill the Jews with horror at the idolatries and abominations of the Canaanites, when they were made to witness the miseries they had brought upon them. And God might with propriety employ the Jews in a way in which it would not be proper to employ men in a higher state of improvement, and under a purer and a fuller law. Exercises which would prove hurtful to men in higher stages of improvement, and under a brighter dispensation, might prove useful to men in a ruder state and under a darker dispensation. We know that God's object was to destroy idolatry and crime, to train a people in the knowledge and service of the true God, and to prepare the way for the spread of light and purity and happiness throughout the world. 7. God did not inflict any other punishment upon the Canaanites for their sins, than he threatened to inflict upon the Israelites, if they followed their evil ways. There was no partiality in the Divine Being. 8. What God commanded the Israelites to do, was not something more cruel than was customary in war in those days, but something much *less* cruel. The common custom of war in those ages, was extermination; and this continued to be the custom among the pagans for many hundred years after, and it continues to this day. But God did not enjoin the entire destruction of the people: he mitigated the horrors of war, and afforded the guilty Canaanites opportunities of preserving themselves either by repentance or by flight.

The Lord commanded the Jews to keep his ordinances, "that the land spew you not out also, when ye defile it, as it spewed out the nations that *were* before you." They did "defile themselves," and the land has "spewed them out." This prophetic threat has been executed to the *letter*, to which the world has been witness for eighteen hundred years, and will be so long as the nation shall exist, and "Jerusalem shall be trodden under foot of the Gentiles."

embodiement as they are. Why did Mr. Barker introduce the words of other men into this volume entitled the "Christian," by Joseph Barker? Answer—Because of the relative position in which these writers stand to him as concurring *with*, or dissenting from him. In this book, we have the inspiration of Joseph Barker. In the Bible we have the inspiration of Jehovah. The inspiration of God and Joseph Barker differ as personages differ from each other, and as the Bible differs from the volume I hold in my hand. But if the inspired portions of the Bible were principles "supernaturally revealed and miraculously attested," these words to which we have referred, such as the words of angels, men, and demons, we must receive as such upon documentary evidence, if at all, for they would not have been transmitted to us but for the inspired portions of the Bible. This will suffice. I hope I am understood.

Second. He farther represents that we hold the preceptive portions of the Old Testament as perfect, and the rule of Christian virtue and piety. We have taken no such position. The Old Testament does not claim to be perfect, and the New Testament does not award perfection to it. Moses says, "another Prophet shall the Lord your God raise up like unto me; to him shall ye harken." Would it appear from this prediction, that Moses expected that all the nation would refer to him for instruction throughout all time? Again—Jeremiah says, Behold, the days come, saith the Lord, that I will make a new covenant with the house of Israel, and the house of Judah: not according to the covenant I made with their fathers; in the day I took them by the hand to lead them out of the land of Egypt." Paul commenting upon this says, (Hebrews 8, 7,) "For if that first convenant had been faultless, then should no place have been sought for the second. But being faulty, the Lord said by the mouth of the Prophet, he would abolish it and make room for a new convenant established upon better promises." Again—Ezekiel says, "I gave them, also, statutes which were not good, and judgements by which they should not live."

This is that sponge that wipes away an hundred of Mr. Barker's objections. They were not good in one sense, and yet in another sense they were good. The word *good* is a relative term. To illustrate my meaning, I will say that when "Solon was interrogated whether he had given the Athenians the best laws? said that he had given them the *best* of which they were capable." So God gave to the Jews the best laws they were capable of receiving in that age of the world.

Who would propose our "Constitution," and complex laws for the government of the American Indians? Or who would propose the Constitution of England with its more complex code for the government of the Greenlanders? Such a proposition would subject a legislator to merited reproach.

Mr. Barker, however, has a few words upon this

point. They are not only explanatory of, but corroborate the views just submitted. On account of the dimness of my vision, I shall call upon Mr. McNeely to read for me. He will read an extract from "Christianity Triumphant," page 428.

Ans. The religion of Christ differs very considerably from the religion of the Jews, and yet God might be the author of both without being changeable. God is the author both of the sun and moon; and the sun and the moon differ widely from one another, and yet it does not follow that God is changeable. He made the sun and moon for different purposes: the sun to rule the day, and the moon to rule the night, and they are both well adapted to their purposes. So with the religion of the Jews, and the religion of Christ. The religion of the Jews was like the moon, or like the morning star, adapted exactly to its place and time; but not adapted for the whole world, or for all times. The religion of Christ is the sun, intended to bring the full light of day, and adapted to all ages, and to all climes.

God is a parent, we are his children, and God is unchangeably attached to his children, and invariably seeks their highest happiness. What course shall we expect his unchanging wisdom and goodness to pursue? Will he treat mankind in one unvarying way from first to last? By no means. While the human race is in its infancy he will exercise their feeble powers with childlike labors, giving them little tasks and easy ones, such as their childish state requires. Thus did God deal with the first generations of men: he laid few burdens on them, and those but light ones. The laws he gave to the Patriarchs were very few and far from strict, but they were as many and as strict as in those rude and infant ages could be of service to mankind. It was necessary that some laws should be give thus early, and it was necessary that those laws should not be many or severe, and the kindness and wisdom of our Father appointed it so. But after a number of generations had passed away, men became intellectually and morally stronger; they were capable of greater exercises, and they needed them; and God, always the same affectionate Father, gave them more work. He gave the law by Moses, and accompanied the law with fuller revelations of his character and providence. Under this new dispensation the human family rose still higher, and gathered more inward strength, and became prepared for greater and better things; and it was then that God, in the same unchanged and unchangeable wisdom and benevolence, abolished former systems, and gave a full and perfect system of truth and duty by Jesus Christ. But in all these changes we see the same unchanging Father, pursuing the same grand end, the greatest happiness of the human race.

God has given us "a perfect system of truth and duty by Jesus Christ." That expresses the second feature of my proposition beautifully and truly. I marvel that Mr. Barker upon his principles should calumniate the Bible; for, if there be no supernatural revelation, if the Bible contains nothing divine, from *whence* flow all the communications found upon its pages? From the same source, the common fountain from which the Shasters, the Koran, all systems of superstition, all the different forms of Paganism and infidelity were derived. Upon his own principles, if there be nothing supernatural, if *all is nature and nature is all*, then, his opposition to the Bible is nothing but the development, the workings of his own nature; and my opposition to him is nothing more nor less than *nature in conflict with nature.* We must hear Mr. Barker on this point also. I engaged in this discussion before I knew that Mr. Barker was the author of such works as I have, and shall read from them. They came into my hands unlooked for, and I had them some weeks in my possession before I opened them. I had used the very argument to which I have just adverted, weeks before I discovered the extract which we shall read in a moment, to which my worthy friend, (the reader,) is witness. Finding that Mr. Barker's writings contained a great amount of matter which I desired to bring before this audience, my health being feeble, not having been able to be out of bed a whole day for some weeks past until within a few days,

I discovered it would save me a vast amount of labor and research to refer to his own writings and present them to the audience. I feel under lasting obligation to my friend for this assistance.

We now ask the reading of the argument to which I have just referred. "The Christian," Vol, 1st, page 19.

"Unbelievers sometimes say that nature never errs; that she is wise and beneficent in all her operations; and that the reason why her children are not happy is because they follow other guides. They especially blame religion and superstition, and represent them as the great occasions of human guilt and wretchedness. But if religion be false, and infidelity true, NATURE is the only power in existence. If religion be false, and infidelity true, then religion is one of nature's productions, one of nature's own children. What else but nature could produce religion on the unbeliever's theory? If the theory of the unbeliever be true, all that unbeliever's complain of, and even the complaints of unbelievers themselves, are the productions of nature. Nature and religion are not at variance; they are one. If the unbeliever's theory be true, there is no such thing as following other guides instead of nature; nor is there any such thing as the transgression of nature's laws. Religion itself, and superstition, and ignorance, and error, and priestcraft, and slavery, and war, and intolerance, and civil government; and all that is black, and unclean, and terrible, as well as all that is fair, and lovely, and glorious, are all so many parts or productions of nature. If religion, then, be wrong, nature is wrong. If nature be right, religion is right. So full of inconsistency is the unbeliever's creed.

It does seem to me that Mr. Barker cannot, with any degree of consistency, as a scholar, or a man of integrity, throw off the responsibility of such arguments. "True," he says, "I have thrown them away. They were mine." This is mine originally; I did not receive it from him. It is his also; therefore the validity of the argument has double support.

Mr. Barker repeatedly says, "I *know* that Mr.

Hartzel cannot prove his position." I would say to my friend as one said of old, "Let not him that putteth on his armor boast himself as he that putteth it off." But this kind of egotism seems to be characteristic of the man. It displayed itself more or less while he was a minister, and it still manifests itself. It is a personal peculiarity for which I will not hold him responsible, nor chide him; but there is no argument in it.

I now commence the train of argument where I left it. In my last address I closed by saying that the Bible is all that civilization is worth to us. I was about to read a beautiful extract from Mr. Barker, which I will read now. "Christianity Triumphant," page 385.

"Obj. 87. The arts and sciences flourished among the Greeks and Romans, before Christianity was heard of."

Ans. 1. Yes SOME of them did; but when earthly arts and sciences flourished most among them, they were a wicked and miserable people. The history of the Greeks and Romans is a proof that Mathematics, Sculpture, Painting, and Poetry may flourish among a people, while war, and pride, and slavery, and intemperance, and licentiousness, are indulged in almost without restraint.

2. There are many important arts in use among us, which were not at all understood among the ancient Greeks and Romans. The most important of all arts, the art of DOING GOOD, appears not to have been at all understood or practised among those nations. They made fine statues, and kept them with the greatest care; but they cared not for the LIVING statues with which they were surrounded; they murdered their brethren without a sigh. They were very clever im imitating with the pencil, flowers, and fruits, and landscapes; but their armies trampled the flowers and fruits which the liberal earth sent forth in the mire; and the landscapes painted by the hand of Heaven—the fields, and woods, and gardens, which were full of life and blessing—they turned to a

desolate wilderness. They studied Mathematics, Logic, and Rhetoric; but they allowed the millions of their brethren, among whom they lived, to suffer all the miseries of ignorance, and error, and vice, without a single effort to enlighten and regenerate them. Sculpture and Painting, Music and Poetry, Mathematics, Logic and Rhetoric, are but childish trifles compared with the multiplied arts of beneficence called forth into being, and kept in active operation, by the influence of the religion of Christ."

You will remember that Mr. Barker, yesterday, made quite a point upon this, that it was impossible that a religion generally adopted by the world could be a documentary religion and rest upon historic basis. We proceed then to the argument.

If, then, Christianity is a blessing, this promise to Abraham was not an empty boast, but God has fulfilled his convenant, and sent the richest blessings upon the nations through Abraham's promised seed. We claim that these promises to Abraham were "supernatural communications," and have received a miraculous confirmation. Abraham is yet a great nation, and his name is still great. The Jews delight to do him honor by naming their sons Abraham. Christians do the same. In almost every Christian family, there are Abrahams, Isaacs, Jacobs, and Sarahs. In my own family I have a Sarah. These names are honorable on account of their connection with blessings conferred upon the world through the Gospel. But who calls his son Esau? I have never found one Esau, etc. The name of Abraham is still a *great* name, and God's promise has been fulfilled: "I will give unto thee a great name." In the exact ratio of the spread and prevalence of the Gospel will the name of Abraham become greater and greater.

Now is it possible that man's human perception, human invention, or foresight could have originated these promises and placed them in that early period of the world? If Abraham had originality enough to devise a scheme, and so control and direct it, to carry it out through so long a period of successive ages, he is the author of an imposition for which the world has no comparison.

MR. HARTZEL'S EIGHTH ADDRESS.

If Mr. Barker had remembered the principles to which we adverted on yesterday, involving the means of acquiring knowledge, whether scientific or religious, it would have saved both him and myself some time, and Professor Hitchcock from the caricature to which we have just listened. I refer to the principle that man is subjected to this necessity—"that he can only know things by things already known."

Mr. Barker.—"I deny doing injustice to the views of Hitchcock. I defy any man to produce proof that I have done so."

Mr. Hartzel.—I wish to make a few detailed remarks respecting these "statutes which were not good." My friend looks at the Bible through the eye of an infidel. I still look at it through the eye of an admirer, a lover, and own that I highly respect its authority. To me there never was a system of things since the world began that is so beautiful. It is true that the *strained* interpretation he puts upon certain parts of the Scriptures, may have weight with some. But you may torture any book and make it say what it does not mean.* With regard to Moses and Jesus,

---

*I shall here give a few examples of Mr. Barker's method of quoting and perverting the Scriptures, and let these represent his course throughout the entire controversy.

First: He said some of the Psalms are beautiful, while others are very different. He then said, "I will read one." This he did not do; he only read from the 9th to the 16th verse of the 109th Psalm, and then exclaimed: "IT IS ENOUGH TO MAKE ONE SHED TEARS OF BLOOD." The Psalmist was here uttering some imprecations against the ungodly, "Because he remembered not to shew mercy, but persecuted the poor and needy man, that he might even slay the broken in heart. As he loved cursing, so let it come unto him, as he delighted not in blessing, so let it be far from him. As he clothed himself with cursing," etc. If he had read the connexion, HE MIGHT HAVE RESTRAINED "his tears of blood."

Second: "Happy shall he be that taketh and dasheth thy little ones against the stones."—Psalm 137. "Strange HAPPINESS that would be," exclaimed Mr. Barker. Why did not Mr. Barker quote the preceding verse; because it did not suit his purpose. "O daughter of Babylon, who art to be destroyed, happy SHALL he be, that rewardeth thee as thou hast rewarded us, happy SHALL he be that taketh and dasheth thy little ones against the stones."

The "daughter of Babylon" was, for many years, the most oppressive power on earth. They carried the Jews, with their consecrated vessels, into Babylon, burned their temple, and left their city in ruins. One of their inspired poets foretold the coming fortune of this tyrannical despotism. "O daughter of Babylon, who art to be destroyed." She was "destroyed." God named the man two hundred years before he was born—called him his "ANNOINTED" to "open to him the two leaved gates of brass," etc. Who was commissioned to perform this service? Cyrus WAS HAPPY in executing the divine denunciation against Babylon. The prophecy against which Mr. Barker has directed his SATIRE, was declarative of the divine purpose and justice, as a judicial proceeding, and Cyrus is yet called "happy."

Third: "Some passages say that God tempts no man; another says he tempted Abraham."

The word "tempt" is sometimes used in an ill sense. To incite to an evil act, in this sense God tempts no man, as the Scriptures say—"Let no man say when he is tempted, I am tempted of God, for God cannot be tempted with evil, neither tempteth he any man. But every man is tempted when he is drawn away of his lusts and enticed." But the word "tempt" is also used in a good sense, to "try," to "prove," to "put on trial for proof." "Thou shalt not tempt the Lord thy God."—Deuteronomy 6th. Matthew 4th, "You shall not put the Lord your God to the proof."—Dr. Campbell's translation. In this sense, God did "tempt" Abraham. He put him to the proof. You may substitute the word TRY in the case of Abraham, and many other passages, and the sense will be the same. "God did TRY Abraham." "There has no temptation (trial) taken you, but such as is common to man."—1st Corinthians 10: 13.

Fourth: "The Bible contains bad morality concerning sacrifice. It recommends human sacrifice. It represents God as commanding Abraham to offer up his son," etc. There were three distinct actions in a sacrificial performance. First, the offering; second, the slaying or sacrificing of the victim; third, the burning of the sacrifice. God gave the command to Abraham in the first, and he obeyed it in its expressed terms; but, when he was about to proceed to its implied terms, the angel said unto him, lay not thy hand upon the lad. Mr Barker committed no small blunder when he said, "the Bible recommends human sacrifice." It did, in this solitary case, command a human offering, but FORBADE a human sacrifice."

This cavil of Mr. Barker's is as old as Voltaire; and we shall let certain Jews, in a series of letters to Monsieur Voltaire on pages 358 and 359, answer Mr. Barker, as they did his worthy predecessor: "If the God of the Jews had approved of such sacrifices, would he have stopped the hand of Abraham who was offering up his son to him? Satisfied with this trial of his servant's faith and obedience, he forbids him to stretch his arm over so dear a victim, and substitutes another in its place. Does not this conduct at a time, when, according to you, the Canaanites were beginning to sacrifice their children to their divinities, show that "the God of Abraham" did not resemble the gods of the idolators, who delighted to see innocent blood flowing. The refusal of this

none would understand by anything in the language, that Jesus was to be like unto Moses in all things. There were remarkable points of similarity between the two personages. These you can examine for yourselves. Jesus, Peter, James, and John, being in

---

victim, under the circumstances, was doubtless a striking lesson by which God, whilst he made a trial of Abraham's faith, meant to give a perpetual lesson to this holy man and his posterity, of his abhorence of those barbarous superstitions."

Fifth: Mr. Barker says, "when I read the parable of the rich man and Lazarus, I am filled with sorrow and amazement. Dives was rich, but no evil is charged against him." Let us see: "There was a certain beggar laid at his gate full of sores; and desiring to be fed with the crumbs that fell from the rich man's table; moreover the dogs came and licked his sores."

The "rich man" in the parable, was the exact personification of a voluptuous, brute-hearted Saducee—more brute-hearted than a dog. HE WAS LITERALLY AN INFIDEL. He neither believed in a resurrection, future life, angel, spirit, heaven or hell. But "no evil is charged AGAINST HIM," says Mr. Barker. No evil implied in this? "A BEGGAR LAY AT HIS GATE, WISHING FOR THE CRUMBS THAT FELL FROM HIS TABLE—DOGS LICKED HIS SORES." Dives was not like the good Samaritan, or he would not have let the dogs dress the poor man's sores, he would have done it himself; he would not have suffered him to lie exposed at his gate; he would have taken him into his house and laid him on his bed; he would have had no occasion to desire crumbs, for the GOOD man would have given him LOAVES.

SENSUALITY, and a WANT OF SYMPATHY for suffering humanity, are no crimes with Mr. Barker. Query; how is it that his benevolent soul can feel so deeply for the neglected slaves? Are not slaveholders, to say the most, as kind to their slaves as this "rich man" was to the "beggar"? Yes; but that such a man should be sent to hell is what fills Mr. Barker with HORROR. No doubt the distinction which shall be visibly displayed in a future state, between the righteous and the wicked, is the chief cause of opposition to the Bible.

Sixth: Mr. Barker referred to the words of Christ in Matthew 5th, "but whosoever shall say, thou fool, shall be in danger of hell fire." He then quoted these words of Christ to his disciples: "O, fools, and slow of heart," etc. If the word "fool" had but one meaning, if it could be used in but one sense, there would be some point in Mr. Barker's remarks. "Fool," as defined by Webster, has six meanings: 1st, an idiot; 2d, a person deficient in intellect, one who acts absurdly; 3d, IN SCRIPTURE, FOOL is often used for a wicked or depraved person; 4th, a weak Christian; 5th, a term of indignity and reproach. In the 5th of Matthew, Christ forbade his disciples to use the word "fool" in its fifth meaning as a term of reproach; but in Luke 24: 25 he applied it to his apostles in its fourth meaning: "O fools (weak) and slow of heart to believe all the apostles have spoken." Ought not Christ to have suffered these things, and to enter into his glory? Now ought not Mr. Barker, a scholar, to know that the words are different in the original.

Seventh: "Some passages say you must not be angry, and if you are you are in danger of the judgment; while others represent Christ himself as being angry." The first meaning of the word "angry," is feeling resentment. Christ forbade his disciples such feeling of resentment as might prompt to murder, or the use of reproachful language, for this was the subject of his teaching in Matthew 5: 21, 22, but in Mark 3d, to which Mr. Barker referred, the Jews "watched Jesus Christ if he would heal on the Sabbath day, that they might accuse him," "And when he had looked round about on them with ANGER, BEING GRIEVED FOR THE HARDNESS OF THEIR HEARTS, he saith unto the man, stretch forth thy hand." Christ's "anger" was a HOLY RESENTMENT, "BEING GRIEVED FOR THE HARDNESS OF THEIR HEARTS."

The above is a fair specimen of Mr. Barker's efforts to pervert the plain and obvious meaning of Bible language. To this infidels have always resorted in their opposition to the Scriptures. That cause must be a bad one, which is driven to such means for support. Mr. Barker, being a master of language, evidently DISSEMBLED when he said, and repeatedly said, "I AM NOT AN ENEMY TO THE BIBLE;" "I DON'T WANT TO DESTROY THE BIBLE," etc. I am happy in the conviction, that although his means were chosen with direct reference to this END, the wise will regard it as another display of infidel folly, and, as "DEAD FLIES cause the ointment of the Apothecary to send forth a STINKING SAVOR, so doth a little FOLLY him that is in reputation for wisdom and honor.

a high mountain—Moses and Elias, from the regions of the dead, appeard in their midst. While engaged in conversation with the Messiah about his death, (see Luke 9: 31,) a voice was heard from the Eternal Heavens, saying: "This is my beloved Son; hear him." Moses then laid his commission down, and resigned his authority as God's oracle and law-giver to Jesus Christ, his successor in office and authority. These formalities, with the imperative hear him, were, doubtless, to satisfy the Apostles that their present law-giver who was to be like unto Moses, was yet superior to Moses, and had authority to change or abrogate his Law, as he *had* done in his sermon on the mount. The Savior there repealed some of those "statutes which were not good." "An eye for an eye, and a tooth tor a tooth," was not a good statute; and Jesus Christ abolished it, and gave this better statute: "*But I say unto you, that you resist not evil.*" Now, Jesus Christ, the last messenger of Jehovah, has taken the place of Moses; and surely the predecessor is honored by the successor.

When the Pharisees asked this question: "Is it lawful for a man to put away his wife for every cause?" He answered: "In the beginning it was not so." "Why did Moses, then, command to give her a writing of divorcement and send her away?" "Moses on account of the hardness of your hearts suffered you to put away your wives," etc. This was another statute which was not "good," but it was the best Divine wisdom and benevolence could do. "Ye have heard it said by them of old time, thou shalt not kill, and whosoever shall kill shall be in danger of the judgment. But I say unto you that whosoever is angry with his brother without cause, shall be in danger of the judgment &c." The letter of this *law* was required at the hand of the Jew—the overt act was the offense. But Jesus Christ forbids the indulgence of the passion, (anger,) which might prompt the act, and make this an offence against his more discriminating *law* of moral rectitude. The Apostle's teaching was in perfect harmony with this: "*Whosoever hateth his brother is a murderer.*"

"Ye have heard, that it was said by them of old time, thou shalt not commit adultery? But I say unto you that whosoever looketh on a woman to lust after her, hath committed adultery already with her in his heart."

The law forbade the act; but the Gospel forbids the passion. God has required of man, under every dispensation, according to the light they had, and the privileges they enjoyed; but his mercy made many abatements, else no flesh could have been saved.

Paul makes a beautiful comment on the Law and the Gospel: "For what the Law could not do, in that it was weak through the flesh, God sending his own Son in the likeness of sinful flesh, and for sin condemned sin in the flesh; that the righteousness of the Law might be fulfilled in us who walk not after the flesh, but after the spirit."

God in the greatness of his mercy did not require the righteousness of the Law from the Jew. The righteousness of the precepts: "Thou shalt not kill," "thou shalt not commit adultery," was more than to abstain from overt action. Moses required obedience to the letter of these great moral principles. Christ to the spirit of them. The one placed his interdict upon actions; the other upon passions first, and second upon actions. The Law was weak for the want of *motive;* hence the Jew was always in bondage on the score of moral principle. The Gospel, or the Law of the spirit of life has *motive*—imparts strength; hence the Christian is "free," and the Gospel is the "Law of *liberty*."

Our friend still talks of contradictions. I must say, and I hope he will not consider this speaking disparagingly of him, for it is my settled conviction, that these contradictions are of his own creation. He asserts that the Gospel says that Christ was angry. Will he bring the passage? I know of no such passage. I wish here to say to Mr. Barker that if he will bring forward some palpable contradictions, such as are important, and cannot be reconciled, I will concede to him that he has accomplished something against the authority of the Scriptures. Let me be understood. Such contradictions as would effect the credibility of witnesses before a court of law. He does say that Jesus Christ never contradicted himself, or contradicted the truth. "Christian," Vol. 1st, page 20.

"Unbelievers cannot prove that ever Christ taught doctrines that were inconsistent with each other; they cannot prove that He ever either contradicted himself, or contradicted the truth."

The argument, that upon infidel principles, *nature is all, and all is nature*, he tried to meet with his notions of human progression.

I wish now to offer my views on the subject of progression. I did not intend to introduce them at present, but it seems to be required.

"Man is progressive." True: So are animals and vegetables, and all things that come to maturity by the law of growth. Still progress is subject to certain limitations. It has its hitherto; and man, as well as other animals, is subjected to the same humiliating "*hitherto shalt thou come, and here shall thy progress be stayed.*" When the law of growth has accomplished its work in the vegetable kingdom, the plant suddenly passes into another state, which we are pleased to call *maturity*. In this state it remains but a short time, then passes into another, which we call *decomposition*. Nor is it otherwise with man, at least in so far as our eyes and ears can follow him through his earthly pilgrimage. Some twenty years will finish his physical progress; and in twenty years more the retrograde begins; and at sixty the *mental* faculties are fully developed, and the retrograde begins. Some of the mental faculties begin to fail, and in a few years more his friends begin to say, "he is getting childish." "Why! how childish he is." Incapable of any important business transaction, he retires from the active cares of life, and from the world,—a superanuated man—a child—an idiot,—he drops into the grave.

This is, indeed, a humiliating picture. No more so, however, than true. It is so, because true.

Now let me ask the infidel: What of your boasted progression—eternal progression? Nothing sounds more ludicrous and imaginative, than to hear an unbeliever talk of his eternal progression. And even while in his progressive state, his progress is subject to some controlling influences, we call circumstances. This is true both of his body and his mind. Some never attain to physical manhood, and others fall short of intellectual manhood on account of adverse circumstances. Some make no progress in art, in science, in government, in religion. It is a fact of history that many nations existed for ages without knowing the use of fire, among whom were the Persians and Phœnicians. Many do not *now* know how to make a hatchet. They cannot read a word, nor form a letter—progression notwithstanding has done nothing for them. From whence, then, comes the propelling power? Ah! that is *the* question. Is it inside of man, or outside of him—to speak in a homely way? It is both. The capacity is within, but the *steam*, the *power*, that drives the machinery, is without.

Our friends, even more speculative than profound, have not discriminated between man's native capacity for improvement, and the instrumental causes effecting it; and hence they speak of man as a *self-*

sharpener, a *self-propeller*, a *perpetual motion*. I have often wondered at Mr. Fowler's tardiness. Perhaps he is one of those gentlemen who do not prize patent honors. Be that as it may, I would certainly advise Henry C. Wright, if he has not progressed out of the region of his resolutions, to make a trip to the Patent Office as soon as convenient. We might suppose that man was capable of making the necessary progress in things pertaining to his present temporal welfare without the Bible. The history of the world, however, declares it to be quite otherwise. Where has humanity developed itself most rapidly and most favorably? In Pagan lands? Will my friend say yes, in heathen lands? And if not there; where then? We answer within those geographical boundaries, where the Bible has been most circulated and read.

Come to our own America. To test this principle, select, if you please, any State in the Union, or we will say any six neighboring States, which have made the most progress in art, in science, in morals, in education and general intelligence, and see if they were not more devoted to the reading and circulating of the Bible than any other six in our political confederacy. Will some one name them? "The six New England States." You are right sir. In this respect Mr. Barker is with us. "The Christian," Vol. 2, page 247.

"I have another fact to state. Those nations, where the Bible is respected, and where it is most read and studied, are the FIRST, the FREEST, the WISEST, the BEST, the HAPPIEST of the nations. There are greater philosophers in those countries, and greater philanthropists, than in other countries where the Bible is not respected or read. There are more examples of temperance and purity in the Bible countries than in others. There is more domestic comfort, there is more respect to marriage and to marriage duties in Bible countries than in others. There is, also, less priestcraft, and more religious freedom in Bible countries than in others. In all respects the lands of Bibles are the first and happiest nations of the earth. I know that in Bible countries there is still much sin and misery; but this vice and misery will be found most prevalent among such as pay least regard to the Bible and its teachings. In Bible countries some forms of vice, perhaps, prevail which do NOT prevail in countries where Bible influences are not felt; but this arises from the abuse of that liberty which the Bible creates. When men are free they necessarily become either better than others, or worse than others. Those who choose to IMPROVE their liberty, excel in goodness; while those who ABUSE their liberty become extravagant in vice. Still the tendency of the Bible is to promote virtue and happiness."

This extract concedes everything we claim. We ask again, have the blessings of civilization advanced without the Bible? Have infidels and atheists plunged into the wilderness of Heathenism, with their Godless and Christless books, educated and elevated the savage tribes of earth? We answer, emphatically, *no! never!* Who, then, has accomplished the little that has been done in that way? The *Christian* with God's Bible in his hand and in his heart. These are eloquent facts,—they speak for themselves. They need no comment.

Finally, upon the subject of eternal progression. We have seen WHAT it is, so far as this life is concerned, and if there is no future life, it is all a dream.

But Christians, with the evidences of the Gospel in favor of a future life of blessedness, may reasonably indulge in this pleasing hope. But infidels must be required to prove first, that there is a future life for man; and then, secondly, that that life will not be as the present. First *progress*, then *retrograde*. For upon their own principles, if God, or nature has placed them in this world, I am sure they can have no reason to offer, that they may not be placed in a worse hereafter. But Christianity is every way favorable to human progress, in all that is valuable to man; but especially in moral excellence, without which, all other advances are of no avail. "But grow in grace and the knowledge of our Lord and Savior Jesus Christ, that favor, mercy, and peace may be multiplied unto you."

The Christian has Jesus Christ before him as the *beau ideal* of all perfection. His examples are of Heavenly type. These are copies for his eyes. He looks at these with admiration and a prayerful desire to imitate. He listens with attention to his precepts; these serve as so many prompters to his eyes. His lessons of Heavenly wisdom and of love are constant food for his soul, and he feels sure that with his best effort he shall not reach that point of mental and moral grandeur to which he himself aspires; and let me say to my friends, that when they have reached this point of moral excellence, and can progress no further, and they are not removed to another world more favorable to their full development, they will then have a right to petition Heaven in behalf of a new and more perfect standard of moral excellence. And if their petition shall be denied them, they will, probably, be excused from further progress.

I now resume my main argument, and I promise

myself a more calm sea and fairer sailing to the end of our voyage. Our friend said yesterday, that he was going to strike out a course for himself. Is he not here to respond? Is it not my place to lead? But if he is not disposed to reply, we are not responsible for his failure.

We shall, then, continue our train of argument on prophecy. Then we shall offer some arguments on miracles, Bible history, and biography, and the perfect adaptation of the Gospel for the removal of slavery, polygamy, and all the other organized and systematized forms of iniquity that afflict and degrade mankind. Had I a guaranty from this audience that they would continue this attendance for eight or ten days, we would follow our friend through all his windings and shiftings, though our proposition does not require it. But lest he should make a solitary child believe that there is argument in his declamations, I would pursue that course. I aver Mr. Barker is an excellent declaimer, but I am not sure he is quite so good a logician.

Mr. Barker. "I used to be a good logician."

Mr. Hartzel. Yes, I admit that; but he has changed, and what a *change!*

Argument five: We have now given *four* arguments. *One*, upon Authenticity—*three*, upon promises and their fulfillment. And now proceed more directly to prophecy. The Jews were the subjects of prophecy during the whole of their national existence, and an examination of these claim a place in our series. Moses says: "And yet for all that, when they be in the land of their enemies, I will not cast them away, neither will I abhor them, to destroy them utterly, and to break my covenant with them: for I am the Lord their God."

I must here read some more *prophetic data* before summing up the testimonies on the subject before us. I read first from Jeremiah, 46: 28. "Fear thou not O Jacob, my servant, saith the Lord; for I am with thee; for I will make a full end of all the nations whither I have driven thee; but I will not make a full end of thee, but correct thee in measure; yet will I not leave thee wholly unpunished." Again, Jeremiah 31: 35, 36, 37. "Thus saith the Lord, which giveth the sun for a light by day, and the ordinances of the moon and of the stars for a light by night, which divideth the sea when the waves thereof roar; the Lord of hosts is his name. If those ordinances depart from before me, saith the Lord, then the seed of Israel also shall cease from being a nation before me forever. Thus saith the Lord: If Heaven above can be measured, and the foundations of the earth searched out beneath, I will also cast off all the seed of Israel, for all that they have done, saith the Lord." We will next read Hosea 3: 4, 5: "For the children of Israel shall abide many days without a king, and without a prince, and without a sacrifice, and without an image, and without an ephod, and without a teraphim. Afterward, shall the children of Israel return and seek the Lord their God, and David their king; and shall fear the Lord and his goodness in the latter days."

"There is nothing in the history of nations so unaccountable on human principles as the destruction and preservation of the Jews." Citizens of the world and yet citizens of no country, subject to kings but not their own, obedient to laws but not of their own framing, oppressed but not oppressing, persecuted but not persecuting, "like the bush that was burning, but not consumed." "They shall not be utterly destroyed," said the Prophet Moses. They shall still exist, but not as they once did—without king, prince, sacrifice, image, teraphim, etc. In this condition they were to "abide many days." For almost eighteen hundred years they have existed in this condition—a people who were so prone to image worship—a people who, for a thousand years, could not be kept from idolatry; but now, when their temptations have been greater, they have existed without an image, for no image or idols are to be found in their synagogues. There are many wicked practices charged upon this nation, but the pen of the historian has not accused them of the sin of idolatry for eighteen hundred years. Once they had kings—once they had princes, sacrifices, ephods, images, and teraphim. But ever since the destruction of their Temple—the breaking up of their priesthood—they have existed without these.

"I will make a full end of all the nations whither

I have driven thee, but I will not make a full end of thee." The *first* has been literally fulfilled.

MR. HARTZEL'S NINTH ADDRESS.

A few words of reply. You remember that Mr. Barker undertook to make a point in relation to the words of prophecy, "*utterly destroyed.*" He says, "to destroy means to kill, and that the nation is still alive, and that we have failed in our last argument." Let him prove that "destroy" necessarily means "to kill," and he will have made a capital argument. "And they shall serve other Gods, which neither thou nor thy fathers have known." Well, they did serve other Gods, as the history clearly shows, while in Babylon.

The Prophecies to which we referred, relate to another period in the history of the Jewish nation, and we have shown that they fully describe their present condition. We have then established our point. The Prophet says they would be in that condition a long time — "for many days." They have been in the condition described for eighteen hundred years, and are so at present. We acknowledge the prophecy to which Mr. Barker referred was literally fulfilled. We also claim a literal fulfillment for those which we have cited.

Mr. Barker says there were no points of likeness

between Moses and Jesus Christ. Let us see: Moses was forty days on the Mount; Jesus was forty days on the Mount. Moses was a law-giver; Jesus Christ was a law-giver. Moses was a Prophet; Jesus Christ was a Prophet. There are many other points of resemblance, but the coincidences we have named are sufficient to justify what we said upon that prophecy, and the accomplishment is plain and undeniable.

Mr. Barker says we thought we had found a point with regard to his saying that Christ was angry. I did not think so. All I thought was that he had not found one. I shall show, then, what a point would be. I only said there was no contradiction in relation to that subject. If Mr. Barker will find a passage which says that Christ was never angry, then he will have made out his case.

Mr. Barker. I did not quote it as a contradiction.

Mr. Hartzel. Then, as to the abolition of slavery and the sects most opposed to it; who hold that slavery is ordained of God and sanctioned in the Bible, who refer with great assurance to "cursed be Canaan, a servant of servants shall he be," &c., we have something to offer on that subject hereafter.*

---

*"And Noah awoke from his wine, and knew what his younger son had done unto him. And he said, cursed be Canaan; a servant of servants shall he be unto his brethren. And he said, blessed be the Lord God of Shem; and Canaan shall be his servant. Gen. 9. 24. 26."

Slaveholders and apologists for American slavery press this scripture into their service, and infidel abolitionists into theirs. They agree as to the meaning of the text. They only differ in the application. They first claim it as a guarantee for Americans to enslave the African race, and the second as an objection against the inspiration of the Bible. I shall briefly examine their respective claims.

First. They claim that Noah's awakening from his "wine," and the malediction pronounced upon "Canaan" were in the order of time, as they stand in the order of history. Is this a legitimate conclusion? surely not in a history so condensed that nine chapters engross a period of 2006 years; where events are connected in the order of words, which were many years apart in the order of time. "And Noah began to be a husbandman, and he planted a vineyard: And drank of the wine and was drunken,"

My friend mentions the Quakers as favorable to abolition, and claims that they are unbelievers. The Quakers are not infidels. They receive the Bible as of divine authority. I have their declaration of faith. I will read from their own official documents to prove my position, at the proper time and place.

With regard to Mr. Barker's caricature upon the subject of marriage, we shall come to this in the regular course of our argument. He quotes from 3rd chapter of Peter: "Likewise ye wives be in subjection to your own husbands, &c." If he had read the whole connection, his objections would have had no force. I will read it: "Likewise, ye husbands, dwell with them according to knowledge, giving honor unto the wife, as unto the weaker vessel, and as being heirs together of the grace of life." I pledge

---

etc. There were some years between these events. There was first, the "planting," second, the growth of the vine, etc. Would it be safe to connect the "planting" of the "vineyard" and the inebriation as following each other in immediate succession? We say no.

"Farther, only "eight" souls entered the ark and "eight" came out of the ark. The "curse" was pronounced upon Canaan, not upon Ham. There is no evidence that Canaan was born at the time that Noah recovered from the influence of his wine, for he was the fourth son of Ham; there may have been many years between Noah's intoxication and his predicting the future fortunes of his sons. We are not at all certain that Ham was the father of Canaan at the time Noah "awoke from his wine;" but we are sure that he was at the time, and long before the history (Genesis) was written.

It is, then, of the most doubtful interpretation that the cursiug of Ganaan had any connection with anything good or bad that Ham had done, or that it resulted from any vindictive feeling either toward Ham or his son "Canaan." Neither does the word "curse" in the text necessarily imply any unkind feeling toward his son or his grandson. Among the many meanings of the word "curse" is this: "devoted to destruction;" "devoted Canaan." "Ah, devoted Canaan."—Thompson's translation. When God made known to Cain his future destiny, he employed the word "curse" in the same sense. "And now art thou cursed from the earth," "devoted to destruction." And this prophecy was as literally fulfilled, for all his descendants perished in the flood which God brought upon the ungodly, just as he subjected to servitude and destruction the descendants of Canaan when the cup of their iniquity was full.

Second. They assume that "Ham's" conduct toward his father was disrespectful. Where is the proof? Did he make a mock of his father? Nay. He informed his "brothers without." The whole transaction on the part of the son shows nothing but FILIAL RESPECT.

The parties have based their claims upon nothing but assumption, which is always the case whenever the Bible is forced into a wrong service. Setting out from the same point, they first say the Bible justifies the relation of "master and slave," THEREFORE SLAVERY IS RIGHT. The others say, we agree with you that the Bible teaches slavery, but slavery is wrong, and the Bible is false.

We will now for the sake of the argument grant all that the advocates of American

myself, if you will be patient, that I will elaborate out of this volume, the principle which has accomplished more for the amelioration of mankind from all despotism, than all that human philosophy or Pagan mythology, or all other good men or systems, outside of the Scriptures, have *ever* accomplished. It is the law of nations that the strong shall oppress the weak — that might gives right. The teachings of our Lord Jesus Christ is the reverse; namely: "that the strong are to bear the infirmities of the weak." If my opponent will be patient I will meet these calumnies in due time. I have now noticed all and more than I deem worthy of a passing remark. I return to prophecy. "I will make a full end of all the nations whither I have driven thee, but I will not make an end of thee." There are two distinct features in this prediction; the first of

---

slavery claim of divine right from this scripture. And then we shall require of them, first; to prove that the American slaveholders were once themselves slaves; (servant of servants shall he be.) Second; That the Africans are the descendants of "Canaan." Third; That the commission God gave the Jews as his executives was not accomplished by them against the sinners, the "Canaanites." Fourth; That God is still carrying on a judicial process against the Africans (Canaanites) by the sons of Japheth, acting under another commission. I say when they shall have settled all these preliminary matters, we shall then be satisfied with their right, and shall only ask for their commission. Then will we make their slaveholding no more a matter of complaint or admonition, provided first; that they will show that the Jewish law (by which the servitude of the Canaanites was regulated,) is yet in full force for the special benefit of the Christian slaveholder, with this amendment; NO JUBILEE TO THE SLAVE FOREVER.

Hebrew slavery being impracticable in America, we will only ask of them this little thing; that they colonize themselves somewhere about central Africa, that they may buy of the heathen "round about them," for in their present location the American Indians are the "heathen round about them;" and when they have righted themselves as to location, that they buy their slaves, unless they have good evidence that another law has been amended or repealed, namely, "he that stealeth a man and selleth him shall surely be put to death." Come you sticklers for law and order, this thing of pleading law only for the right, and then managing the balance without, or in opposition to law don't look just right. You seem to have a great veneration for the Bible; you would not hold slaves if the Bible did not justify you in doing so. Your consciences are as tender upon the simple question of RIGHT TO BE MASTERS as were the Pharisees about the tithing of "mint, anise and cummin, and like them you reject the weightier matters," and violate every precept of the Hebrew law, regulating their domestic servitude. You do not yourselves (being Gentiles) acknowledge the obligations of that law any farther than as its moral principles have been transferred to the New Testament. Suppose the law of Moses were your standard of moral obligation to your slaves; now would the decision stand in that day when God will judge the secrets of man by Jesus Christ? "As many as have sinned in the law shall be judged by the law."

which has been literally fulfilled. I wish to refer you to McIlvaine, pages 205, 206:

"Where are the nations among whom the Jews were scattered? Has not the Lord, according to his word, MADE A FULL END OF THEM? While Israel has stood unconsumed in the fiery furnace, where are the nations that kindled its flames? Where the Assyrians and the Chaldeans? Their name is almost forgotten. Their existence is only known to history. Where is the empire of the Egyptians? The Macedonians destroyed it, and a descendant of its ancient race cannot be distinguished among the strangers that have ever since possessed its territory. Where are they of Macedon? The Roman sword subdued their kingdom, and their posterity are mingled inseparably among the confused population of Greece and Turkey. Where is the nation of ancient Rome, the last conquerors of the Jews, and the proud destroyers of Jerusalem? The Goths rolled their flood over its pride. Another nation inhabits the ancient city. Even the language of her former people is dead. The Goths! where are they? The Jews! where are they not? They witnessed the glory of Egypt, and of Babylon, and of Ninevah; they were in mature age at the birth of Macedon and of Rome; mighty kingdoms have risen and perished since they began to be scattered and enslaved; and now they traverse the ruins of all, the same people as when they left India—preserving in themselves a monument of the days of Moses and the Pharaohs, as unchanged as the pyramids of Memphis, which they are reputed to have built. You may call upon the ends of the earth, and will call in vain for one living representative of those powerful nations of antiquity, by whom the people of Israel were successively oppressed; but should the voice which is hereafter to gather that people out of all lands, be now heard from Mount Zion, calling for the children of Abraham, no less than four millions would instantly answer to the name, each bearing in himself unquestionable proofs of that noble lineage."

I will also read an extract from "Volney's Ruins," page 23:

"Here, said I, here once flourished an opulent city; here was the seat of a powerful empire. Yes! these places now so desert, were once animated by a living multitude, a busy crowd circulated in these streets, now so solitary. Within these walls, where a mournful silence reigns, the noise of the arts, and shouts of joy and festivity incessantly resounded; these piles of marble were regular palaces; these prostrate pillars adorned the majesty of temples; these ruined galleries surrounded public places. Here a numerous people assembled for the sacred duties of religion, or the anxious cares of their subsistence; here industry, parent of enjoyments collected the riches of all climates, and the purple of Tyre was exchanged for the precious thread of Serica; the soft tissues of Kachemire for the sumptuous tapestry of Lydia; the amber of the Baltic for the pearls and perfumes of Arabia; the gold of Ophir for the tin of Thule.

And now a mournful skeleton is all that subsists of this powerful city! Nought remains of its vast domination, but a doubtful and empty remembrance! To the tumultuous throng which crowded under these porticos has succeeded the solitude of death. The silence of the tomb is substituted for the bustle of public places. The opulence of a commercial city is changed into hideous poverty. The palaces of kings are become a den of wild beasts; flocks fold on the area of the temple, and unclean reptiles inhabit the sanctuary of the Gods! Ah! how has so much glory been eclipsed? How have so many labors been annihilated? Thus perish the works of men, and thus do empires and nations disappear!

And the history of former times revived in my mind. I recollected those distant ages when many illustrious nations inhabited these countries: I figured to myself the Assyrian on the banks of the Tigris, the Chaldean on those of the Euphrates, the Persian reigning from the Indus to the Mediterranean. I enumerated the kingdoms of Damascus and Idumea, of Jerusalem and Samaria, the warlike states of the Philistines, and the commercial republics of Phœnicia. This Syria, said I, now so depopulated, then contained a hundred flourishing cities, and abounded with towns, villages, and hamlets. Every where were seen cultivated fields, frequented roads, and crowded habitations. Ah! what are become of those ages of abundance and of life? How have so many brilliant creations of human industry vanished? Where are those ramparts of Nineveh, those walls of Babylon, those palaces of Persepolis, those temples of Balbeck and Jerusalem? Where are those fleets of Tyre, those dock-yards of Arad, those work-shops of Sidon, and that multitude of sailors, of pilots, of merchants, and of soldiers? Where those husbandmen, those harvests, those flocks, and all the creation of living beings in which the face of the earth rejoiced? Alas! I have passed over this desolate land! I have visited the palaces, once the theater of so much splendor, and I beheld nothing but solitude and desolation. I sought the ancient inhabitants and their works, and could only find a faint trace, like that of the foot of a traveler over the sand. The temples are fallen, the palaces overthrown, the ports filled up, the cities destroyed, and the earth, stripped of inhabitants, seems a dreary burying-place. Great God! whence proceed such fatal revolutions? What causes have so altered the fortunes of these countries? Why are so many cities destroyed? Why has not this ancient population been re-produced and perpetuated?"

I have given, for the consideration of my friend

and the audience, not the testimony of a corrupt Christian priest, but I have brought the testimony from the other side of the house. You have heard his testimony to the point in the argument, for which we read him. This testimony must have its full weight on the subject, for surely Volney cannot be suspected of having any partiality in favor of Christianity. It cannot be supposed that this apostle of infidelity would have written for the confirmation of prophecy. We then say, upon the testimony of a competent witness, and he an avowed enemy of the Bible, that God has made an end of these nations who were once the oppressors of the Jews, and honored the truth of his prophetic word.

"But I will not make a full end of thee." "The Jews, where are they," or rather, "where are they not?" "The laws of nature have been suspended in their case." "A stream has held on its way through a lake without losing the color and the characteristic marks of its own current." A mighty river, issuing from the mountain sides of Judea, has poured its contents into the ocean of life, where it has been broken and lashed into spray, hundreds and thousands of times; yet, strange to tell, every drop may be separated and identified as having passed into the sea of human existence through that particular channel. We would call this a miracle. All that is marvelous in this imaginary case, is literally true, with respect to this extraordinary people, the Jews.

Again, Jeremiah: "If these ordinances depart

from before me saith the Lord, then the seed of Israel shall cease to be a nation before me forever." The facts respond to the prophecy and say the Jews are still a nation separate and distinct from all other nations. If any nation on earth could have reason to run out its separate national existence, it must have been the Jewish. For eighteen hundred years their very name has been a badge of disgrace, and the signal for persecution. They have been the victims of popular fury and massacre. They have not only outlived their cotemporary nations, by whom they were oppressed in their dispersed condition, but also those who took their rise subsequently. They have seen the words of their Prophets fulfilled, in the entire destruction of these nations, and their own miraculous preservation. What is this but miracle connected with prophecy which it fulfills? It is a double miracle!

"Whether testimony can ever establish the credibility of a miracle, is a question of no importance here. This miracle is obvious to every man's senses. All nations are its eye-witnesses." The Jews are still among our richest pedlars, merchants, bankers and brokers, and possess a vast amount of floating wealth. Once they were the greatest agricultural people in the world. Such is the testimony of history: yet, now they are exclusively engaged in commerce. So far as I know there is but one Jew under Heaven who depends upon the productions of the soil for subsistance and wealth. This is Meshullem, who purchased from the Sultan a beautiful and fertile plain, some six miles from Jerusalem, and is carrying on extensive and successful farming operations; so much so, that it has excited the cupidity of the English Hierarchy.

They will not cultivate the lands belonging to the Gentiles, either for themselves or as hirelings. If there are exceptions, they are so few that they do not affect the general result.

How strong must be that bond of union which has bound them together through so long a period of time, and so many fearful revolutions! No national policy can explain this *phenomenon*, for they have none. Their local position will not solve the wonder, for this has been most unfavorable to their union. Nothing will solve it, but the peculiarities of their religion, and the superintending care of the Almighty. And the anticipation of their precise condition for so long a period, can only be solved by acknowledging "that the Bible contains communications supernaturally revealed." "*They are still beloved for their father's sake!*"

I shall now ask your attention to those prophecies which relate more directly to Jesus Christ, and his coming. These are numerous, varied and minute. "To him give all the Prophets witness." "The spirit of Prophecy is the testimony of Jews."

Argument 6*: On the time of the coming of Christ. Prophetic date.*

The sceptre shall not depart from Judah, nor a

law-giver from between his feet, until Shiloh come." Dr. Adam Clarke gives "*sent*" as the definition of Shiloh. The *sceptre* as the ensign of royalty. The point in this prophecy is, that the kingship should still be in the tribe of Judah till the coming of Christ; and so it was, "Judah grasped the sceptre with a feeble hand." But the Jews were still a united people. A king ruled over them. They were governed by their own laws, and their judges were from among their own brethren. The power of life and death was in their hands, until about twelve years after the birth of Christ. The same year that Jesus, the Son of Mary, made his first public appearance, Archelaus, their King was banished. Caponius, a Gentile, was appointed *Procurator*, and the kingdom of Judea, the last remnant of its regal glory, was debased, and became a part of the Province of Syria.

Absolute princely power has not been exercised by a Jew from that day to the present, save by David's Son, and David's Lord; and this in fulfillment of a prophecy uttered nearly three thousand years before! What an overwhelming proof of inspiration! How improbable, at the time this prophecy was delivered, that Judah would ever furnish a king! At that time he was a *slave* and continued so for many years after; and after his emancipation, and taking possession of the land of promise, the Jews were governed by Judges for the space of four hundred years; their government was a Theocracy—a most beautiful social arrangement—supposed by many to have been one of the best forms of republicanism ever enjoyed by any people. Now the Jews desired a king. (1st Saml. 8th chap.) Samuel came before the Lord, and the Lord said: "Hearken unto the voice of the people, in all that they say unto thee, for they have not rejected thee, but they have rejected me, that I should not rule over them." He ordered Samuel to tell them what manner of king they should have. That he would take their sons and make servants of them, and of their daughters he would make confectioners, bakers, cooks, etc. All these things were faithfully submitted for their consideration. Still the people were clamorous and would not hearken to Samuel. "We will have a king to rule over us." A king was given them. "I gave them a king in my anger and took him away in my wrath." This shows an important principle in the divine government. When the heart of an individual or of a nation is determined upon a certain thing, and they cannot be dissuaded from their purpose, God will even let them have it, that they may be taught a lesson by their own devices. He, therefore, gave them a king, that they might learn a lesson by experience, which they refused to learn from the divine counsel.

When finally a kingship was orignated in Israel, it was not in the tribe of Judah, but in the tribe of Benjamin. How discouraging and dark everything appeared thus far with respect to the sceptre passing into the hand of Judah! Saul, a Benjaminite, wears the crown royal. But he is unfaithful. God removed him, and appointed David, the son of Jesse, of the tribe of Judah, to be head over Israel. David is annointed king and now the sceptre passes into the hand of Judah. Judah now became the royal family, and continued to be from David until Archelaus, the son of Herod, was removed by order of a Heathen Emperor.

Who can tell who shall be our next President? Who has sufficient political sagacity and forecast to foretell who shall fill the Presidential chair in three years from now? Who can tell into what family the Presidency will pass at next election? No one. We are utterly unable, with all the data we have, and surely there is not a little from which a far-sighted politician might make some calculation, and yet no one would run a hazard or stake his reputation upon his foreknowledge. But infinite wisdom could foretell, that after so many hundred years, the "sceptre" should pass into the hand of Judah, and should continue in that tribe until the coming of "Shiloh," *two thousand years* distant from the date of the prophecy.

Again: "I will shake all nations and the desire of all nations will come: and I will fill this house with glory, saith the Lord."

MR. HARTZEL'S TENTH ADDRESS.

Mr. Barker, in answer to some remarks we made with reference to the great promoters of civilization, claimed that the Quakers, with many others he named, were infidels.

Mr. Barker. "I said only that most of them were unbelievers."

Mr. Hartzel. Joseph John Gurney, an orthodox Quaker, says, (page 5 of a pamphlet, entitled "A Declaration of his Faith respecting several points of Christian Doctrine :)

"The Holy Scriptures. My belief respecting the Scriptures of the Old and New Testament may be stated in the words of George Fox : 'Concerning the Holy Scriptures, we believe they were given forth by the Holy Spirit of God, through the holy men of God, who spake as they were moved by the Holy Ghost. We believe they are to be read, believed, and fulfilled, (he that fulfills them is Christ ;) and they are profitable for reproof, for correction, and for instruction in righteousness ; that the man of God may be perfect, thoroughly furnished unto all good works, and are able to make wise unto salvation, through faith in Christ Jesus. We believe the Holy Scriptures are the words of God.'"

We might give other testimonies on the same point, and shall if called for.

Mr. Barker referred to the Law in Deuteronomy, chap. 14: 21, as something exceedingly objectionable; namely, that the Jews were allowed to give to the stranger and sell to the alien, the meat of animals that had died by disease. The Jews had been accustomed to eat such flesh, or why prohibit it? The prohibition is evidence that they had done so hitherto.

They were to be a peculiar people, from henceforth, for important purposes; therefore the Lord forbade them the use of this kind of flesh in the future. Here was some progression. The custom of eating such flesh was universal at that time, and among the nations surrounding the Jews. It may have been esteemed a luxury. The Jews were prohibited, but their laws could not, of course, operate upon the heathen. It is somewhat strange, I must say, that my friend should prefer such charges against this Old Testament law, since during his own life-time—within thirty years—the custom of eating such flesh has prevailed in many parts of civilized England. We have living witnesses to this fact, whom I could name, but will not at present. Some Germans, and those of other nations whom we call civilized, do so to this day.

Geology again: If Mr. Barker had only read Hitchcock, and let us judge of its contents without perverting the text with his comments, there would have been no occasion for my referring to it again. If God had spoken to man in the language of physical science, it would have been impossible to have made them understand what was meant, unless he had also given them instruction in physical science, which appears to have formed no part of his design. God does nothing for man that man can do for himself.

The argument of Mr. Barker this morning, upon nature, is answered by a reference to his own writings; for, if there had never been any "supernatural communications," I could see no propriety in his reasoning against the Bible; for, if there is nothing supernatural—if it be true that nature is *all*, and *all* is nature—then slavery, priestcraft, infidelity, atheism, sectarianism, can neither be called bad nor good: they are but so many manifestations of nature. This was my argument. How did he meet it? He did *not* meet it. He gave us his views of progression. I made an argument on progression in reply. Did he meet it?

I shall proceed.* "I will shake all nations; and the desire of all nations shall come, and will fill this house with glory saith the Lord: Again, and the glory of this latter house shall be greater than the former." Haggai 2: 7—9. Sometime previous to this prophecy, the Samaritans made propositions to

---

*Mr. Barker has now taken this position, "That the nations who do not progress will be destroyed—and destruction becomes a means of progression." Is not this giving up the question that man is, by the laws of his own nature, a "progressive" being? It is conceded that some nations do not "progress." If we had accurate statistics of the nations who make no advance in art, in science, in morals, etc., we would doubtless see that a vast majority of the mighty whole are doomed to destruction, on Mr. Barker's plan, and HIS MEANS OF PROGRESSION."

Now, what of the "progression" of the race collectively, when some have retrograded into a state of CANNABALISM, and yet are not "destroyed?" "Is Saul, also, among the prophets?" Is the "progression" of the "race" a matter of CALCULATION, or is it a matter of PROPHECY? If "progression" was universal, if all "progressed," if it were but the millionth part of an inch, in knowledge and virtue in a million of years, it might be a matter of feasible calculation. What is characteristic of the species is common to the individuals. (Fury is characteristic of the lion as a species, because common to the individuals.) In the light of this TRUISM, let us look at man. If "progression" were a characteristic of the "race," it would be common to ALL UNDER ALL CIRCUMSTANCES. But the truth is, as Mr. Barker says, some nations "progress" not at all. The experience of every individual, nay "the record of history fails to trace the movement of the index of the HUGE DIAL." "The hand of the great clock moves so immeasurably slow, that it is impossible to note it," and a philosopher might modestly doubt the truth of the theory, and say no. As it now is, so it always has been. Some nations advance, while others RETROGRADE. And even among the nations who do advance in knowledge and virtuous excellence, there are many individuals on the descending scale—with all the help of the most favorable circumstances, are waxing WORSE and WORSE continually. It is most certain that this golden age, to come for the "race," in the CONCRETE, is not "calculation," for the index of the world's history points the other way. It is then a matter of prophecy? Yes; and the truth is, (if it be a truth,) for which progressionists contend, that as with other parts of their system, "it is but a PLAGIARISM from the ABJURED Bible." And, if I must believe prophecy, I prefer the sublime strains of the Hebrew and Christian prophets, to the visionary prose of any OMNISCIENT CLAIRVOYANT or my friend Joseph Barker. I do most sincerely disbelieve their prediction about their infidel MILLENNIUM, and their means by which it is to be brought about.

the Jews, to unite with them in the rebuilding of the Temple, as they "worshipped the same God, and especially prayed to him," and were desirous of their religious settlement, etc. But they declined their offer, and in their response offered them the privilege common to others, "to come to the Temple and worship God there." The Samaritans now wrote an epistle to Darius to stop the building. At this time the Governor of Syria and Phœnicia sent a deputation to Jerusalem for the purpose of embarrassing the Jews in this enterprise. The Sanhedrim referred this deputation to the edict of Cyrus, under whose direction they had commenced the work, and challenged their adversaries to investigate the matter. They accordingly wrote to Darius. Darius sent them a copy of Cyrus' edict to rebuild the temple, etc.—Josephus, book 11, chap. 4. "During the period of the troublous times the Jews became disheartened—their workmen relaxed their energies for a time—but, when Haggai delivered his predictions they resumed the work with great energy."

"The glory of this latter house shall be greater that the former, saith the Lord of hosts, and in this place will I give peace saith the Lord of hosts." We claim that this is a prediction of the coming of the Messiah. This latter house, however, was not to be greater than the former on account of its magnificence. Josephus relates the facts as to its inferiority. I believe they are every way reliable; that when the young men saw the temple they rejoiced;

but when the old men looked upon it, they wept: for they saw how much inferior it was, when compared with the former, in which the tribes were wont to rejoice before God. The remembrance of which made them weep in Babylon, as described in the beautiful language of one of their prophets in the 137th Psalm: "By the rivers of Babylon there we sat down; yea we wept, when we remembered Zion. We hanged our harps upon the willows in the midst thereof. For there they that carried us away captive required of us a song; and they that wasted us required of us mirth, saying: Sing us one of the songs of Zion. How shall we sing the Lord's song in a strange land? If I forget thee, O Jerusalem, let my right hand forget her cunning. If I do not remember thee, let my tongue cleave to the roof of my mouth; if I prefer not Jerusalem above my chief joy."

But wherein *did* the superiority of this latter house consist? Let Malachi answer: "Behold I will send my messenger, and he shall prepare the way before me; and the Lord whom ye seek, shall suddenly come to his temple, even the messenger of the covenant, whom ye delight in; behold he shall come, saith the Lord of hosts." Let us examine the points in this; first: "The Lord whom ye seek"—whom ye look for—whom ye desire—"and the desire of all nations." I intend to introduce a considerable amount of reading to this point. I shall open the "Debate" between Campbell and Owen, part 2d, pages 74–76:

"But so clearly was the event predicted, and so general was the knowledge of it, through the Septuagint version of the Jewish Scriptures, then read through the Roman Empire, that the expectation became general, that at this time some wonderful personage was to be born, who would put the world under a new government. This singular fact shows that the prophecies concerning the time in which the Messiah should be born were so plain, in the estimation of all who read them, as to preclude all doubt as to the time of the appearance of the Messiah. But some will ask, Where is the proof of the fact that such an expectation was general? I answer, the history and poetry of Rome prove it. We shall summon some of their historians and the Manteran bard to give their evidence in the case:

"Suetonius, in the life of Vespasian.—An ancient and constant tradition has obtained throughout all the East, that in the fates it was decreed, that about that time, 'some who should come from Judea would obtain the dominion of the world.'

"Cornelius Tacitus speaks to the same effect, when speaking of the prodigies which preceded the destruction of Jerusalem. He says, That 'many understood them as forerunners of that extraordinary person, whom the ANCIENT BOOKS of the priest did foretell should come about that time from Judea and obtain the dominion.'

"From the Jewish prophets, the Pagan sybils gave out their oracles, so that the expectation was universal. The same year that Pompey took Jerusalem one of the sybil oracles made a great noise, 'that Nature was about to bring forth a king to the Romans.' Suetonius says, this so terrified the Roman Senate that they made a decree that none born that year should be educated. And in his life of Augustus he says, that 'those whose wives were pregnant that year did each conceive great hopes, applying the prophecy to themselves.'

"Appian, Sallust, Plutarch, and Cicero, all say that this prophecy of the sibyls stirred up Cornelius Lentulus to think that he was the man who should be king of the Romans. Some applied it to Cæsar. Cicero laughed at the application, and affirmed that this prophecy should not be applied to any one born in Rome.

"Even Virgil the poet, who wrote his fourth Eclogue about the time of Herod the Great, compliments the Consul Pollis with this prophecy, supposing it might refer to his son Salonimes, then born. Virgil substantially quotes and versifies the prophecies of Isaiah, and applies them to this child Salonimes:

"The last age decreed by Fate, is come;
And a new frame of all things does begin.
A holy progeny from Heaven descends.
Auspicious be his birth! which puts an end
To the iron age! and from whence shall rise
A golden state far glorious through the earth!

"Then the poet alludes to Isaiah 65: 17: 'The wolf and the lamb shall feed together, and the LION shall eat straw like the ox. They shall not hurt nor destroy in all my holy mountain:'

"Nor shall the flocks fierce lions fear,
Nor serpent shall be there, nor herb of poisonous juice.

"Then the expiation of Daniel is referred to:

"By thee what footsteps of our sins remain,
Are blotted out, and the whole world set free
From her perpetual bondage and her fear.

"The very words of Haggai, last quoted, are by the poet next referred to:

"Enter on thy honors! Now 's the time
Offspring of God! O thou great gift of Jove!
Behold this world! Heaven, Earth and Seas do shake!
Behold how all rejoice to greet that glorious day!

"Virgil, as if he were skilled in the Jewish Scriptures, goes on to state that these glorious times should not immediately succeed the birth of that wonderful child:

"Yet some remains shall still be left
Of ancient fraud; and wars shall still go on.

"Now the question is not, whether Virgil applied this partly to Augustus, Pollis, or Salonimes then born; but, whether he did not apply it to the general expectation everywhere prevalent, that a wonderful person was to be born, and a new age to commence?

"The Jews have been so confounded with these prophecies and events, that such of them as did not believe, have degraded Daniel from the rank of a great prophet to one of the inferior prophets; and others have said, that there were two Messiahs to come—one a suffering, and one a triumphant Messiah. But the excuses of mankind for their unbelief are so frivolous and irrational, that they deserve pity rather than argument. It is worthy of remark, however, that not only the Gentiles, the proselytes to the Jews' religion, the Eastern magi; but myriads of the Jews themselves recognized these evidences, and bowed to their authority."

"One was to prepare his way." Jesus says: "I was daily in the temple." "The Lord shall suddenly come to his temple," after his way was prepared. He must first be introduced as the son of that Father whose house they had desecrated. The Queen of Sheba had come from a far-distant country to see the glory and hear the wisdom of Solomon. But Jesus said, "behold a greater than Solomon"—"the builder of the former temple is here."

To sum up this prophetic data, Christ was to come before the second temple had gone into decay—at the time when all nations were expecting him. He was to come immediately after the coming of John the Baptist. "Prepare ye the way of the Lord," etc. All these predictions meet in the reputed son of Joseph. The desire of all nations did come, when the expectation was prevalent. When he came, the temple stood in all its glory—not one "stone" was removed. "The voice of one crying in the wilderness, prepare ye the way of the Lord, make his paths straight," was heard; and, soon after his death, every mark of his coming was erased. Therefore the Jews look in vain for a Messiah yet to come. Who but the Spirit of God could have foretold all these events? Who but God could have justified his own word, and brought about the fulfillment of prophecy by corresponding events; events which have no significance, if we deny God's predetermination.

Argument seven: Still further with regard to the time of Christ's coming, and the setting up of his kingdom." I shall read from the prophecies of Daniel 2: 35–45: "Then was the iron, the clay, the brass, the silver, and the gold, broken to pieces together, and became like the chaff of the summer threshing floors; and the wind carried them away, that no place was found for them; and the stone that smote the image became a great mountain, and filled the whole earth. This is the dream; and we will tell the interpretation thereof before the king. Thou, O king, art a king of kings: for the God of Heaven hath given thee a kingdom, power, and strength, and glory. And wheresoever the children of men dwell, the beasts of the field, and the fowls of heaven, hath he given into thine hand, and hath made thee ruler over them all; thou art this head of gold. And after thee shall arise another kingdom inferior to thee, and another third kingdom of brass, which shall bear rule over all the earth. And the fourth kingdom shall be strong as iron; forasmuch as iron breaketh in pieces and subdueth all things, and as iron that breaketh all these, shall it break in pieces and bruise. And whereas thou sawest the feet and toes, part of potter's clay and part of iron; the kingdom shall be divided, but there shall be in it of the strength of the iron, forasmuch as thon sawest the iron mixed with miry clay. And as the toes of the feet were part of iron and part of clay; so the kingdom shall be partly strong, and partly broken. And whereas thou sawest iron mixed with miry clay, they shalt mingle themselves with the seed of men; but they shalt not cleave one to another, even as iron is not mixed with clay. And in the days of these kings shall the Lord of Heaven set up a kingdom which shall never be destroyed; and the kingdom shall not be left to other people, but it shall break in pieces and consume all these kingdoms, and it shall stand forever. Forasmuch as thou sawest that the stone was cut out of the mountain without hands, and that it brake in pieces the iron, the brass, the clay, the silver, and the gold; the great God hath made known to the king what shall come to pass hereafter: and the dream is certain, and the interpretation thereof sure."

Nebuchadnezzar, a Gentile, had the dream; and Daniel, the Jew, gave the interpretation. "Babylon and Jerusalem attest its truth." Gentiles and Jews combine in making the revelations, and both are concerned in their future consummation, and are equally interested in the setting up of the fifth kingdom, symbolized by the "stone cut out of the mountain without hands, that should fill the whole earth." Daniel says, the "head of gold" is the *Chaldean* dynasty. This lasted fourteen hundred years, and was subverted seven hundred and seventy years before the coming of Christ. The "silver shoulders" are the Medo-Persian dynasty. This continued two hundred years, and fell three hundred and thirty-six years before the Christian era. The "brazen body" was the Macedonian Empire. This continued only ten years, and ended three hundred and twenty-four years before Christ. The "iron legs" were the Roman Empire. This was the last of the four great Pagan Empires, which held in turn the supremacy of the world; and make out the three "overturnings" of Ezekiel's prophecy. In the last overturn he was to come "whose right it was;" and he should wear the crown and the diadem. And in the days of these kings, symbolized by the iron part of the image shall the God of Heaven set up a kingdom which shall never be destroyed. Thus prophecy joins prophecy in fixing in advance the time of Christ's coming, and the beginning of his earthly reign.

Now we must consult the historic portions of the New Testament: "And it came to pass in those days, that there went out a decree from Cæsar Augustus, that all the world should be taxed." While this tax-law was in operation, Joseph and Mary went up to Bethlehem to enrol their names: while there, the Messiah was born. This fact meets one point. Jesus Christ then was born while the Roman Cæsar Augustus was upon the throne; not before the iron kingdom was brought into existence, nor after it had passed away; but while that part of the kingdom, symbolized by the "iron" part of the "image" was in existence: now it was that Christ the Messiah was born. For the sake of brevity we pass. But nothing is heard about the setting up of a new kingdom yet; all is moving along quietly. The strong "iron" kingdom holds the supremacy of the world; while the Jews are under the Governorship of one of their own nation, and their courts are formed of their brethren. They yet exercise the right of trying offenders by their own courts, and executing the sentence of law upon the culprits.

Some twenty-eight years after the inquiry was made in Jerusalem, "Where is he that is born king of the Jews?" a singular personage appeared in the wilderness of Judea. His personal appearance was grave and solemn. His mode of subsistence abstemious. His costume that of the ancient prophets. His voice was heard on the banks of the Jordan—"Repent ye, for the kingdom of Heaven is at hand." Tiberius Cæsar was now upon the throne of universal empire. The Jews went out to hear this voice crying in the wilderness, "prepare ye the way of the Lord, make his paths straight." "Repent ye, for the kingdom of Heaven is at hand." While John was baptizing such as professed repentance, came Jesus also. You may see the account in Matthew, 3d chapter. When this stranger appeared for baptism, the Baptist forbade him, saying "I have need to be baptized of thee, and comest thou to me?" And Jesus answering, said unto him "Suffer it to be so now; for thus it becometh us to fulfill all righteousness: then he acquiesced." "And Jesus, when he was baptized, went up straightway out of the water; and lo, the Heavens were opened unto him, and he saw the Spirit of God descending like a dove, and lighting upon him: and lo, a voice from Heaven saying, This is my beloved son in whom I am well pleased." The "Holy Spirit," in the form of a "dove" identified his person. Now there could be no misunderstanding as to the person recognized by the voice and introduced to the audience, as the Son of God. John the Baptist preached, "the kingdom of Heaven is at hand." The Lord Jesus proclaimed the same, "repent ye, for the kingdom of Heaven is at hand." He commissioned the twelve, and sent them to the "lost sheep of the house of Israel." Then he commissioned "other seventy," and sent them forth on the same mission. The prayer and the sermon were in perfect harmony. The prayer was—"Thy kingdom come." The sermon—"The kingdom of Heaven is at hand." Meanwhile, in the mighty contest between Jesus Christ and his countrymen, the Heaven-appointed king of that kingdom which was soon to be set up, was brought to trial. One of his Judges asked the question, "Art thou king of the Jews?" Jesus answered, "To this end was I born, and for this cause came I into the world, that I should bear witness unto the truth." He was tried and condemned. The prospect of his becoming a king was doubtful. When the king falls in battle, the kingdom is subverted or passes into other hands. The hope of the Disciples was blasted. How natural, how artless their communication with each other! "We trusted it was he that should have redeemed Israel." But the Savior rises from the grave, and hope revives. So strong was the expectation of the Jews, that their Messiah would be a king, that when he was crucified and buried, the unbelieving portion of them supposed they had triumphed, and his Disciples were disappointed in their expectation of having a deliverer in Jesus of Nazareth. Peter says, "I go a fishing." But no sooner did they see him alive again, than their former hope revives, and then fondly ask, immediately before his ascension, "wilt thou at this time restore again the kingdom to Israel?" How can we account for this expectation, that the Messiah would come? How can we account for the fact, that both Jews and Gentiles expected such a personage, upon any other than their prophetic writings? "Yet have I set my king," says David, "upon my holy hill of Zion"—the king whose right it is to reign. "The God of Heaven shall set up a kingdom." The preaching of John the Baptist greatly strengthened this expectation; and the expectation was gaining strength all the time until Messiah was cut off. The unbelieving Jews, with their ancient oracles in hand, are still looking for their promised Messiah. But when Jesus Christ arose from the dead, the disciples had the fulfillment of promise and prophecy "miraculously attested." The resurrection of Christ was the greatest and most convincing of all the New Testament miracles. After this, his Disciples doubted no more; for here they had now a double miracle. The delivery of the prophecy was an *intellectual* miracle, and his literal rising from the dead, was a *physical* miracle.

MR. HARTZEL'S ELEVENTH ADDRESS.

The reading and study of the prophetic writings have not, as yet, had the effect predicted by Mr. Barker. The more I have read, compared and examined prophecy with history and seen its fulfillment, the more I have been confirmed in the inspiration of the Bible. I must read again from Haggai. You will remember that the Jews were engaged at this time in rebuilding the temple. Haggai 2: 1–9:

"In the seventh month, in the one and twentieth day of the month, came the word of the Lord by the prophet Haggai, saying: Speak now to Zerubbabel the son of Shealtiel, governor of Judah, and to Joshua the son of Josedech, the High Priest, and to the residue of the people, saying: Who is left among you that saw this house in her first glory? and how do ye see it now? is it not in your eyes, in comparison of it as nothing? Yet now be strong, O Zerubbabel, saith the Lord; and be strong, O Joshua son of Josedech, the High Priest; and be strong all ye people of the land, saith the Lord, and work: for I am with you saith the Lord of hosts. According to the word that I covenanted with you when ye came out of Egypt, so my spirit remaineth among you: fear ye not. For thus saith the Lord of hosts; Yet once, it is a little while, and I will shake the Heavens and the earth, and the sea and the dry land; And I will shake all nations, and the desire of all nations shall come; and I will fill this house with glory saith the Lord of hosts. The silver is mine, and the gold is mine, saith the Lord of hosts. The glory of this latter house shall be greater than of the former, saith the Lord of hosts: and in this place will I give peace saith the Lord of hosts."

I do not like to animadvert upon my friend's intelligence or candor. The "*little while*" did not refer to that part of the prophecy, "*the desire of all nations*," but to the "shaking of the Heavens and the earth," which, metaphorically, in the Bible, mean governments; and the connection must determine whether ecclesiastical or political. And was there not a tremendous shaking of the political heavens for the next five hundred years? To that the "*little while*" referred. It stands in connection with these events. "And I will shake all nations and the desire of all nations shall come: and I will fill this house with glory, saith the Lord of hosts." I will first "shake all nations" then the "Desire of all nations shall come." Who does not know that for some time before the coming of Christ there had been the greatest political agitation. The Emperor Augustus was upon the throne. He administered the government with so much prudence that it was a time of universal peace, when *the* Christ was born.

"The silver is mine, and the gold is mine, saith the Lord of hosts." I will be forthcoming to you and supply you with materials necessary to accomplish the work. "The glory of this latter house shall be greater than the former, saith the Lord of hosts, and in this place will I give peace saith the Lord of hosts." The word "peace" was in those days used in a sense different from now. We now understand by the word "*peace*," quietness, a kind of repose. But the word "*peace*" in those days meant, not only that, but almost every blessing, comfort, consolation.

This is what we understand by the word "*peace*" in this passage.

The same, shall I say, disingenuousness or ignorance of prophecy appears in his remarks upon this passage: "Behold I will send my messenger, and he shall prepare the way before me: and the Lord whom ye seek, shall suddenly come to his temple, even the messenger of the covenant, whom ye delight in: behold he shall come saith the Lord of hosts." Mr. Barker grounds his objection to my argument on the wrong feature in this prophecy. "Suddenly come to his temple." That is, immediately after the coming of John the Baptist. There are two "messengers" in this prediction. One was to "prepare" the way of the Lord. The Lord was the "messenger" of the "covenant." Jesus Christ is styled "mediator of the new covenant." "He shall suddenly come." How "suddenly" did he come? I cannot tell exactly how many days or months it was after his baptism before he was seen in the "temple." It was not long, only forty days after, that he entered upon his public ministry. He first took a tour into the land of "Zebulon." He was seen in the "temple" soon enough to justify the language of Malachi.

I am sorry that Mr. Barker is dragging in so much irrelevant matter, and will not reply to my arguments. Why this waste of time? What was the testimony of Gibbon, one of his own side of the house, in regard to Christianity, in its going forth in its begining? I read from a book entitled, "Infidelity Refuted by Infidels." We have here the testimony of a number of infidels who wrote against Christianity in the early ages of the church. I have the same list of witnesses by Mr. Barker in favor of Christianity. The testimony which I am about to read and the testimony found in his own book do agree, and therefore depose to the same important events concerning the spread of the Christian religion. Gibbon says, page 257, 258:

"A candid but rational inquiry into the progress and establishment of Christianity may be considered as a very essential part of the history of the Roman Empire. While the great body was invaded by open violence or undermined by slow decay, a pure and humble religion gently insinuated itself into the minds of men, grew up in silence and obscurity, derived new vigor from opposition, and finally erected the triumphant banner of the cross on the ruins of the Capitol. Nor was the influence of Christianity confined to the limits of the Roman Empire. After a revolution of thirteen or fourteen centuries that religion is still professed by the nations of Europe, the most distinguished portion of human kind in arts and learning, as well as in arms. By the industry and zeal of the Europeans it has been diffused to the most distant shores of Asia and Africa, and by the means of their colonies has been firmly established from Canada to Chili, in a world unknown to the ancients.

Our curiosity is naturally led to inquire by what means the Christian faith obtains so remarkable a victory over the established religions of the earth. To this inquiry an obvious but satisfactory answer may be returned; that it was owing to the convincing evidence of the doctrine itself, and to the ruling providence of its great Author. But as truth and reason seldom find so favorable a reception in the world, and as the wisdom of Providence frequently condescends to use the passions of the human heart, and the general circumstances of mankind as instruments to execute its purpose, we may still be permitted, though with becoming submission, to ask, not indeed what were the first, but what were the secondary causes of the rapid growth of the Christian church."

This is right good evidence for an infidel. This same Gibbon says, "a great and powerful state grew up in the heart of the Roman Empire;" having reference to the Christian church. It was called the "Kingdom of Heaven," because a "kingdom" is the most splendid of all human organizations, and the prefix "*Heaven*," distinguished it from the kingdoms of this world.

I left off in my last address with the argument on the death and resurrection of Christ. Our Lord Jesus Christ took an appeal from those wicked courts where he was tried and unjustly condemned. He was not willing to rest the case there. Where would a man seek to regain his reputation but where the robbery had been committed? Our Lord, therefore, appealed from the decision of the Jews and the Gentiles to the high court of eternity. That appeal stands written out in the 2nd epistle of Peter, chapter 2: 23.—"Who, when he was reviled, reviled not again; when he suffered, he threatened not; but committed himself to Him that judgeth righteously."

In a few days after the Lord Jesus Christ had referred his case for another adjudication, a report was sent down from Heaven. We have an abstract of that report in Act[illegible] [illegible]d chapter. It embodies the decision of tha[illegible] [illegible]uestion. They said he was a "blasphe[illegible] [illegible] "worthy of death." That was the d[illegible] [illegible] judges. Another made an effort [illegible] have the former decision reversed. [illegible]s not guilty of the charge alleged [illegible] this man," *he said*, "and I fin[illegible] [illegible]ut Pilate gave him into the ha[illegible] [illegible]d then, in their presence, took a basin of water and "washed his hands," saying, "I am innocent of the blood of this just person; see ye to it." Alas! poor Pilate! all the waters in the Pacific could not have washed from his guilty soul the stain of murder. He had incurred the awful responsibility of delivering an innocent man to be crucified. We shall next hear the decision of the Supreme Court of the universe with reference to the crucified one.

"Ye men of Israel, hear these words: "Jesus of Nazareth, a man approved of God among you by miracles, and wonders, and signs, which God did, by him in the midst of you, as ye yourselves also know: Him being delivered by the determinate counsel and foreknowledge of God, ye have taken and by wicked hands have crucified and slain: Whom God hath raised up, having loosed the pains of death; because it was not possible that he should be holden of it. For David speaketh concerning him: I foresaw the Lord always before my face; for he is on my right hand, that I shall not be moved."

Then Peter cites David upon this point. He reminds them, that David spoke not of himself, but of the resurrection and ascension of Jesus Christ. He told them that "David's sepulchre was with them to that day." That God fulfilled his pledge, that He would raise up Christ to sit on his throne. Now, be it understood, that this decision in regard to the personal righteousness of Christ, was not only satisfactory but was so overwhelmingly convincing, that *three thousand* of these very people, who were accessory to his murder, were satisfied with regard to the claims of Jesus to the Messiahship, and cried "men and brethren, what shall we do?" Peter's reply was, "repent and be baptised every one of you in the name of Jesus Christ, for the remission of your sins, and ye shall receive the gift of the Holy Ghost. For the promise is unto you, and to your children, and to all that are afar off, even as many as the Lord our God shall call." And as many of the literal descendants of Abraham who received Jesus of Nazareth as the promised seed, and the Messiah, were baptised. "And the same day there were added unto them about three thousand souls." The "kingdom" was small in its beginning. According to prophecy it was the "little stone" that was cut out of the "mountain;" but it was to become a great "mountain," and fill the whole "earth." It was a rapid growth for "*three thousand*" to be added to the little "kingdom" at one time." "*One hundred and twenty*" counted in a day. The number was now rapidly increasing. "*Five thousand*" were added soon after. Multitudes of Jews believed. They were not only satisfied with the demonstration they had received, but they also were satisfied with regard to that frightful difficulty about the "*genealogies*" of Christ. If they had not been convinced that Jesus Christ had descended through the progenitorial line, they would not have received him as their "promised Messiah, specified in the Old Testament. They had the records, and could have as good an opportunity of examining His genealogy as you have of going to your recorder's office and examining your land titles.

My friend seems to intimate that he had very little confidence in prophecy while he was a preacher.

Mr. Barker. Not so. I had very little confidence in it as an argument to prove the authenticity of the Scriptures.

Mr. Hartzel. I think I see in *that* one cause of his sliding. He stood upon an *avalanche* that in a very short time would slide from under him,—or rather bear him down in its awful descent. But he did refer to prophecy while a Methodist preacher. Hear his answer to an infidel objection:

Obj. 71. "Christianity destroyed the Roman Empire."

Ans. "Christianity did, in one sense, destroy the Roman Empire, and the fact that it did so, is a most striking proof of its truth and divinity. It was foretold by Daniel, several hundreds of years before Christianity made its appearance in the world, that it should break in pieces the Roman Empire, as well as all similar empires: See Daniel, 2nd chapter 34: 35—44, 45; chapter 7: 12—28." And it is a most striking thing that the prediction should have been so plainly and wonderfully fulfilled; that even infidels themselves should be heard stating the facts as a matter beyond doubt. Thus does God make his own enemies to bear witness to his truth.

Christianity will destroy all Governments or Empires founded in force, and leave no other authority on earth but that of truth and charity; but this is to me a recommendation of Christianity. What harm will it be to have all men living in love with each other; all nations voluntarily disarmed, confiding in each other as brethren, and rejoicing in each other's welfare. We have had terror, and violence, and blood enough surely; we ought to rejoice in the prospect of the universal reign of love."

His kingdom then began with "*one hundred and twenty* subjects." Behold! how it grows like a grain of mustard seed! As the Redeemer himself said:

"The kingdom of Heaven is like unto a grain of mustard seed, which is the smallest of all seeds; but when it is grown it is the greatest among herbs, and becometh a tree, so that the birds of the air come and lodge in the branches thereof." The "kingdom" of Jesus Christ then was the smallest of all the "kingdoms" of the earth. It began with "*one hundred and twenty*." We have the testimony of Gibbon, and if more is needed it can be had. The history of the whole world from the time of Tiberius Cæsar to the present day is full of testimony to the same point. It is a difficult matter to give anything like a correct history of our own day without having much of Christianity incorporated with it.

As the death and resurrection of Christ are intimately connected with the setting up of his "kingdom," which occurred in the days of the Roman Cæsars, we next call attention to a few prophecies upon these awfully sublime and interesting Gospel propositions. I will read as introductory from the 15th chapter of Corinthians, 1, 2, 3, and 4.

"Moreover, brethren, I declare unto you the Gospel which I preach unto you, which also ye have received, and wherein ye stand. By which also ye are saved, if ye keep in memory what I preached unto you, unless ye have believed in vain. For I delivered unto you, first of all, that which I also receive, how that Christ *died for our sins according* to the *Scriptures;* And that he was buried, and that he *rose* again the *third day* according to the *Scriptures.*"

That my auditors may see the point in these three propositions, I must make a few remarks. The point in this seems not to be that Christ did die. There was nothing extraordinary in his dying; for his connection with human flesh subjected him to mortality. It was to be expected then that he would die. Neither was it remarkable even that he should die for sin.

Men have died for their own sins, and people for the sins of others; "yet peradventure for a good man some would even dare to die." This is the divinity of the proposition, *that Christ died for our sins "according to the Scriptures."* Among the many thousands who had died, there was but one whose death was "according to the Scriptures"—the subject of previous prophecy.

Secondly. "*He was buried according to the Scriptures.*" It was the custom of the barbarous and civilized to bury their dead; but of all that were buried *only one was buried "according to the Scriptures."* Again, Christ *rose from the dead according to the Scriptures.*" Some had arisen from the dead before, but *not* one of them "*according to the Scriptures,*" as we shall show by reference to historic facts. The many events connected with the death of Christ were the subjects of prophecy. This will be seen by comparing the history of his death as recorded by the Evangelists, with some of the predictions of the Old Testament. We select Mathew, 26, 31. The Lord Jesus, the night on which he was betrayed, used this language: "All ye shall be offended because of me this night; for it is written I will smite the shepherd, and the sheep of the flock shall be scattered abroad." Did they believe it? Not a word of it. Peter said unto him: "Though all men shall be offended because of thee, yet will I never be offended." What an expression of the most unflinching steadfast adherence! Christ knew Peter better than Peter knew himself.

MR. HARTZEL'S TWELFTH ADDRESS.

It is true, indeed, that Christianity has, in one sense, given rise to an amount of "fanaticism," and to that which has been evil in the world. But why is it so? Have these evils been the natural result of Christianity? If Mr. Barker had opened the New Testament, and shown that the teachings of Jesus Christ and the Apostles had justified slavery and falsehood, and those many evils of which he complains, then he would have gained a point. He referred to certain delinquent churches and individuals, and called them Christians. Were they really so? Did they practice the precepts of the New Testament?

Mr. Barker. I did not say so. You, yourself, said they were Christians. You referred to them as a proof of the spread of Christianity.

Mr. Hartzel. One reason that the Christian religion has given rise to such extremes, is the following:

No religion, since the world began, has set the human mind into action as this has done. No religion has all those motive powers and mighty stimulants to apply to the human soul — to develope all that belongs to human nature, either for weal or for woe. Such a religion going forth amid ignorance and heathenism would, indirectly, lead to many extravagancies.*

I did not say the "kingdom of Heaven" began in the fourth century, but that Christianity had extensively prevailed in the fourth century.

---

*Mr. Barker has done merited justice to the subject, he has accounted for many of the errors and wrongs connected with the Christian profession upon rational principles, and fully defended Christianity from all those unjust and libelous imputations with which he now assails the Gospel. If he could have extenuated the imperfections of professors, by showing that their wicked conduct was legitimate and in harmony with Christianity, he would have done so. His position in the discussion required this at his hand.

But you shall hear him where he occupied my ground, and somebody else his. Christian, Vol. 1st, pages 139, 140.

INFIDEL.—No religion has produced such abundance of enthusiasm, fanaticism, false doctrines and intolerance as Christianity.

CHRISTIAN.—Because no religion has roused, awakened, set in motion, so many ignorant and untutored minds. Most other religions have allowed men's minds to slumber; they have allowed men to be brutal, animal; to pass through life without thinking on the great subjects of God and providence, of duty and immortality. And if men never think on these subjects, they cannot think wrong: if men never move, it is impossible for them to go astray; if they never act, it is impossible for them to act amiss. Christianity will not allow men's minds to slumber; it will have them awake and active. Its object is to make men intelligent and godlike; to make them think, and judge, and feel, and act. It aims at raising men to God; at making them sharers of his nature, partakers of his wisdom, his purity, and his love. And it is impossible to do this, without being the occasion of many and mournful excesses. Children are sure to stumble, when they first begin to walk; and the mind will stumble, when it first begins to think. We, none of us, should be able to thread our way through a wood with ten thousand false tracks, without getting, at times, a little out of our way: and the mind cannot find its way through a world of errors and delusions, without at times being led astray. It is impossible to conduct a multitude of free and thinking creatures, through the measureless distances between the cradle of a child and the mansions of the Cherubim and Seraphim in Heaven, without tremendous risk. When I think of man's nature, and consider the object and character of Christianity, I cannot wonder that the Gospel, in the accomplishment of its great, and godlike, its infinitely benevolent, but infinitely difficult task, should prove the occasion of many, and strange, and mournful tragedies.

But the Gospel does not CAUSE the evils which appear in its spread; it only reveals them. It does not MAKE the weaknesses and faults of its disciples: it only makes them manifest. It draws forth man's soul in all varieties of circumstances, in the midst of all kinds of difficulties and trials; and thus reveals its powers and its weakness, its noble capacities of what is good and great, and its terrible liabilities to what is bad and fearful. It is a moral or spiritual influence, making a new creation, forming a vast universe of bright and fair, of beautiful and godlike creatures; and it is not to be wondered at, if, in its difficult and perilous operations, it should, at times, give rise to strange disorders, to terrible and dark catastrophes. The creation of a universe of great and godlike souls, is inconceiveably more difficult than the creation of the earth and heavens; and if the first creation had its chaos, no wonder that the second should have one too.

Mr. Barker. I did not represent Mr. Hartzel as saying so; I say he referred to it.

Mr. Hartzel. I have some arguments for the defense of the Christian religion from all these imputations of favoring slavery, etc. If the Christianity of the New Testament is a pro-slavery religion—if it is favorable to slavery, you shall have the benefit of that objection, Mr. Barker. But honor us with a candid hearing. My friend will be good authority for me on that subject.

I will now proceed with my argument:

It is said by Matthew that Jesus Christ was "betrayed by Judas, one of the twelve." *This was "according to the Scriptures."* "Yea mine own familiar friend in whom I trusted, which did eat of my bread, hath lifted up his heel against me." When Jesus had pointed out Judas as the man who should betray him, he turned his back upon the Savior, and went to the temple, and said to the chief priests: "What will you give me and I will deliver him unto you?" How apposite the metaphor, "lifted up his heel" against me. In following out the history of this traitor—he returned the thirty pieces of silver to the chief priests and elders and made this confession: "I have sinned in that I have betrayed the innocent blood." The chief priest had some qualms of conscience about this price of blood, and with it purchased the "Potter's Field." Zechariah 11: 12, 13.

Now we look at Peter, the *bold* Peter. "Though

all men forsake thee, yet will I not forsake thee." "Then *all* his Disciples forsook him."

The first thing in a legal process against an offender is the arrest. He is then taken to court for trial. The next thing is to find witnesses. "Many came," but their testimony was irrelevant. At the last came "two false witnesses," upon whose testimony he was condemned. And what was their testimony? Almost true. But he had not quite said what they testified. They said: "This fellow said, 'I am able to destroy the temple of God, and to build it in three days.'" Christ did not say so. When Christ rebuked the Jews for their desecrations of the temple, (as one having authority,) they asked him for a sign. "Destroy this temple, and in three days I will raise it up." By comparing these words of Christ with those of the witnesses you will see that they made some changes and additions. "Forty and six years," said the Jews, "was this temple in building, and wilt thou rear it up in three days?" There was a law in Israel, that if any man should speak or prophecy against the temple, he was considered worthy of death. See "Bishop Porteus' lectures on Matthew." This was speaking contemptuously of the temple. But Jesus spoke, really, not of the Jewish "temple," but the "temple of his own body." Well do the Scriptures say: "False witnesses did rise up; they laid to my charge things that I knew not." The high priest asked him: "Hearest thou what these testifiy against thee?" Christ answer-text. Then the inquiry arises, why these forgeries? What was to be gained by them? Let my opponent answer. Many writing at different periods, with long intervals between them—by men who could not have conferred together—could not have acted by intelligent concert, or any system of enlightened selfishness. Can we account for these predictions upon any known principle of human policy? Why are they in the Book? How came they there? Has their genuineness ever been questioned by the Jews?

Or Secondly: It must be claimed that their application to Jesus of Nazareth was a mere matter of accident or chance. But this is assuming that the Prophets spoke without an object. These prophecies which are supposed by thousands of intelligent persons, to be clear and lucid predictions concerning the suffering of Christ, were nothing but random sayings,—that they were neither inspirations of the divine spirit, nor preconcerted frauds. But that all these predictions could have met in one person—predictions so numerous, so complex, so minute, as the result of blind chance, *beggars* all credulity, even that of a *sceptic.* And that such a coincidence of things should only have been brought about once in twenty five hundred years! Was it a lucky hit? Would it not have been strange that all these should have met in the person of the son of Joseph? The probabilities are as a *million* to *one* against it. I refer you to an extract from the writings of Dr. Gregory, published in "Campbell and Owen's Debate, page 77, 78; Vol. 2.

"Suppose, says he, that instead of the spirit of prophecy breathing more or less in every book of Scripture, spreading events relative to a great variety of general topics, and delivering besides almost innumerable characteristics of the Messiah; all meeting in the person of Jesus; there had been only TEN men in ancient times, who pretended to be prophets, each of whom exhibited only FIVE independent CRITERIA as to place, government, concomitant events, doctrine tought, effects of doctrine, character, sufferings, or death—the meeting of all which in one person should prove the reality of their calling as prophets and of his mission in the character they have assigned him. Suppose moreover, that all events were left to CHANCE merely, and we were to compute, from the principles employed by mathematicians in the investigations of such subjects, the probability of the fifty independent circumstances happening AT ALL. Assume that there is, according to the technical phrase, AN EQUAL CHANCE for the happening or failure of any one of these specified particulars; then the probability against the occurrence of all the particulars in ANY way is that of the 50th power of 2, to unity; that is, the probability is greater than ELEVEN HUNDRED AND TWENTY FIVE MILLIONS OF MILLIONS TO ONE that all of these circumstances do not turn up even at distinct periods. This computation, however, is independent of the consideration of TIME. Let it be recollected farther, that if any one of the specified circumstances happen, it may be the day after the delivery of the prophecy, or at any period from that time to the end of the world; this will so indefinitely augment the probability against the contemporaneous occurrence of merely these FIFTY circumstances, that it surpasses the power of numbers to express correctly the immense improbability of its taking place."

Jesus, the Nazarene, has had many civil claimants to the Messiahship of Israel. Most of them were tried and condemned to death as he was. Why have not these predictions met at least in *one* of the "*twenty-seven*" that have appeared from the first to the sixteenth century.

Thirdly: There is but one other position to be taken; namely, that these were genuine predictions—"That holy men of old spake as they were moved by the Holy Ghost"—that God made use of their vocal organs and their pens to make known beforehand the "sufferings of Christ and the glory that should follow."

That a Jew left to his own meditations should have had any notions of a suffering Messiah, is wholly out of the question. According to their religion, health, wealth, and victory over enemies were indications of divine power,—and the opposite of these, manifestations of the divine displeasure. That a Jew, therefore, should have spoken of their coming Redeemer as a root out of dry ground, without form or comeliness—"as despised and rejected of men"—"as a man of sorrows and acquainted with grief," from his own impulses, is contrary to reason and fact. And because these predictions, so descriptive of the deep humiliation of Jesus the Son of Mary, were so literally fulfilled in him, the nation, *as a nation*, rejected him. Yet many were convinced that Christ's degradation to the cross and the grave was according to their Scripture, and received him as their Messiah.

So overwhelming were the arguments of the Apostles, that on their first effort they convinced "*three thousand*," and on the second "*five thousand;*" and soon a "multitude of the priests became obedient to the faith;" and myriads of the Jews believed and obeyed the Gospel.

Argument 9: *Christ was buried according to Prophecy.*

We will read from Isaiah, 53 chapter: "And he

made his grave with the wicked, and with the rich in his death; because he had done no violence, neither was any deceit in his mouth."

I will give you Bishop Lowthe's translation, (I quote from memory. There are some translations more clear and lucid than others.) "He was with the wicked in his death, but his grave was with the rich man." I think this the more correct reading. Was Christ buried "according to the Scriptures," is the present inquiry?

There are many different things connected with a burial. First: The persons engaged. Second: The dressing of the corpse. Third: The grave. One might be with the rich in his burial, in one of these and not in all. In that case the prophecy would be but partially fulfilled. Jesus Christ was with "the rich" in his burial, in every sense of the proposition. We can imagine no application of the prophecy which is not justified in the burial of Jesus Christ. The body was given to "Joseph of Arimathea." But he must dress the corpse. Did he call a servant to his side? No. Nicodemus, a rich man, who brought with him "myrrh and alloes, a hundred pounds weight," to embalm the body of Jesus, as was the custom of the Jews. The first of these, Joseph, went to Pilate, as it is said by one of Christ's biographers, and "begged the body." They took it down from the cross—clothed the body in clean new linen. Thus far he was with "the rich" in his burial. The body was now clothed according to the

made his grave with the wicked, and with the rich in his death; because he had done no violence, neither was any deceit in his mouth."

I will give you Bishop Lowthe's translation, (I quote from memory. There are some translations more clear and lucid than others.) "He was with the wicked in his death, but his grave was with the rich man." I think this the more correct reading. Was Christ buried "according to the Scriptures," is the present inquiry?

There are many different things connected with a burial. First: The persons engaged. Second: The dressing of the corpse. Third: The grave. One might be with the rich in his burial, in one of these and not in all. In that case the prophecy would be but partially fulfilled. Jesus Christ was with "the rich" in his burial, in every sense of the proposition. We can imagine no application of the prophecy which is not justified in the burial of Jesus Christ. The body was given to "Joseph of Arimathea." But he must dress the corpse. Did he call a servant to his side? No. Nicodemus, a rich man, who brought with him "myrrh and alloes, a hundred pounds weight," to embalm the body of Jesus, as was the custom of the Jews. The first of these, Joseph, went to Pilate, as it is said by one of Christ's biographers, and "begged the body." They took it down from the cross—clothed the body in clean new linen. Thus far he was with "the rich" in his burial. The body was now clothed according to the taste and means of these Jewish Grandees. They did not carry it to some obscure place as the "*potter's field*," but to the "*rich man's garden*," in which was a "new tomb," hewn out of a solid rock, in which no man had ever been laid, and in this "sepulchre" they laid the poor man, the crucified one.

What wide extremes in this mysterious person join.

Who can say that this prophecy was not literally fulfilled? "He shall be with the rich in his burial." But why was he to be with "the rich in his burial?" Let the Prophet answer: "Because he had done no violence; neither was any deceit in his mouth." These honorable senators would not have conferred this honor upon the body of Christ if he had been justly condemned. They were conscious of his innocence or they would not have conferred upon him this last tribute of respect. These honorable rulers of Israel were not avowed converts. One of them took a lesson in the "night;" the other was a disciple, "but secretly for fear of the Jews." *Poor, weak humanity!* Still it is evident that they held him in the highest veneration; if not convinced that he was the Messiah, they were of his innocence and moral worth. I ask now, in view of these facts, whether such a coincidence could be the result of chance? If fact, with prophecy, could possibly have happened by mere accident? The Jewish people looked for something different. They had raised their expectation to a person of military and princely character, clothed in regal pomp and splendor. One who would carry out their political designs in the character of an earthly conqueror. He did not come in this character, and they rejected him, "*according to the Scriptures.*" The Scriptures said they should reject him.

None but the omniscient spirit could have enabled men to have foretold such events so many hundred years before they came to pass. We claim that these prophecies were "communications supernaturally revealed and miraculously attested." How improbable that an individual who was condemned to suffer death—who was "crucified between two thieves"—who was condemned before two courts—suffering death in a form too ignominious for the vilest citizen in the empire—a form reserved for aliens and slaves only, (see Bishop Porteus again;) how improbable we say, that such an one should have been with "the rich" in his burial. This incident stands by itself in the history of the world. Its parallel is not known. The reason assigned is, also, without a parallel in the history of mankind:—"*because he had done no violence.*"

But he also arose from the dead "according to the Scriptures." There were some resurrections before the resurrection of Christ; but none of them were the subject of prophecy. Such as Elisha raising an individual to life (the widow's son,) and Jesus raising the daughter of Jairus, and Lazarus. But these were only miraculous demonstrations of divinely appointed missions. But the resurrection of Christ had a higher aim. It entered into the original design of his whole scheme—was indeed an essential part of it, and therefore the worthy subject of prophecy. Psalms 16—"For thou wilt not leave my soul in hell, neither wilt thou suffer thy holy one to see corruption." There are two distinct features in this prophecy. First, the subject of it, or his "flesh should not see corruption." If Jesus Christ had continued in the grave till the fourth day, decomposition would have begun. But he was not to "see corruption." "I will rise again the third day." He was in the grave, but did not "see corruption." And immediately or soon after his resurrection, he should appear in the presence of the Lord, and sit at his "right hand." This expresses a station of dignity and honor. This will not apply to David. It will not apply to any of those who rose from the dead before Christ arose. All these were still men in the flesh, and were as liable to death as before. The man Christ Jesus was the "first fruits of them that slept." The first that went from the grave to the skies. He has gone to Heaven with an immortal, a glorified body—" the man Christ Jesus, now upon the throne." Humanity exalted in the person of Jesus Christ. " Sit thou at my right hand," is an oracle of great significance in Christianity, and should fill every heart with the highest and holiest aspirations.

To sum up the argument deduced from this comparison let me say, that the incidents recorded in the biographies of Jesus Christ, in regard to his trial, death, burial, resurrection, and ascension, form a series of predictions with corresponding facts, which never could have been the work of collusion or fraud.

His Disciples did not believe that he would suffer. He repeatedly told them that he must "suffer many things from the scribes and Pharisees"—that he must be put to death, and "rise again the third day." But they believed it not. Peter on one occasion could not suppress his feelings, but said, in the language of rebuke, "These things shall not happen unto thee." And when he was buried it did not enter into their hearts, that he would rise from the dead. This is evident from their own artless story. They are not to be suspected for acting in concert to get him out of the grave. They could have had no motive for doing so. If they had done so, they would have acted contrary to all rational motives. And if his enemies acted intelligently in bringing about his death, they must have acted with reference to the fulfillment of their own prophecies.

MR. HARTZEL'S THIRTEENTH ADDRESS.

It is indeed humiliating to be required to notice such an address as we had near the close of last session. I do not like to call it a tirade—perhaps that would be too hard—but I will pay to it this melancholy tribute of respect, to read a few prophecies, in which more than all that was detailed in that speech was anticipated by two New Testament prophets.

Much that is now history was once prophecy. Much that is now becoming history; and, much that will follow in the future history of the world, till time shall be no more, stands upon the prophetic page. I wish time and other engagements, and matters over which we have no control, would permit us to elaborate this point more extensively than we can under present circumstances. We read from 2 Timothy 3: 1–7:

"This know also, that in the last days perilous times shall come. For men shall be lovers of their own selves, covetous, boasters, proud, blasphemers, disobedient to parents, unthankful, unholy; without natural affection, truce-breakers, false accusers, incontinent, fierce, despisers of those that are good; traitors, heady, high-minded, lovers of pleasures more than lovers of God; Having a form of Godliness, but denying the power thereof; from such turn away. For of this sort are they which creep into houses and lead captive silly women laden with sins, led away with divers lusts; ever learning, and never able to come to the knowledge of the truth."

These had forgotten the injunction given to the primitive churches—to abandon all "foolish jesting" and *unprofitable pleasures*, which obtained throughout the Pagan world—which were so incongruous to Christianity. "Having a form of Godliness, but denying the power thereof: from such turn away.

For of this sort are they which creep into houses and lead captive silly woman." This, from Paul the Apostle to his son Timothy, is of transcendant importance. But you ask, to whom does it refer? We answer, to some who proposed to be Christians. Those who have "a form of Godliness," but deny the power of that form in its purifying and ennobling influence. We had the matter most sadly detailed in the address of last evening.

Voltaire claimed to be a Christian. Some of the most black-hearted villians in the world have claimed to be Christians. Some of the vilest men seek to cover their deformity under the Christian name, because they know it is honorable. If they can appropriate that name to themselves; *if* they can get the world to award it to them, they can use Christianity as a hiding place. It is true, we often find worse men within the circulation of the Bible than any where else. There have been greater giants in wickedness in Christian lands, than in pagandom. We account for this, upon the same ground that the sweetest wine will make the sourest vinegar. The richer the soil the more abundant will be the crop, whether of wheat or of weeds. I know you will understand that.

The next prophecy to which we refer, is in Peter 3: 3, 4. We will break into the connection:

"Knowing this first, that there shall come in the last days scoffers, walking after their own lusts; and saying, Where is the promise of his coming? for since the fathers fell asleep, all things continue as they were from the beginning of the creation." The phrase "last days," is in both of these prophecies, and it is not in these two passages only that the phrase occurs. It is applied to the gospel dispensation, not only because it was the last system of divine communication to man, but because it was to continue so till time shall be no more. The next revelation will be the personal appearance of Jesus Christ. This dispensation will continue till that revelation shall supersede this. How marvelous, my dear friends, that the Jewish people should have transmitted a book that is a standing reproach against their character. A book that records the disgrace of the nation. But they have kept that oracle, and keep it still. And what shall we say of both Papists and Protestants? Have they not done the same? Did not my friend say, the "Scriptures have come down to us from a source most corrupt"? We admit it. Why did not Mr. Barker accept the proposed issue, with respect to his supposed contradictions in the Scriptures? Was it not a fair one? Some of the audience may have forgotten it. We proposed to him to select a few palpable contradictions, if any there were, and present them in due form and order, and we would attempt a reconciliation of them; if we did not reconcile them so as to show that there was no important discrepancy between the statements, he should be entitled to the benefit of his contradictions when he had proved them to be such. Why has he not done so? I will give you the reason. I will refer you to the "Christian," by Joseph Barker, vol. 1, pages 394, 395:

"The Sacred Scriptures are a collection of writings, written by different men, in different ages and countries, all tending to throw light on God's character and will, and all tending to awaken and cherish the spirit of piety in man, and adapted to promote the improvement and perfection of men in knowledge and true holiness. They are not a creed, but helps to understand and believe the truth. They are not a law, but helps to a right understanding of God's law, and helps and encouragements to obedience. They are helps to religious knowledge, to true piety, and to everlasting blessedness. When they were written, where they were written, and, in some cases, by what persons they were written, are matters not certainly known. Nor is it certainly known, with respect to several of them, in what form they at first appeared. Nor is it certainly known what changes they have undergone since they were first written. The original copies are lost, and what WE have, are translations, translations of translations, translations of translations of transcripts, of transcripts of transcripts.

And every translation, and every transcript which has ever been made of those writings, was made by men who were liable to err, by men, all of whom, we have reason to believe, did err more or less. There is, however, reason to believe, that the principal translators and transcribers, and the principal printers and publishers also of the sacred writings, have been persons who, like the original writers, were, in a great measure, under the influence of the spirit of God, the spirit of truthfulness and piety. And there is reason to believe that, in general, the Scriptures retain their original character, and are fair expressions and correct revelations of the righteous souls that gave them forth. That passages have been added, and that passages have been taken away, and that other passages which remain have been altered and marred, is beyond all doubt. Still there is abundant reason to believe, that the general character of the writings remains, and that they are calculated, when read and interpreted, and applied, in the spirit of truth and piety, and in reliance on that light enkindled by our heavenly Father in our own souls, to answer the great end for which they were designed. They came from God, and God has graciously preserved them for our good."

We ask, who was the writer of the communication just read? Joseph Barker. How long since he wrote it? In 1844. Who was Joseph Barker? Was he a novice, or was he a man of mature years? He was in the prime and vigor of life. Was he a scholar? So far as I am competent to judge of scholarship, he was. He has examined the Scriptures, not only in the different versions, but also in the original languages, from which they were translated. We regard him then as a competent witness. What then does he declare the facts be? He says, "that there is reason to believe that, in general, the Scriptures retain their original character, and are fair expressions and correct revelations of the righteous souls that gave them forth." He says, "they came from God, and God has graciously preserved them for our good."

His remarks upon transcripts and translations appear to me extravagant. Our friend says, *all* we claim. It is satisfactory to me; and, we believe most Christians would endorse the sentiments contained in this extract. Is not this enough? If the Scriptures bring us into intimacy and fellowship with God, from whom they have been derived, is not that enough? That is all we claim.

I will resume the series of argument where I left it. The words of Christ are but the re-echo of prophecy. "I came not to be ministered unto, but to minister, and to give my life a ransom for many." We have before hinted that the death of Christ was according to prophecy, and an important part of his earthly mission—I will add to this his resurrection and ascension. Before the death of Christ, while in conversation with his disciples, he staked all his pretensions to the Messiahship on the fulfillment of these prophecies uttered by himself. These predictions are recorded in the testimony of Matthew, Mark, Luke and John. We will refer only to two recorded in Matthew, and one in John."

Matthew 16: 21.—"From that time forth began Jesus to show unto his disciples how that he must go unto Jerusalem, and suffer many things of the elders, and chief priests, and scribes: and be killed, and be raised again the third day."

Matthew 20: 18, 19.—"Behold we go up to Jerusalem; and the son of man shall be betrayed unto the chief priests and unto the scribes, and they shall condemn him to death. And shall deliver him to the Gentiles, to mock, and to scourge, and to crucify him: and the third day he shall rise again."

We open to John 6: 62.—"What and if ye shall see the son of man ascend up where he was before."

These were the most fearful tests that could have been imagined. Why were they so? 1, because of their complexity; 2, because of the kind of co-operation essential to their accomplishment. When a series of items enter into the constituency of any thing, we call it complex. Our Lord, therefore intended to make this test of the most precarious character on which he would rest his claim to the Messiahship of Israel. We shall give them numerically: 1, that the son of man should be betrayed 2, that he should be betrayed to the chief priests and scribes; 3, that he must suffer many things before he should be put to death; 4, that he should be condemned of the Jews; 5, that they should deliver him to the Gentiles; 6, that the Gentiles should mock him; 7, that they should scourge him; 8, that he should rise again. Is not this complexity? It would not have been strange that he should have foretold that he would die, or that he should die by violence. Sometimes a man may foretell that his death will be brought about by violence, especially if he should be surrounded by malignant foes, and was himself unflinching in his principles, bent upon his purposes, with fearful odds against him. A man might predict under such circumstances, that his death would be by violence. But to predetermine that he would be "betrayed"—that he would be betrayed into the hands of the "chief priests and scribes"—that he should "suffer many things" before his death—that he would be condemned by the Jews—that he would be "delivered unto the Gentiles"—that they would "mock him"—that he would "rise again the third day." No human foresight could have anticipated all these events, so unprecedented, occurring in connection with his own death, or the death of another; neither is it possible for a man so to influence his enemies as to inflict upon him all the sufferings foretold by Jesus Christ. Nothing can solve these difficulties but Christ's prescience, and no agencies could have brought them about but unrelenting foes, and the interposition of the Almighty. If Christ had been betrayed into the hands of the populace, or if he had not been betrayed at all — or if he had been mocked but not scourged, etc., these would have been but a partial accomplishment.

It is a rare occurrence that a culprit suffers much before his execution. There is something in human nature that calls for sympathy in behalf of those under the sentence of death. I have seen the most hardened sinners weep, when the Judge sentenced an offender to the State's prison. But the sympathy natural to men was restrained, when Pilate delivered him up to be crucified. They "*mocked*" him—they "*scourged*" him. He suffered all these indignities before they crucified him. The crucifix was not the most common mode of punishing culprits. Socrates was not nailed to the cross. Seneca was permitted to choose in what way he would die. The crucifix was reserved for slaves and aliens, and these of the vilest character only. But Jesus Christ had said, "the son of man must be crucified." The apostles heard their Lord foretell all these things concerning himself, so very improbable, and so unwelcome to their ears; but they saw their literal accomplishment. What a proof of his integrity and Messiahship!

2. "And in three days he shall rise again." He did "rise again." So that this test was also literally fulfilled. If he had risen on the second day, there would have been some doubt about the matter. If he had remained in "the tomb" till the fourth day, it would have been the same.

3. The third and last test of his Messiahship was

his ascension. "What and if ye shall see the son of man ascend up where he was before." Our Lord had fed a multitude the day before he spoke these words. The second day, they came again from base motives, when he gave them this gentle rebuke: "Ye seek me not because you saw the miracle, but because you ate of the loaves and were filled." Jesus now spoke of himself as the bread of heaven, and said, "except ye eat my flesh and drink my blood, ye have no life in you." Many of the disciples said, "this is a hard saying." Who can bear it? He said unto them, "Doth this offend you?" "What and if ye shall see the son of man ascend up where he was before." Will not that settle the question? Will not that test my pretensions as the Messiah of God? These proofs dispelled all doubt, and they were satisfied. I say, having these demonstrations they were satisfied and did not doubt the fact thereafter. *All their former doubts were now removed.* Peter once so faint-hearted, could no longer be intimidated. No officer could alarm him. He was in great terror when Christ was arrested, and when accused with being one of his company, he said, "I know not the man." The fearful now became bold as the lion. When Peter and John stood before an infuriated council, the people "marvelled at their boldness, and took knowledge of them that they had been with Jesus." They disregarded the menaces of their rulers, and answered their threatenings by an appeal to themselves: "Whether it be right in the sight of

God, to hearken unto men more than unto God, judge ye, for we can but speak of the things we have seen and heard." The future fortunes of the cause of Christ depended upon his success with the apostles. To make these "able ministers of the new covenant," was essential to the propagation of the Gospel. He knew the kind and the amount of evidence they required to fit them for the work, and he was able to give it. Having seen all the things accomplished upon which he staked his pretensions even to his rising from the dead and ascension, they doubted no more.

MR. HARTZEL'S FOURTEENTH ADDRESS.

Before proceeding, I will call for the reading of an article from the "Christian," published A. D. 1848, vol. 4, pages 276, 277:

"The finest specimen of moral greatness on record, is Jesus Christ. There is something in the character of Christ unspeakably sublime. There is something in his character infinitely great. I cannot describe the feelings with which I contemplate his life at times. Nor can I describe the reverence with which I regard him I feel, while I look on his character, that if there be one thing under heaven more worthy of my wishes than another, it is tc share his god-like spirit, and to be conformed to his glorious likc ness. Compared with the greatness which I see in Jesus, al physical greatness, all mere intellectual greatness, all the splendo of talent, all the stores of learning, all the mighty achievements all the wondrous discoveries in science, all the improvements in art look little; appear as nothing. Christ was not without intellectua greatness. On the contrary, his intelligence was unusual. Bu his goodness is the most striking, the most touching, the mos enchanting, the most transporting. I cannot imagine an objec more lovely than Christ. I cannot conceive greatness more divine or glorious than his.

We have specimens of moral greatness in the characters of some of the apostles, and especially in the apostle Paul. He gave up his reputation for learning; he sacrificed his Jewish friends and connections; he relinquished the honors of his sect; he renounced whatever he had prized of a worldly character, and gave himself up to a life of hardship, of reproach, of suffering and of loss, out of regard to the truth, and for the welfare of mankind. His labors were most abundant. His sufferings were great and almost constant, yet he thought himself abundantly repaid for them, in the good which he was able to do to his fellow-creatures. When he was told on one occasion, that bonds and imprisonments awaited him in every city through which he was likely to pass, he replied, 'None of these things move me, neither count I my life dear unto myself, so that I may finish my course with joy, and accomplish the service to which I have been appointed by the Lord Jesus, to testify the glad tidings of the goodness of God.' And as he lived, he died. When writing to a friend near the close of his life, he says, 'I have fought a good fight, I have finished my course, I have kept the faith: henceforth there is laid up for me a crown of righteousness, which the Lord, the righteous judge shall give to me, and not to me only, but to all them that love his appearing.' We have other striking examples of moral greatness in the reformers of later ages. We see something of it in Wickliffe. We see something of it in Luther. We see more of it in Fox and Penn. We see something of it in Priestley and Channing. We see something of it in Whitfield, and Wesley, and Fletcher. But in none do we behold so rich, so full a revelation of true greatness, as in Jesus. And shall we not labor to share his greatness? This is a kind of greatness which all can appreciate. It is a kind of greatness which we all admire in the departed. And shall we not seek to emulate this greatness ourselves? The greatness of which we have been speaking will endure for ever. It will never cease to be admired. It will never cease to be glorious. It will be loved and honored as long as God himself shall live, or eternity endure."

From what source did Mr. Barker derive these views of the character of Jesus Christ and the Apostles? He certainly received his information from these "fabulous," corrupt Scriptures. If they could give him such exalted views of moral excellence and grandeur, exhibited not in imaginary or fabulous personages, but in real life—characters more exalted and holier than have been presented by the best and most enlightened of moral reformers of later ages, I am sure these facts are a refutation of his notions of the progress of our race. If he finds the best examples of moral greatness, and human perfection, eighteen hundred years back in the history of mankind,—where has been this glorious progression, of which we have heard so much boast by some minute modern philosophers?

Primitive Christians refer us back to the time of Christ and his Apostles. Ancient Christians to the fathers—the days of St. Cyprian, St. Augustine, Crysostem, etc. Modern Christianity brings us down to our own times. Into these periods Christianity is divided by the celebrated D'Aubigne. It is not ancient or modern Christianity, but primitive Christianity for which we plead. We can only be held responsible for the character and teachings of Jesus Christ and the Apostles. We have nothing to do with the professors, whose characters our friend has painted so darkly. Mr. Barker has shown the entire fulfillment of the prophecy read, and has so far been proving the truth of our proposition. I am glad he has performed this service, as the task was one we did not like to perform. There are, however, many exceptions to this terrible picture he has drawn. I wish there were more. My friend admits there were good priests, and has placed Christ at the head of all of them. "Luther," he says, "was a good priest." I believe he did honor Campbell, by placing him in the list. After these were expelled, we believe there were yet some good ones left in the churches. I am persuaded of one thing however, that it is after all an exaggeration on the part of Mr. Barker: still his testimony justifies the prophecy. The prophecy does not apply to the church universal, but that there should be such men claiming to be Christians, having "*a form of godliness;* (not *the* form,) they were apostates. The genuine Christian has *the* "form of godliness," and the power with it. I sympathize with Mr. Barker. I have ten volumes of his writings, covering thirteen years of his life, and I have no doubt but that my friend has been instrumental in part, in bringing upon himself the persecutions to which he has been subjected. Somehow or other he seems not to have a proper respect for the feelings of others, or the treatment due to them. Christians are required to be "courteous." He seems to have taken this view of humanity when a preacher, that men are like iron, to be operated upon when hot. When iron is hot it is soft—when men are hot they are hard. I see in my friend's case fulfilled the saying of Jesus Christ—"with what measure you meet it shall be measured to you again." Had he observed this precept of the Savior—"Whatsoever ye would that men should do to you, do ye even so to them"—in his intercourse with men, he would not have experienced the ill-treatment of which he complains.

But to proceed with the argument. I was broken

off in my last address while speaking of the complex character of the tests to which our Savior submitted his claims to the Messiahship. I had only examined those accomplished by human agency, and began to remark upon those which called for supernatural interposition. When the Jews had crucified the Lord, they had done all they could do. Human agency could go no farther. When they had laid him in the grave, the only thing they could do farther was to keep him there. They go to Pilate, the Roman Procurator, and ask him for a guard. They obtain it; and a band of Roman soldiers are placed around the "sepulcher." Now, another agency must be introduced to bring him out of the grave, or Christ must fail in the testimony offered to the apostles. Two miracles must now be performed to meet the pledge Christ gave to his disciples. First, "And rise from the dead the third day." Behold, the morning of the third day begins to dawn! All Heaven, Earth and Hell are in a state of anxiety and suspense! There was a reason for the Jews to use the precaution they did, to keep him in the grave. Mighty "signs" had showed themselves in him. They would not feel easy about the probable results. Ah! this was an eventful morning—the immortality of a world suspended on the issues of a moment! But, before the sun had shaken his golden locks over the hills and valleys of creation, the Redeemer had risen and secured "life and immortality," for man. Jesus had risen from the dead. It did not hence follow that his disciples must see him ascend up to Heaven. But he had referred them to his ascension as evidence that he was the "bread of life." Second, "What and if ye shall see the Son of Man ascend up where he was before." That will settle the question, that the man who obeys my voice shall never die. In "forty days" after his resurrection, he ascended to the skies, and, like a kind father, full of affection for his children, he pronounced upon them a parting blessing. While thus engaged, he began to rise. He ascended higher and higher—and, as they were gazing after him, a "bright cloud" bore him rapidly out of their sight—like the high-soaring eagle, its form diminishes as it ascends till finally it is lost in the expanse above. But God gave them consolation in this trying moment. An "angel" descended and said unto them, "Ye men of Galilee, why stand ye gazing up into Heaven? This same Jesus, which is now taken up from you into Heaven, shall so come in like manner as ye have seen him go into Heaven."

I defy Mr. Barker to call in question these facts. Gibbon knew better than to attempt it. I challenge our friend to show on rational principles, how the death, resurrection, and ascension of Jesus Christ can be regarded as false without disregarding every item of the evangelical history. These enter into the frame-work of the entire system, and are to Christianity what the foundation is to the superstructure. The apostles being witnesses to these, we can easily account for their zeal in propagating the Gospel, and the present existence of the Gospel history.

I know we are traveling slowly; but the man who attempts a short answer to so long a question, will not make his answer satisfactory. I also ought to say, that the question in debate is one of transcendant importance. I have come here for the purpose of benefitting those who may attend this discussion. I will ask the audience to be patient, and when you have given us a faithful hearing, and we have not redeemed the pledge, then yours will not be the blame. You shall next hear Mr. Barker on these interesting facts. In his discussion with W. Cooke, page 600, he says:

"I believe that Jesus was (in Hebrew,) the Messiah; (in Greek,) the Christ; (in English,) the most favored and exalted of mankind; the beloved Son of God. I believe that Jesus was endowed by God with power and wisdom, that God wrought many "signs and wonders" by him, and set him forth as a teacher of truth, as an example of goodness, as the guide, the Savior, and the judge of mankind. I believe in the general truth of the Gospel history. I believe that in the Gospels we have, in general, a truthful and satisfactory history of the Savior's life; of his teachings and labors, of his trial and death. I believe that Jesus rose again from the dead, and that he still lives to labor for the good of mankind."

Before closing my serial argument, offered in defence of the affirmation, that the "Jewish and Christian Scriptures contain a series of communications supernaturally revealed and miraculously attested"—let me bring the whole to bear upon a single New Testament proposition: namely, "*Thou art the Christ, the Son of the living God.*" See Matthew 16th chapter. After this is done, we shall proceed to the second feature of our proposition. We have now offered ten independent arguments; any one of which is sufficient, in itself, to sustain the first feature in my proposition:

First. Upon the authenticity of the Old Testament. Suppose we take out of these ancient records all the prophecy relating to Jesus Christ, what would their credibility be worth to us? Would they be worth contending for? Surely not. The hope of a coming Messiah was the soul of these ancient oracles; as the testimony they now bear to Jesus of Nazareth, as the "Christ of God," is still the heart and life of them. "The testimony of Jesus is the spirit of prophecy."

Second. The promise to Abraham. "I will make of thee a great nation." Is there anything appreciable in the election of Abraham, and the making of him a great nation, independent of Christ and Christianity? The Gospel gives a thousand good reasons for God making of Abraham "a great nation."

Third. "I will make thy name great." God never elected men to distinctions and honors for their own sake—always for relative purposes. Paul gives a good reason for this. See Galatians 3: 14: "That the blessing of Abraham might come upon the Gentiles through Jesus Christ."

Fourth. "In thee shall all families of the earth be blessed." This promise, though grand in its conception, and benevolent in its design, is yet without any significance or meaning, unless we receive Paul's words as true: "God, who at sundry times and in divers manners spake in *times* past unto the *fathers* by the *prophets*, hath in these *last* days spoke unto *us* by his *Son*, whom he hath appointed heir of all things, by whom also he made the worlds." Let this basis of the Christian religion be repudiated; let Mr. Barker show it unworthy of rational belief, and we will readily admit that the promises to Abraham are without any importance. We do not see any enlightened system of selfishness or fraud in them. But when this promise was fulfilled in Christ, what untold blessings are contained in it!

Fifth. The preservation of the Jews. Why was this nation so long under the protection and chastening of the Lord? It is inexplicable from any other ground than this, that Jesus who was declared to be the Son of God when emerging from the baptismal grave, is also the son of Abraham according to the flesh—that he is both the "root and the offspring of David." All the greatness, and all that has given consequence to this extraordinary family is in some way connected with this more extraordinary personage.

Sixth. And why should prophet have united with prophet in fixing the time of his coming so definitely, that the expectation at the time of his birth was general, both among Jews and Gentiles. All this, to introduce to the nation of Israel one of its *own* children! To introduce Jesus, the carpenter's son, to his own nation!! Wonderful!!!

Seventh. Why should the time of the setting up

of his kingdom have been determined so many hundred years in advance, if he was not the "Prince of peace"—the "Prince of life"—the Son of God—and his kingdom that of "peace and righteousness," differing from all other organizations under heaven?

Eighth, ninth, tenth. To speak in a more summary way—why should his death, burial, and resurrection, have received so much attention? No satisfactory answer can be given but this—he died "for our offences, and rose again for our justification;" and hence his resurrection was a demonstration of his mission.

"And declared to be the Son of God with power, according to the Spirit of holiness, by the resurrection from the dead."—Romans 1: 4. This is a corroborative proof of Peter's confession: "Thou art the Christ the Son of the living God," and that the revelation he had received was reliable. "Flesh and blood have not revealed it unto thee, but my father which is in Heaven." When did he receive this revelation? At the time of his baptism. What was it? "This is my beloved Son in whom I am well pleased." "The Holy Ghost shall come upon thee, and the power of the Highest shall overshadow thee." "Therefore that holy thing [offspring] which shall be born of thee shall be called the Son of God." This was the announcement of "Gabriel" to the virgin—mother of the Messiah. It is always the prerogative of the parent to name the offspring. There is then a beautiful decorum in this, as well as a most simple and unostentatious introduction of the Son of God, by his own Father, to the people of Israel.

We now enter upon his ministry. He called certain individuals from their humble vocations to be his Disciples. He took them under his special care and teaching for a time, and then sent them out as missionaries to the Jewish nation. These were instructed in the doctrines of his "approaching reign." These were entrusted with all his secrets. They had rival feelings and jealousies among themselves. They were often reproved by their Master. On one occasion he called the most bold and decided one among them, "Satan." On another occasion they asked him, "shall we call down fire to destroy these?" Shall we do as Elijah did—burn them up? How beautiful, how benevolent, the response! "The Son of Man is come not to destroy men's lives, but to save them." The freedom with which our Lord reproved the Disciples, *never* elicited from them an unfavorable report of him.

MR. HARTZEL'S FIFTEENTH ADDRESS.

A formidable list of difficulties truly! A very few words by way of reply. The speaker who has just taken his seat says, "it is strange that the Disciples of Jesus Christ should have been so ignorant." We answer, this is not strange. If they understood the

Savior no better than they did, would they not have been too ignorant to fabricate such a religion? How can Mr. Barker impeach the testimony of the first article we read from his pen this morning? Will he show that the character of Jesus Christ which we have in the Gospel, is not a genuine protraiture? He knew better than to assail it, after having written an eulogy, so true, so beautiful! If it be a true portraiture—if the Evangelists drew it from real life, from practical life—if they described the character and moral excellence of any one individual, then it is a true protraiture. It is for him to show that it was not a portraiture, but a fiction. Then he would have done something. He would have changed the difficulty, but would not have removed it; then the inquiry would arise, how could the human mind invent such a character without a model?—*so he let it alone most cautiously.* In regard to these indelicacies in the composition of the Bible, I will respond in the language of the Apostle Paul, in his epistle to Titus, 1: 15: "Unto the pure all things are pure: but unto them that are defiled and unbelieving is nothing pure; but even their mind and conscience is defiled." False modesty awakens suspicion. The chaste and pure in heart, of all ages, have employed familiar language, when there was occasion for it. Having noticed all worthy of reply, I proceed.

And after his separation from them, they were more faithful than before. See "Christianity Triumphant," page 22:

"After the ascension of Jesus into heaven, the principles of his religion took a wider spread, the number of his disciples was greatly multiplied, and the blessed effects of the Gospel were more clearly seen. The Apostles, in the true spirit of their religion, gave themselves, in the face of danger and death, to the work of instructing and regenerating the world. They renounced all selfish interests, abandoned all prospect of earthly gain, and against a world of opposition and persecution, they went forth toiling and suffering for the salvation of mankind. Wherever they went, the Gospel proved the power of God to the salvation of their hearers. Fornicators, idolators, adulterers, effeminate, abusers of themselves with mankind, thieves, covetous persons, drunkards, revilers, and extortioners, were washed from their impurities, and made holy and useful and happy.—(1 Cor. vi. 10, 11.) Men and women, that had wallowed in licentious pleasures, and taken the lead in the wanton and riotous disorders of abominable idolatries, became patterns of sobriety and chastity.—(1 Peter iv. 3, 4.) Magicians, soothsayers, and sorcerers were arrested by the power of the truth, and gave up their impositions; and 'many that believed came and confessed, and showed their deeds. Many of them also, which used curious arts, brought their books together, and burned them before all men: and they counted the price of them, and it amounted to fifty thousand pieces of silver. So mightily grew the word of God, and prevailed.'—(Acts xix. 18, 19.)"

The Apostles had the world to contend against—all the priesthoods and governments, both Jewish and Pagan. "We have not followed cunningly devised fables when we made known to you the coming of our Lord Jesus Christ," said Peter, near the close of his life. They acknowledged both his authority and his wisdom, while he was with them. "The multitudes were astonished at his doctrine, for he taught them as one having authority and not as the scribes." How can this report be accounted for, without acknowledging the truth of the evangelical history? How, I ask, can we account for the existence of these biographies, without the subject of them?—the variety of detail, without any irreconcilable contradiction or falsehood? But what is most astonishing, is that they should differ in the subject matter of their narratives, yet all succeed in drawing a picture of moral perfection which has secured the respect of the good, and extorted homage from the bad; and that they have all succeeded in this portraiture so admirably, that we know not to which of them the *palm* should be awarded. That a man should have one biographer who is a living witness is *rare*. That he should have two is *extraordinary*. That he should have three is *unparalelled*. And a fourth, who drew upon the testimony of those who were eye and ear witnesses of the things they reported — who was himself a cotemporary with the subject of these narratives, is something *unheard of, and without* a parallel in the history of our world. The wonderful doings of Jesus Christ have come down to us well attested; and the evangelical history can furnish the only solution of a religion superhuman in its conception — a religion miraculous in its developement and propagation.

I shall now proceed directly to the task before me, which is to prove, "*that in the New Testament we have a perfect rule of life.*" And first: to give such a law of life is itself a work most onerous. We would be naturally led to this conclusion, from the many who have undertaken it and have utterly failed, that no mere man or set of men possess the necessary qualifications to ensure success. Competency to give to our ignorant and erring race a perfect code of ethics required more than the highest degree of human wisdom.

Second. Such lawgiver must have a perfect knowledge of all the diversified relations, both religious and political, that now are or shall be in the future. Relations must be understood before duties can be defined. At this point the wisdom of the world has always failed. "The world by wisdom knew not God" the creator, and, therefore, could not know man the creature.

Third. To adapt a system of moral instruction to man—universal man—required a knowledge of more than the present and the local. It required a knowledge of the distant and the future. As no man could be acquainted with the condition of society in districts unknown to himself, and as no finite being can know the changes of after ages, therefore it required Omniscience to give such a "rule of life" as we possess in possessing the New Testament.* If my affirma-

---

* Are man's powers creative and inventive, or inventive only? This inquiry will bring to light his utter inability to contrive a religion equal to his wants. No man of a sound head will claim for himself or others, physical creative powers, and none will deny to man physical inventive powers. The mechanic invents, he does not create. When the jeweler has worked up his material, he must cease to operate. When the manufacturer has exhausted his stock, his machinery stops, and his hands are discharged. He is subjected to this necessity because he cannot create—creative powers imply omnipotence.

These reflections are only introductory to the question. Does man possess moral creative powers? We answer, NO, without fear of contradiction. He can no more create the material of thought than the cabinet-maker his lumber, or the smith his iron and steel; but from his stock of mental types and images, by which we mean all he can know by his own observation and all he has learned from the experience of others, from conversations, books, etc.; all that comes within the domain of knowledge, faith and opinion, constitutes, both to the savage and the sage, all the material for his mental operations. From this store he may invent a thousand new fancies, associations and combinations. This leads out two conclusions: First, when man desires to perform some mental operation for which he has no mental images, he is compelled to abandon the enterprise; second, when he has exhausted all his capital upon a given subject, his moral machinery stops until he obtains a new supply; but, if the mind could by its natural fecundity originate the types of things unknown, there would be no bounds to our mental progress. But the mind like the "hand" has its metes and boundaries. It may not be so easy to decide upon the HITHERTO, still every man's experience says, there is an UNCOMPROMISING HITHERTO.

The mind may elaborate from its available capital many new associations, theoretical

tion is true, and I trust we shall prove it so, is not Christianity adapted to all countries? I answer yes. Where men can live by honest industry. Are not the moral precepts of the Gospel as well calculated to promote the best interests of mankind *now*, as they were *eighteen hundred years ago?* We answer yes—progression notwithstanding.

Fourth. Such an one must possess authority to command—otherwise the duties specified will not, or may not be regarded as imperious. Then there must be some sanction to inspire with motive to do some things, and not to do certain other things. The requisite qualifications to give to man "a perfect

---

and practical; they may be right, true and good, or they may not. All knowledge may be classified under two comprehensive headings—the FINITE and the INFINITE. We apply these terms to "time," to "motion," to "power," etc. The mind may grasp a period of fifty years—or, say one hundred—say one thousand, then it feels burdened—say one million of years, and the mind becomes MULISH—but say ETERNITY, time without end, here I am lost. "Complex ideas" relate to the first class, or things finite, and may be defined; but "simple ideas" belong to the second, or things infinite, therefore cannot be defined. To illustrate farther, a strong man can raise three hundred pounds, a horse can carry five, a locomotive will move at the rate of forty miles per hour, with a train carrying many hundred tons burden. The greater the power the more vague the conception. Indeed, the mind is bewildered long before it arrives at the INFINITE, the OMNIPOTENT. Man has power to build a palace when furnished with tools and material. The reader can form tolerably distinct notions of his strength and inventiveness. But God made the universe without hammer or saw, without tools or materials, whatever he may have employed of the one or the other, he first made it. "He said, let there be light and light was." THIS WAS THE EFFECT OF POWER INFINITE, OMNIPOTENT. This is the God of the Bible—the God whom the Christian delights to honor. To this God, as revealed in the Bible, are ascribed a class of infinite perfections, such as the human mind never did, nor ever could originate, for the want of sensible SIGNS OR IMAGES. Though revealed (supernaturally,) they are only addressed to our powers of apprehension; with this we must be satisfied. We are! If our God was of our own creation, we could comprehend him as we do all our inventions; and, therefore, he could not be an object of rational worship. To specify, our God is ETERNAL, OMNIPOTENT, OMNISCIENT, OMNIPRESENT. While writing these words, my mind is lost in their awful significance. Here I feel my HITHERTO; perhaps better felt than told. Yes; but let me try. Of things most immediately connected with the finite, the mind forms the most distinct conceptions; and the nearer we approach to the infinite, the more indefinite the conceptions: therefore, when we arrive at that point where the mind can go no farther for the want of DATA; where it cannot form another idea from such material as it may possess, however vague—we would say that is the TERMINOUS—all beyond this must be revelation. I do not say that nothing else is, but this must be.

From this stand point let us look at the revealed God of the Bible, and the invented gods of the heathen. David gives this striking contrast; "He that planted the ear shall he not hear? He that formed the eye shall he not see? He that chastiseth the heathen shall he not correct? He that teacheth man knowledge SHALL NOT HE KNOW?" Psalms 94—"Their idols are silver and gold, the work of men's hands. They have mouths but they speak not: eyes they have but they see not." "They have ears but they hear not;" "hands they have but they handle not; feet they have but they walk not. They that made them are like unto them," etc.—Psalms 105. Man can invent no better God than this, for he never did.

rule of life," and to make it in any degree efficient and effectual, are manifestly superhuman and divine.

To sum up in few words. The author of "a perfect rule of life," must first have a perfect understanding of the relations of the persons or parties involved, in order to make known to them their mutual obligations; and to accompany the same with sufficient motive power to secure respect and obedience. Relation, duty, and destiny, are three essential elements in what we call "a rule of life." Bless God, we have found one who is competent to the task of giving to man such a rule of moral right;

Man's ability to originate a god worthy of his homage, whose moral character when transferred to the worshiper would tend to his improvement and happiness, has been tested upon a broad scale. The heathen world has had time, learning, science, talent—enough of every facility to exhaust all human resources. What of her inventions? "Lords many, gods many." The VICE that has not been deified would be a new one in the catalogue of crime. THEREFORE the heathen, by common consent of infidel and Christian, escape CENSURE AND THE CHARGE OF HYPOCRISY. Let their ignorance and crimes be what they may, they are yet the objects of commiseration. Their gods neither "planted the ear nor formed the eye." To their invented gods they neither ascribed infinite purity, holiness or ubiquity; hence there was no "fear of God before their eyes," neither can there be without the abiding conviction of an all-pervading, everywhere present Divinity, with whom we have to do, and to whom we are accountable. The man that does not feel this is not to be trusted at all times. The fear of man can only restrain when in his presence, and self-respect is not always strong enough to keep tumultuous passions in obeyance. Perhaps in these facts we have the reason why an Atheist cannot be a witness in law; an avowed infidel cannot become a member of the LODGE, according to the Canons of the brotherhood, and this is the legal decision of one of our ablest jurists. "Many things may be reproved in sound morals, which are left by the law without remedy. except by an appeal to the conscience of the party himself." "It should therefore always be borne in mind, that he who adopts the law of the land, as the only guide in his dealings, or the only rule for his moral conduct, is neither a good neighbor nor an honest man."—Judge Swan.

Why appeal to a man's conscience who has no realizing faith in the Divine presence? It may be safely questioned, whether such a man has any conscience beyond self-interest. Moses appealed to the conscience of such an one in behalf of some slaves, but he stoutly answered. "I know not the Lord, neither will I let Israel go." I am told that some of the heathen moralists believed in the unity of God, his omnipresence, etc. Grant that they had some light upon these subjects. Did they receive it? or, did they create it? "Moses was born more than a thousand years before Pythagoras, Socrates, Plato, or Seneca." He could not have borrowed from them; but they may have borrowed from him. "Genesis, and the whole of the Jewish law, antedate Solon, Xenophon, Zeno," and all these philosophers of infidel boast. "Hiram, king of Tyre, was in habitual intercommunity with Solomon, whose fame for learning and wisdom was in all nations round about." Some of these distinguished Pagans lived in the days of the prophets, and were blessed with many facilites to learn the knowledge of the true God. Our only marvel is, that they learned so little, and so confounded that little with such a mass of corruption, ignorance, idolatry, etc., as to destroy all its practical utility. Whatever worthy views they had of the INFINITE ONE they did not invent, for where in all creation could they get the types to print the words OMNISCIENCE, OMNIPRESENCE? Let the learned infidel Volney say, "Moses created INSTITUTIONS whose influence extended to the WHOLE human race."

"even Jesus of whom Moses and the Prophets did write." See Matthew 11th chapter. "Come unto me all ye that labor and are heavy laden, and I will give you rest. Take my *yoke* upon you, and *learn of me;* for I am meek and lowly in heart, and ye *shall* find rest unto your souls." I must look at this Scripture in its connection and practical signification. Christ here assumes the office of a teacher—"*learn* of me." He prefaced this claim and invitation to the humble, to learn of him, by a few words of adoring praise: "I thank thee, O Father, Lord of Heaven and earth, because thou hast hid these things from the wise and prudent, and hast revealed them unto babes. Even so, Father; for so it seemed good in thy sight. All things are delivered unto me of my Father; and no man knoweth the Son, but the Father; neither knoweth any man the Father, save the Son, and he to whomsoever the Son will reveal him."

Here is something beautiful, decorous, orderly. Jesus Christ accommodated his language to human weakness. Man can only know divine relations, by his knowledge of human relations. It is in the divine as in the human—the father knows the son and the son knows the father. Therefore the Father knew the competency of the Son to reveal the "*all things*" delivered to his charge. "And as no man knows the Father but the Son—*therefore* no man can know the Father but "he to whomsoever the Son will reveal him." God withheld these honors from the worldly, "wise and prudent, and revealed them unto babes." Christ was a "babe," and so were his present Apostles "babes" in the learning of the schools—the literature of this world.

God determined that the Gospel of his grace should not be valued on account of the worldly consequence of the messengers employed to develop and propagate it. Nothing but its intrinsic worth should recommend it. The *diamond* should not be valued because of the *casket that contains it.* Hence said an Apostle, "we have this treasure in *earthen vessels*, that the excellency of the power may be of God and not of us." Jesus Christ says to all who desire to know God—"learn of me." "No man hath seen God at any time; the only begotten Son, which is in the bosom of the Father, he hath declared him."—John 1: 18.

All antecedent revelations of the divine character, were to some extent imperfect—they wanted *fulness.* To the Jews God was but partially revealed. They had no "*Emanuel.*" To them God was not manifested "in the flesh." When God revealed himself on "Sinai," they were filled with terror. When God threw over himself the vail of humanity, they could converse with him without fear—could approach him as a friend—could recline on his bosom, etc.

The Pagan forms of idol worship, and legalized immortalities, (of which we have something to say hereafter,) show clearly their utter ignorance of God and his moral perfections. The knowledge of God possessed by the Christian is as vastly superior to that possessed by the Jews, as Jesus Christ was superior to Moses and the Prophets; and theirs as superior to that of the Gentiles, as Moses and the Prophets were superior to the Heathen oracles and moralists.

The knowledge of God is the only basis of ethical science. From this stand-point let us look at our second affirmative—"In the New Testament we have a perfect rule of life."

Arg. 1.—As the matrimonial alliance lies at the basis of all the relations of society, I shall proceed with this; and shall specify first, *that marriage is from Heaven.* In man's creation we have the origin of this institution. Woman taken from man's side, near his heart, contains a volume upon this subject. From this every intelligent Bible reader would infer, that woman was not designed to be at the head of man, nor yet at his feet, but under his protecting arm and near his loving heart—that she was intended by the Creator to be a help-meet to man and not to be her husband's slave or lord. So Adam understood it. Said he, "this is now bone of my bone and flesh of my flesh." "No man ever yet hated his own flesh," is a New Testament maxim; and in perfect harmony with this grand fact. A single verse from Paul is all we need in the form of precept or of law upon this subject: "Nevertheless let every one of you in particular so love his wife even as himself; and the wife see that she reverence her husband."—Ephesians 5: 33.

The duties here specified are strictly philosophical, because in harmony with the natural and differential peculiarities of the parties. Farther: Christianity has given birth to a principle, (for it rules more by principle than by statute law,) which has broken the arm of oppression, and will do it so far as the Gospel is understood and obeyed. "We then that are strong ought to bear the infirmities of the weak, and not to please ourselves."—Romans 15: 1.

This precept is enforced by Christ's own example; for even Christ pleased not himself—therefore one of his Apostles commands the Christian husband to give honor unto the wife as the weaker vessel. See 1 Peter 3: 7: "Likewise, ye husbands, dwell with them according to knowledge, giving honor unto the wife as the weaker vessel, and as being heirs together of the grace of life; that your prayers be not hindered."

Woman's weakness entitles her to respect. This must secure to woman her rightful portion when her lots falls under the influence of the Gospel. Hence it is that Christianity has merited our everlasting gratitude, for bringing woman back again to her rightful position—to her husband's side and heart—to his affection and esteem. Yes, but the wife is commanded to be subject to her husband as the church is to Christ. True, and the husband is commanded to "love the wife as Christ loved the church." And how was that? He "gave himself for her"—laid down his life for the church. What is right in principle, cannot be wrong in practice. If Christianity, as then taught and practiced, brought about such a happy change for woman, it will do so now, and forever. That Christianity is most favorable to woman is admitted by infidels. Gibbon says, (See "Decline and Fall of the Roman Empire," vol. 4, page 274:) "The dignity of marriage was restored by the Christians." Heathenism had robbed woman of her rights. Christianity gave them back to her again, and will now protect her in possession of them. Hence, wherever Christianity has prevailed, woman is intelligent, virtuous, lovely.

We claim, therefore, that the Christian husband and wife have in the book manual of their profession, "a perfect rule of life." If the husband will treat his wife with that tender affection, required by the New Testament, the wife will reverence him. And if the wife will return the proper respect to her husband, her husband will love her. Let the parties in wedlock carry out these specified duties in all the details of practical life, and they will not fail to receive from each other that which will be in harmony with what may be peculiar to each. The duties to love and revere, are perfectly philosophical. They grow out of the relation. Man feels that there is a degree of respect due to him. God has implanted this feeling within his nature; as he has implanted into the breast of woman the desire to be treated with tender, loving fidelity.

MR. HARTZEL'S SIXTEENTH ADDRESS.

I am required to prove a proposition. This can only be done by presenting testimony bearing upon the proposition, and showing its connection with, and relation to the proposition to be proved. We know what the audience want. They want evidence, not declamation. Declamation does all for my friend; but unsustained assertions will not do for me. If I were simply to affirm that my proposition is true, would you, therefore, believe it to be so? What does Mr. Barker mean by this, viz: "All your evidence in favor of the Bible is brought from the Bible—from the friends of the Christian religion—from those interested." If Christianity is true, Christians have always been interested in the defense of it. If it is not true, their interests would be in disavowing it. It is no new thing for infidels to take this false position. It is saying that men can have an interest in maintaining known, conscious, unprofitable falsehood. Why these insinuations? Why not prove the New Testament writings untrue? A new order of things must be introduced to suit unbelievers; namely, that no witnesses shall be heard in court, who believe what they testifiy. When a man has espoused a cause as right and true, he must be regarded as a liar in what he may say in its defence. When a man has avowed his friendship for another he is incompetent to testifiy in his case. The best qualification a witness can have is, that he believes the testimony he offers. This demand of unbelievers is a departure from all legal and historic investigation, to meet the necessities of a wayward cause. They are, in this respect, as hard pressed as my friend was when he referred to Hitchcock — manufactured a man of straw, and then asked us to protect him. Arbitrary and unjust as this demand is, my friend still insists upon it. I will bring witnesses from his own side of the house before we close; and if I fail Mr. Barker will have the benefit of that failure. We resume, then, our argument.

The religion of Christ has always been the friend of woman. I will refer to Gibbon to show the condition of woman in the Roman Empire, in the Augustan age — the most enlightened period in Roman history. vol. 4, pages 273, 274.

"Experience has proved, that savages are the tyrants of the female sex, and that the condition of women is usually softened by the refinements of social life. "By his (husband's) judgment or caprice, her behavior was approved, or censured, or chastised; he exercised the jurisdiction of life and death; and it was allowed, that in the cases of adultery or drunkenness, the sentence might be properly inflicted. She acquired and inherited for the sole profit of her lord; and so clearly was woman defined, not as a PERSON but as a THING, that if the original title were deficient, she might be claimed, like other movables, by the use and possession of an entire year."

I will next read some historical testimonies from Mr. Barker. I read from "Christianity Triumphant," pages 118, 119, 120, 121.

"In the first place, woman was not honorably and justly treated. In almost all the nations of the earth where the religion of the Gospel has been unknown, woman has been regarded as a being of inferior order, and treated with the greatest indignity and cruelty. Among savages it appears to be the uniform lot of woman, to be treated with unkindness and contempt. "Through the continent of America," says Robertson, referring to the time of its discovery, "their condition is so peculiarly grievous, and their depression so complete, that servitude is a name too mild to describe their wretched state. A wife, among most tribes, is no better than a beast of burden, destined to every office of labor and fatigue. While the men loiter out the day in sloth, or spend it in amusement, the women are condemned to incessant toil. Tasks are imposed on them without pity, and services are received without complacency or gratitude. Every circumstance reminds women of their mortifying inferiority. They must approach their lords with reverence; they must regard them as more exalted beings, and are not permitted to eat in their presence. There are districts in America, where this dominion is so grievous, and so sensibly felt, that some women, in a wild emotion of maternal tenderness, have destroyed their FEMALE CHILDREN in their infancy, in order to deliver them from that intolerable bondage to which they knew they were doomed." "The North American tribes," says Home, "glory in idleness, the drudgery of labor degrades a man in their opinion, and is proper for women only. It would be unpardonable meanness in the bridegroom, to show any fondness for the bride. Young men among the Hottentots," says he, "are admitted into society of their seniors at the age of eighteen; after which it is disgraceful to keep company with women. In Guiana, a woman never eats with her husband; and in the Carribbee islands she is not permitted to eat even in the presence of her husband." Dampier observes in general, that among all the wild nations that he was acquainted with, women carry the burdens, while the men walk before, and carry nothing but their arms. Women even of the highest rank are not better treated. The sovereign of Giaga, in Africa, has many wives, who are literally his slaves: one carries his bow, one his arrows, and one gives him drink; and while he is drinking, they all fall on their knees, and clap their hands and sing. The Giagas subject their wives to every sort of drugery, such as digging, sowing, reaping, cutting wood, grinding corn, fetching water, &c. These poor creatures are suffered to toil in the fields and woods, ready to faint with excessive labor, while the monsters of men will not give themselves the trouble even of training animals for work. Among the wandering Arabs of Africa, the men leave the women to card, to spin, to weave, as well as to manage the household affairs. The women milk the cattle, grind the corn, dress the victuals, bring home wood and water, and even take care of their husbands' horses. Every thing like drudgery is thrown upon the women, while every thing like honor and respect is withheld from them. The poor wives are dragged along with one infant at the breast, and another in a basket, and in the evening, though tired with the march and their burdens, they are not permitted to sleep, but must spend the long night in providing for their haughty and unfeeling husbands. To complete the wretchedness of the woman, a young wife is taken by the husband, who is permitted to abuse her and her children, because she is no longer regarded." — Sketches of the History of Man, by H. Home.

The condition of woman, even among nations reputed civilized, was one of great degradation and misery. Among the Greeks and Romans woman was considered as the property of man, to be treated and disposed of in all cases as he might think fit. She might be sold, or lent, tortured, or destroyed, returned to her parents, or turned adrift upon a wide unfeeling world, without protection, without compassion, and without hope. Fornication was regarded as a thing altogether allowable among the Gentiles generally, and was actually encouraged both by the laws and by the religious ceremonies both of Greeks and Romans. In many cases licentiousness was sanctioned or commanded by law, and crimes were perpetrated, and customs were established, of the most awful description, tending directly to the entire corruption and degradation of the female sex. "In the purest ages of Greece and Rome," says Ryan, "it was lawful to put female infants to death, and on the decline of the Roman empire, Heathen matrons were degraded creatures. According to the system of oppression, which generally prevailed when the Gospel was promulgated, the husband, instead of being the friend of his wife, was a tyrant over her; and the wife, as might naturally be expected, obeyed from a principle of fear, instead of love or gratitude. Callicratidas, a Heathen philosopher, exhorted wives to bear with the unfaithfulness of their husbands patiently, "since the liberty of fornication," says he, "is allowed to men but not to women." Some of the laws of Lycurgus in reference to women were most shameful, and the principles of Plato and Aristotle were no better. It would be a shame even to repeat some of the vile regulations of those renowned philosophers."

Again: to see what Judaism did for woman, see pages 125, 126, 127, 128, of the same book.

"The religion of Heaven has always, in all its dispensations, been distinguished from other religions by its regard to the interests of women. In the account of creation as given in the sacred writings of the Jews, every thing is calculated to inspire respect and tenderness toward woman. She is created to be man's companion in holy duties and enjoyments, she is formed out of man's own flesh and bone, she is animated with the same living breath, she bears the same image of the Deity, engages in the same employments, and inherits the same anticipations of glory and immortality. Marriage is represented as the institution of God, it is made to consist in the union of one male and one female, and that union is made to consist in a close, and cordial, and an inviolable friendship, and in the ceaseless interchange of loving offices. In this state all was delight and harmony; and the Jews were taught by the sacred writings, that in this delightful and harmonious state it was God's original purpose that mankind should live.

The entrance of sin introduced disorder: the original law of marriage was disregarded, and at length forgotten; adultery and polygamy were introduced, licentiousness prevailed and overran all bounds, and the rights and privileges of woman were trampled in the dust. Woman became a slave, a drudge, the sport of man's caprice, the victim of unholy passions, and the miserable inheritor of every form of shame and bitterness. It was in those lowest depths of misery and degradation that woman was found by the religion of Heaven, as established in its earliest and imperfect dispensation by the instrumentality of Moses. Under this dispensation a number of regulations were introduced with the manifest intention of rescuing woman from her degradation, and of restoring her to happiness and honor. Man was not stripped of all his usurped authority at once, nor was woman restored at once to all her rightful portion; but many important steps were taken in the way of moral improvement. Importance was given to woman by a law which made females capable of inheriting property, and which constituted daughters, where there were no male heirs, the inheritors of the entire possessions of their fathers. Adulteries and rapes were punished with death; licensed prostitution was abolished, and a number of regulations were established with a view to the abolition of prostitution altogether. Men were no longer allowed to sell their wives as had been previously the case, but the husband, who was bent on turning his wife away, was required to give her a bill of divorcement, and send her forth among her people free. A number of other laws were instituted, all tending to protect woman from injury, and to promote her comfort and independence. Children were required to honor their mothers as well as their fathers, and all were required to show kindness to the widow. God proclaimed himself the judge of the widow, and the father of her fatherless children; and he threatened the most awful judgments against such as should injure or oppress them. In those numerous and wonderful regulations which were made for the relief and comfort of the poor, the widow and the fatherless were especially remembered. The wealthy were required to assist them in all their distresses, and to give them or lend them as much as their necessities required. And though pledging was allowed in may other cases, yet no one was allowed to take the WIDOW'S GARMENT to pledge. When the people gathered in their harvests, they were not allowed to reap the corners of their fields, or to glean the scattered ears; these were to be FOR THE STRANGER, THE FATHERLESS, AND THE WIDOW. If in cutting down the harvest they forgot a sheaf in the field, they were not allowed to return and fetch it; it was to be FOR THE STRANGER, THE FATHERLESS, AND THE WIDOW. When they were beating their olive trees, they were not to go over the boughs a second time; what was left after the first time was to be FOR THE STRANGER, THE FATHERLESS, AND THE WIDOW. When they gathered the grapes of their vineyard, they were only to go over the vineyard once; the remnant was to be FOR THE STRANGER, THE FATHERLESS, AND THE WIDOW. The produce of the land, during the years of rest, was to be left FOR THE WIDOW AND THE FATHERLESS, and every third year an extra tithe was demanded, that out of the produce THE STRANGER, THE FATHERLESS, AND THE WIDOW MIGHT EAT AND BE SATISFIED. A number of other benevolent regulations intended for the benefit of the poor, which may be mentioned in future pages of this work, were all calculated to exert a happy influence on the character and lot of woman.

The account of the creation prefixed to their law, presenting such an instructive and affecting account of the origin of man and woman, of the nature and design of marriage, and of its institution by the Deity, could hardly fail to lead such as were religiously disposed, to behave toward their wives with respect and tenderness. The prediction that of one of the daughters of Israel the Messiah was to be born, would tend to excite feelings of interest and respect in the minds of men, exceedingly favorable to the happiness of their partners. All these things, as well as others which cannot now be mentioned, tended to render the condition of woman among the Jews far happier than among the rest of the nations of the earth. And notwithstanding the imperfections of this early dispensation, it had the effect of mingling in the cup of woman no inconsiderable measure of felicity, and of diffusing through the dwellings of Jacob a degree of purity and happiness not to be found in the dwellings of any other race of people then existing on the face of the earth."

To show the effects of Christianity in favor of woman, we read again from "Christianity Triumphant," pages 142, 143, 144.

"And as for woman, no where does she appear so lovely and so glorious, as in lands where the light of the Gospel shines around her, and where the influence of its principles is extensively felt. Look at woman as she is found among the tribes of American or African savages, and look at woman as she is found among those who rejoice in the light and blessings of the gospel, and behold the difference. Look at woman as she is found amidst the influences of irreligion and licentiousness, even in our own land, and look at her as she is found under the influences of the religion of truth and purity;—look at her as courted and beguiled, as dishonored and cast away by the infidel sensualist, and look at her as revered and loved, as cared for and comforted by the faithful Christian husband; look at her, in a word, under all the forms of wretchedness and shame in which she is placed by impiety and sensuality, and then look at her clothed in the garments of purity, adorned with the fruits of the Spirit of God, employed in her labors of love, and rejoicing in the fulness of her heart in the hopes of a blessed immortality, and you will then have some idea of the happy influence of the Gospel on the character and condition of woman. From the depths of pollution and shame—from the wreck of her glory and joy—from the sorrows and phrenzies of a broken heart, and from all the miseries and fears of guilt, it raises her to loveliness and purity—to joy and dignity—to all that is dear and delightful on earth, and to all that is glorious in Heaven.

From the first institution of Christianity to the present times, the church of Christ has presented a large and unbroken list of living instances of the happy influence of the Gospel upon the character of females. We cannot look through a single age of the church, in which we do not find women who have been raised by the Gospel to a height of knowledge, and piety, and charity, of which the ancient Pagans could have formed no conception. We find them employed in instructing the ignorant in the principles of religion, training the young in knowledge and piety, nursing and rearing orphan and outcast children, tending the sick, helping and comforting the prisoners, preaching the Gospel, building hospitals, forming themselves into societies for the exercise of charity, founding benevolent institutions, and distinguishing themselves by a forwardness to every good work. Some have distinguished themselves as authors, and many, in times of persecution, have stood forward as confessors of their Lord, and nobly earned the honors of martyrdom."

The first testimony we offered was Gibbon. He was an infidel, one of Mr. Barker's party. The series of testimonies which followed are from the pen of Joseph Barker. Neither do they rest upon his own authority. He has drawn freely upon the history of Robinson, Ryan, and Home for some of these important facts. He knows the respectability of these authors, and the credit due to them. They are worthy of respect; if not he will impeach them now. We proceed with our argument.

Argument 2d: Christianity having set to rights

the relation of husband and wife, it went forward in correcting the whole domestic circle. "And, ye fathers, provoke not your children to wrath; but bring them up in the nurture and admonition of the Lord." Ephesians 6: 4. "Fathers provoke not your children to anger, lest they be discouraged. Collossians 3: 21.

Under these instructions and divine laws they could not expose their offspring, as the universal custom was among the Heathen, and is nearly so yet;—"*but bring them up in the nurture and admonition of the Lord.*" "Do not discourage them." What a reversing of heathen laws and customs! In the state children were mere things; the father could kill them in infancy, or in manhood, or sell them into slavery. In evidence of this I read from Milman's Gibbon's Rome, vol. 3, pages 169, 170.

The law of nature instructs most animals to cherish and educate their infant progeny. The law of reason inculcates to the human species the returns of filial piety. But the exclusive, absolute, and perpetual dominion of the father over his children, is peculiar to the Roman jurisprudence, and seems to be coeval with the foundation of the city. The paternal power was instituted or confirmed by Romulus himself; and after the practice of three centuries, it was inscribed on the fourth table of the Decemvirs. In the forum, the senate, or the camp, the adult son of a Roman citizen enjoyed the public and private rights of a PERSON: in his father's house, he was a mere THING; confounded by the laws with the moveables, the cattle, and the slaves, whom the capricious master might alienate or destroy, without being responsible to an earthly tribunal. The hand which bestowed the daily sustenance might resume the voluntary gift, and whatever was acquired by the labor or fortune of the son, was immediately lost in the property of the father. His stolen goods (his oxen or his children) might be recovered by the same action of theft; and if either had been guilty of a trespass, it was in his own option to compensate the damage, or resign to the injured party the obnoxious animal. At the call of indigence or avarice, the master of a family could dispose of his children or his slaves. But the condition of the slave was far more advantageous, since he regained by the first manumission his alienated freedom: the son was again restored to his unnatural father; he might be condemned to servitude a second and a third time, and it was not till after the third sale and deliverance that he was enfranchised from the domestic power, which had been so repeatedly abused. According to his discretion, a father might chastise the real or imaginary faults of his children, by stripes, by imprisonment, by exile, by sending them to the country to work in chains among the meanest of his servants. The majesty of a parent was armed with the power of life and death; and the example of such bloody executions, which were sometimes praised and never punished, may be traced in the annals of Rome beyond the times of Pompey and Augustus. Neither age, nor rank, nor the consular office, nor the honors of a triumph, could exempt the most illustrious citizen from the bonds of filial subjection: his own descendants were included in the family of their common ancestors; and the claims of adoption were not less sacred or less rigorous than those of nature. Without fear, though not without danger of abuse, the Roman legislators had reposed an unbounded confidence in the sentiments of paternal love; and the oppression was tempered by the assurance that each generation must succeed in its turn to the awful dignity of parent and master.

Christianity makes it the duty of parents to bring up their children, and to treat them with paternal kindness. If the members of the "church" refused obedience to the Apostolic injunctions, they were to be further instructed, exhorted, and rebuked; and if they would not reform, they were expelled from the communion of the "church." There are some important allusions in the New Testament which can never be understood without a correct view of the condition of children under the influence of Paganism and Idolatry. I will refer to one. 1 Timothy 5: 9. Paul in making certain benevolent regulations with regard to superanuated widow members of the "church," specifies among other things, that "she must have brought up children." We would understand this to have reference to the children of others, but as the exposing of infants was a common practice of mothers then, and is to this day in many countries where Christianity does not prevail; hence we understand the Apostle to refer to her own offspring. If she had been an infanticide, she would not have been entitled to this church beneficence. The Christian religion has abolished this inhuman practice throughout the civilized world. And where infancy and childhood are uncared for, unprovided for, Christianity is not. That which was then common and approved is now rare and condemned. Again: Such widow must have been THE wife of one man," not A "wife of one man." This was a stroke at polygamy which has always been proverbially unfavorable to the offspring of one man and many wives.

These inhuman laws prevailed in the Augustan age,—the most enlightened and refined age of the Roman Empire. They were as old as Romulus, who was himself exposed when an infant, but found by some one and rescued from his exposed condition, otherwise he would never have been the founder of Rome. These laws were perpetuated by their senators, and approved by their philosophers and moralists. It is the law and order of nations for the strong to oppress the weak; and from its universality, I believe it is a law of our nature—natural religion—Deism.

MR. HARTZEL'S SEVENTEENTH ADDRESS.

We shall call attention to the reading of a scripture alluded to by Mr. Barker; 1st Corinthians 14: 34.

"Let your women keep silence in the churches: for it is not permitted unto them to speak; but they are commanded to be under obedience, as also saith the law. And if they will learn anything, let them ask their husbands at home: for it is a shame for women to speak in the church. What! came the word of God out from you? or came it unto you only?"

These are regulations given to "the church"—"the church" as an organization. This implies order, and order implies rule. Women are commanded to "teach." Every competent mother of Israel is commissioned to "teach the young women to love their children," to be virtuous, "chaste," etc. The only prohibition placed upon woman is, that she is not to go forth as a missionary or preacher. "What! came the word of God out from you (women?) or came it unto you only?" If Mr. Barker had discriminated between these New Testament terms, the "*word*" and "*teaching*," he would not have committed this blunder.

The subject matter of the New Testament divides itself into two chapters sufficiently marked by inspiration. "Go ye therefore and teach all nations, baptizing them in the name of the Father, and of the Son, and of the Holy Ghost. Teaching them to observe all things, whatsoever I have commanded you; and lo! I am with you always even unto the end of the world."

"Go teach the nations" was to preach the "word" to the unconverted, to make known to them the "Gospel," and accompany the same with supernatural demonstrations, and to "baptize" the "believers." "Teaching them to observe all things whatsoever I have commanded you," was to teach the baptized the duties of the Christian life. This distinction is every where expressed or implied. "Then they that gladly received the *word* were baptized."—Acts 2: 41. "And they continued steadfast in the Apostle's *doctrine*."—Acts 2: 42. Again: 1st Timothy 5: 17—"Let the elders that rule well, be accounted worthy of double honor, especially they who labor in *word* and *doctrine*." Some "elders ruled well." Others preached the "*word*" to sinners and taught the saints the "*doctrine* of Christ." In this latter department woman may work; nay, she is commanded to work.

"Moreover, brethren, I declare unto you the Gospel which I have preached unto you; which also ye have received, and wherein ye stand, by which ye are saved." "For I declared unto you first of all, that which I also received; how that Christ died for our sins according to the scriptures"—"that he was buried and rose again the third day according to the scriptures." The proclaiming of these facts to the world is "preaching the word." Christ chose men only, for "this work." Hence Paul asked those aspiring sisters, "What! came the word of God out from you, (woman?) or came it unto you only? Woman is proscribed upon that subject. Is this degrading to woman? She is graciously exonerated from a duty from which she is not qualified. Why not quarrel with Jesus Christ for not having made some female Apostles.

Now, I venture to affirm, there is not a single passage that our friend will take up, from which he might expect to make some capital against me, but will militate against him, and aid the argument in my favor. Let me inquire into the circumstances connected with the Apostle's language in 1st Corinthians. The women had become too aspiring. This is a trait of human character, that when individuals have been degraded and oppressed, and are suddenly elevated, they will feel a degree of exaltation, injurious both to themselves and others, and will have to be restrained to preserve order. It was so in the primitive churches with the men, as well as the women. Therefore, Paul had to command the men to obey their Heathen "magistrates," because they themselves were once "foolish," etc. Mr. Barker speaks of these terrible men professing to be Christians in England. Were they Christians? Did they give honor to "the wife" as unto the "weaker vessel?" If not, then they were not Christians. As a matter of course, if they did not honor woman, they were heathen, not Christians. My friend must not suppose that because he came from England, that every one living there is therefore a Christian. Many of them are no nearer to Christianity than those living in South Africa. Did these men love their "wives" as "Christ loved the church?" If not they were no Christians. "Christ gave himself for the church." Did the people of Salem know that the Protestant Christians were polygamists? that polygamy was favored in Christendom? If so, I can only say that such as favor the practice are not Christians. Christ forbade polygamy, and it was driven out of the world so far as Christianity prevailed. But Mr. Barker says the Mormons are polygamists. Well, they are about as much entitled to the name of Christian as himself.

Mr. Barker.—As yourselves.

Mr. Hartzel.—They are not Christians.

Mr. Barker.—But they receive the New Testament as their "rule of life."

Mr. Hartzel.—I deny it, sir. They have another Bible, called the "book of Mormon." They appeal to their own book. That contains their "rule of life," church order and practice. The Old and New Testaments have no authority with them. I know what I say, and speak advisedly upon the subject. I lived near the very hot-bed of Mormonism when the delusion began in northern Ohio. I know their religious peculiarities.

But polygamy is in the Old Testament. It is true polygamy existed among the Jews to some extent. I must make a few passing remarks upon this subject, that Mr. Barker may see where the evil began. "And Lamech took to himself two wives." This was the first departure. Polygamy is of human origin, not of divine appointment.

Look at the origin of marriage in the Old Testament. God made *one* man and *one* woman; "and for this cause shall a man leave his father and mother, and cleave to his wife, and they twain shall be one flesh." Suppose, now, that the book of Genesis had been a forgery for the purpose of defending the religion of the Jews; would not the writer have anticipated that sometime or other, some sharp-sighted, clear-headed Joseph Barker would read it, and would discover that the God of the Bible in the latter part of the book had departed from the law of marriage, as taught in the first part of the book? To make the book justify the practice, the writer would have said, in the beginning God made one man and three or four women. He would have said, for this cause shall a man leave his father and mother and cleave unto his wives. That a man should forge a book for a people that would be a standing reproof to them, and that they should receive it and transmit it to posterity, would be paradoxical enough. We do not say Abraham was a perfect character, but we simply say he was a patriarchal saint. Neither are we bound to defend the morality of the Old Testament, either in principle or practice. It is a free will offering on my part. My proposition does not require it at my hand; and all my opponet's animadversions on polygamy are off the premises in the present discussion. With whom did polygamy begin? "And Lamech took unto himself two wives." If polygamy is of divine appointment, God must have instituted it. It filled the writer with surprise, He made it the subject of a special note,—"*And Lamech took unto himself two wives.*"

After "the flood," the people went off into idolatry. Abraham was an idolator when God called him. His father was an idolator. Polygamy was a human device, originated in the family of Cain, and after "the flood" practised by idolaters. The evil had spread far and wide among the nations, and could not be rooted out at once. God gave pure and holy lessons to the people—taught them principles that would ultimately destroy the evil. *Reformation is a progressive work.* God's plan has succeeded where his word is the man of counsel. Abraham had great trouble with his wives, and the same was the case with Jacob. The Christian religion shows no favor with polygamy. If Mr. Barker can find anything either in the teachings of Christ or his Apostles to favor poylgamy—why not bring it out? We call for it. As relates to American slavery, we have a chapter for him; it will be forthcoming in due time.

Argument 3. Next in order will be filial duty. In

this subject the decalogue is like a light shining in a dark place. "Honor thy father and thy mother." "Children obey your parents." This in the elevation of woman was of transcendant importance, for it assigned to the mother her rightful place in the family compact—claiming equal honor for the father and the "mother." These filial obligations extended even farther than to parents. They were required of "nephews." "But if any widow have children or nephews, let them learn first to show piety at home, and to requite their parents; for that is good and acceptable before God."—1st Timothy 5, 4. The inhuman laws and practices of Heathen fathers had their influence upon their children. Whenever the children became the strong, and the parents the weak, the parties changed sides; but the practice was the same. The parents were now the sufferers. In proof, see "Christianity Triumphant," page 152.

"The brutality of the Romans to their offspring, says Henry Home, was glaring. Children were held, like cattle, to be their father's property; and so tenacious was this power of the father, that if a son or a daughter sold to be a slave was set free, the son or the daughter fell again under the father's power, to be sold a second or even a third time. A son being a slave could have no property of his own. In Athens a man had power of life and death over his children. So late as the days of Dioclesian, a son's marriage did not dissolve the power of the Roman father over his son.

The effect of such unnatural powers was to destroy natural affection between parents and their children. When the children, who had been thus cruelly used by their parents, were at length set free from their power, IT WAS NO UNCOMMON THING FOR THEM TO REPAY THE CRUELTY OF THEIR PARENTS BY CONTEMPT AND HATRED. Hence the parent, if he were allowed to live, would frequently be left to groan under the infirmities of age without sympathy, and allowed to die of want, while his children were rolling in abundance. The description of them by the Apostle was no more than truth: they were disobedient to parents, without understanding, without natural affection, implacable, unmerciful,—hateful, and hating one another."

A very important testimony against Paganism and in favor of Christianity. How vain the boast of infidels,—that reason, with the helps of science, is sufficient to make known to man his relations with their corresponding duties! This doctrine is false, or the history of the world is a lie. Look at Pagan Rome in her best days; when she had made some advances in science, art, and literature; great advancement in the development of talent and genius. Look at the family compact. The husband and father is the despot. His power is absolute. His wife and children are *chattels.* He sells them as he does his *horses*, or *kills* them as he does his *pigs.* "The examples of such bloody executions were often praised and never blamed," says the historian Gibbon."

If the history of the world proves anything, it proves this,—that in the ratios of man's intellectual improvement, without moral culture, does he become wicked and abandoned. This is true of all ages, and of all nations. Hence it is that in Christian lands we have some of the greatest giants in wickedness, that have ever afflicted and cursed mankind:—because when man is unprincipled but intellectual, he is capable of higher degrees of wickedness. His moral nature loses that balance of power so essential to goodness—the better sentiments of the soul become dormant, and he becomes a monster in wickedness—a demon.

Argument 4. The superiority of the teachings of the New Testament on the subject of benevolence is the superlative of all excellence. Jesus Christ was sent "to preach the Gospel to the poor." "The spirit of the Lord is upon me, because he has annointed me to preach the Gospel to the poor. He hath sent me to heal the broken hearted, to preach deliverance to the captives; and recovering of sight to the blind, to set at liberty them that are bruised, to preach the acceptable year of the Lord."—Luke 4; 18.

When John the Baptist sent a deputation to inquire of Jesus,—"Art thou he that was to come, or look we for another?" He gave them this in reply: "The blind receive their sight—the lame walk—the lepers are cleansed—the deaf hear—the dead are raised up, *and the poor have the Gospel preached unto them.*"

Jesus was the ever faithful friend of the "poor." He had a treasury for their special benefit. He taught the Apostles both by precept and example. He communicated himself to them. *He lived in them.*—See Galatians 2; 9, 10. When the Apostles made some distributions, in regard to their labors among the Gentiles, James, Cephas, and John went to the Jews: Paul and Barnabas to the Gentiles. Paul says, "this only, they would that we should remember the poor, the same which I also was forward to do." Christians are, then, to aid the "poor" and the "weak." Those who neglect and oppress them are *not* Christians. We want no proof but that of my worthy friend, who says "the poor in England are kept in mines to toil for the rich." Are these oppressors Christians? Do they practice the precepts of Christianity? If not, what did Mr. Barker mean by referring to English tyrants? Paul says, "I have showed how you ought to support the weak, and remember the words of the Lord Jesus,"—"it is more blessed to give than to receive."

The Apostles appointed the weekly "contribution" not for the support of the ministry, but for the relief of the "poor." They got up, at one time, an extensive system of co-operation, for the relief of the poor saints of Judea. "If any seeth his brother have need and shutteth up his bowels of *compassion* from him, how dwelleth the love of God in him."—John.

The religion of Heaven, under every dispensation, was friendly to the "poor." They were the objects of special legislation under Moses. I refer you to "Christianity Triumphant," pages 187 to 193.

"And God has inculcated the exercise of benevolence upon his people, under every dispensation of religion which he has given to mankind. Even under the Mosaical dispensation, imperfect as it was, the exercise of benevolence formed the principal part of what God required of those who were placed under it. Some of the regulations of Mosaic dispensation on this subject, we have noticed already, when speaking of the influence of the religion of Heaven upon the interests of woman; but the subject deserves to be noticed in the present place more at large. The provisions which were made for the poor by the law of Moses, will be admired as long as reason and tenderness shall have a place in the souls of men. This regard for the poor and friendless runs through the whole law. We can hardly read a single chapter without meeting with something intended to protect them from oppression, or to oblige their brethren to seek their comfort and welfare. "Thou shalt not vex a stranger, nor oppress him." saith the Lord; "for ye were strangers in the land of Egypt." The master was forbidden in the most solemn manner to deprive the hireling of his wages, or to put him to inconvenience by neglecting to pay him at the proper time. "Thou shalt not oppress an hired servant that is poor and needy, whether he be of thy brethren, or of the strangers that are within thy gates. At his day thou shalt give him his hire, neither shall the sun go down upon it: for he is poor, and setteth his heart upon it; lest he cry against thee unto the Lord, and it be sin unto thee."

The Almighty cautioned them, when a question was to be tried before the judges in which the rights of the poor were concerned, to take care that they did not suffer the poor to be wronged. "Thou shalt not pervert the judgment of the stranger nor of the fatherless. Thou shalt not wrest the judgment of thy poor in his cause. Keep thee far from a false matter; and the innocent and the righteous slay thou not: for I will not justify the wicked." The sternest and most awful words almost that ever God spoke, were against such as should oppress or injure the fatherless and widow. "Ye shall not afflict any widow or fatherless child. If thou do in any way afflict them, and they cry at all unto me, I will surely hear their cry: and my wrath shall wax hot, and I will kill you with the sword: and your wives shall be widows, and your children shall be fatherless." Exod. xxii. 22. When God would introduce himself as the patron and protector of the needy, he assumes the loftiest titles, and clothes himself in the most terrible majesty. "The LORD your god is god of gods, and Lord of lords, a great God, a mighty, and a terrible, which regardeth not persons, nor taketh a bribe. He doth execute the judgment of the fatherless and the widow, and loveth the stranger, and giveth him food and raiment. Love ye therefore the stranger: for ye were strangers in the land of Egypt." Deut x. 17, 19. The Lord taught them to be tender of the poor man's feelings, as well as of his rights. "When thou dost lend thy brother any thing on a pledge, thou shalt not go into his house to fetch his pledge. Thou shalt stand abroad, and the man to whom thou dost lend shall bring out the pledge abroad unto thee. And if the man be poor, thou shalt not sleep with his pledge, in any case thou shalt deliver him the pledge again when the sun goeth down, that he may sleep in his own raiment, and bless thee; and it shall be righteousness unto thee before the Lord thy God." Deut. xxiv 10, 13.

God established a number of regulations with respect to property, which were both calculated to prevent people from becoming poor, and to secure to such as did become poor their share of the blessings of Providence. In the first place the land was divided equally among all the tribes, except the tribes of Levi; and to the Levites was given such a measure of the produce of the land in sacrifices, tithes, and offerings, as made their portion equal to the portions of the other tribes. If any family were obliged through poverty to sell their land, they could not sell it out of the family for ever; for at the end of every fifty years the land returned to its original owners: so that few families could remain without their share of the land for any great length of time. Lev. xxv. And even while the land was in possession of others, the poor were still entitled to a portion of its produce. The poor were always at liberty to go into their neighbors' fields and gardens, and to eat of the grain and fruit at their pleasure, to their fill. Every seventh year the land was to have rest, and what was produced during that year was not to be reaped by the owners; it was to be for the poor, the fatherless, and the widow. And so it was with the vine-yards and the olive-yard. The fruit which they produced every seventh year, was not to be gathered by the owners, but left for the poor, the fatherless and the widow. Exod. xxiii. 10, 11. During the other six years, the owners of the soil were not to reap the whole of the produce. "Thou shalt not reap the corners of thy fields, saith the Lord, thou shalt leave them for the poor and for the stranger." Lev. xxiii. 22. "Nor shalt thou gather the gleanings of thy harvest, saith the Lord; it shall be for the poor, the fatherless and the widow. And if in gathering in thy harvest thou shalt forget a sheaf, thou shalt not turn back to fetch it; it shall be for the poor, the fatherless, and the widow; that the Lord thy God may bless thee in all the work of thy hands. When thou beatest thine olive tree, thou shalt not go over the boughs a second time; it shall be for the stranger, the fatherless, and for the widow. And when thou gatherest the grapes of thy vineyard, thou shalt not glean it afterwards: it shall be for the stranger, for the fatherless, and for the widow. Thou shalt remember that thou wast a bondsman in the land of Egypt, saith the Lord: therefore I command thee to this thing." Deut. xxiii, 24, 25. The poor and friendless had also assigned to them a portion in the tithes and offerings: and they were, also, to be present at all the feasts which were appointed as occasions of rejoicing and thanksgiving to God, that they might eat and be satisfied, and that their souls might bless the Lord. At the end of every third year the children of Israel were to bring forth the tenth part of all their produce for that year, that the Levite, and the stranger, and the fatherless, and the widow, might come and eat and be satisfied. Deut. xiv. 28, 29; xvi. 9, 11.

The Israelites were commanded to assist their poor brothren by loans, but they were not allowed to take interest from them for what they lent, and at the end of every sixth year came the year of release, when the debtors were all set free. "If thy brother be waxen poor with thee, and fallen into decay, then thou shalt relieve him; yea, though he be a stranger, or a sojourner: that he may live with thee. Thou shalt not give him thy money upon usury, nor lend him thy victuals for increase." Lev. xxv. 35. And again; "If there be among you a poor man of one of thy brethren within any of thy gates, in the land which the Lord thy God giveth thee, thou shalt not harden thy heart, nor shut thy hand from thy poor brother; but thou shalt open thine hand wide unto him, and shalt surely lend him sufficient for his need, in that which he wanteth. Beware that there be not a thought in thy wicked heart, saying the seventh year, the year of release is at hand: and thine eye be evil against thy poor brother, and thou givest him nought; and he cry unto the Lord against thee, and it be sin unto thee; thou shalt surely give him, and thine heart shall not be grieved when thou givest unto him: because that for this thing the Lord thy God shall bless thee in all thy works, and in all that thou puttest thine hand unto. Therefore I command thee, saying, thou shalt not open thine hand wide unto thy brother, to thy poor, and to thy needy in thy land." Deut. xv. 1–11. Better laws for the prevention and relief of poverty could have not have been imagined.

The laws of the Mosaical dispensation on the subject of slavery, were equally friendly to the interests of the poor. They were not only calculated to lesson the bitterness of slavery, but to prepare the way for its complete and everlasting overthrow. Man-stealing was punished with death: "He that stealeth a man, and selleth him, or if he be found in his hand, shall surely be put to death." Exod. xxi. 16. No one could be made a slave against his will, and so many provisions were made for the poor, that few could be under any necessity to sell themselves into bondage. Then the power of the master was so restricted, that but few men could be disposed to buy a slave, and those who did buy slaves had such a feeble hold of them, that it was impossible for them to keep them in their possession without the exercise of great kindness. Six years was the longest term for which a man could sell himself. "If thy brother, an Hebrew man, or an Hebrew woman, be sold unto thee, and serve the six years: then in the seventh year thou shalt let him go free from thee." While they held them, the masters were not allowed to use them as if they were their property, or to rule over them with rigor, as was the general custom of slavery. "When thy brother is sold unto thee, thou shalt not compel him to serve as a bond servant: but as a hired servant shall be with thee. Thou shalt not rule over him with rigor, but shall fear God." "And if a man sell his daughter to be a maid-servant, and she please not her master, he shall have no power to sell her unto a strange nation. And if he have betrothed her unto his son, he shall deal with her after the manner of daughters." And when a man was sold to a stranger or a sojourner, though sold for six years, he was not bound to remain in bondage the whole of that time, provided his brethren or any of his near kindred were able and willing to redeem him. "And if a sojourner or stranger wax rich by thee, and thy brother that dwelleth by him wax poor, and sell himself unto the stranger or sojourner by thee; after that he is sold, he may be redeemed again; his brother may redeem him, or any that is nigh of kin unto him, or if he be able, he may redeem himself. And if he be not redeemed, then he shall go out in the year of Jubilee, both he, and his children with him. And as a yearly hired servant shall he be with him; and the other shall not rule with rigor over him in thy sight. For unto ME the children of Israel are servants; they are MY servants, whom I brought forth out of the land of Egypt." One object for which labor on the Sabbath was prohibited, was to lessen the hardships of those who were in service, and lighten the labors of the poor. "Six days thou shalt do thy work, and on the seventh day thou shalt rest: that the son of thy handmaid, and the stranger may be refreshed." It was further commanded that all servile work should cease on all their festivals, that both the servants and the laboring poor generally might not only be relieved from a portion of their toil, but have the privilege of attending the feasts and the holy convocations. If a servant found the master to whom he had sold himself, cruel, and in consequence of ill-treatment ran away from his place, the cruel master had no power to lay hold of him and drag him back again. "Thou shalt not deliver unto his master the servant which has escaped from his master unto thee; he shall dwell with thee in that place which he shall choose, in one of thy gates, where it liketh him best; thou shall not oppress him." And when the time of deliverance came, the slaves were not to be sent away empty; but the masters were commanded to let them go away well furnished with a portion of those good things which God had given to them. "And when thou sendest out thy servant free from thee, thou shalt not let him go away empty; thou shalt furnish him liberally out of thy flock, and out of thy floor, and out of thy wine-press; of that wherewith the Lord thy God hath blessed thee, shalt thou give unto him. It shall not seem hard unto thee when thou sendest him out free from thee, for he hath been worth a double hired servant unto thee, in serving thee six years: and the Lord thy God shall bless thee in all that thou doest." It was impossible that slavery should flourish under such laws as these. These laws amounted in fact to a prohibition of slavery, and both their object and their tendency was to prepare the way for the abolition of slavery throughout the whole world. Accordingly the system of slavery appears to have died away under those regulations among the Israelites, and thus the fonndation was laid for the entire and universal destruction of the system. Such were the first laws given to mankind by God; such were the manifestations of benevolent regard to the interests of the poor and friendless in the religion of Heaven, even under its earlier and less perfect forms. Well might Moses exclaim, while he contrasted those regulations of Heaven with the systems of selfishness and cruelty which everywhere prevailed among surrounding nations: "What nation is there so great, that hath statutes and judgments so righteous as all this law?" If those laws were not the best that God could give, they were the best that men in the ruder ages of the world were able to receive."

These pages are interesting, both because they are true, and the source from whence they came. But Mosaic benevolence was too sectional. It was too much confined to their own "brethren." Jesus Christ made it as wide as the family of man. The doctrine taught in the parable of the unfortunate man that went down from Jerusalem to Jericho, shows the extent of Christian benevolence. The question had been asked "who is my neighbor?" The savior then put that beautiful imaginary case before the inquirer. A Jew, going down to Jericho, saw one of his brethren in the flesh and religion in trouble, but passed by on the other side. But a Samaritan came that way, dismounted, dressed his wounds, lifted him up and set him on his "own beast," bore him to an "inn," made the necessary provision for his comfort during his sickness, left some money, and promised to defray whatever expense was incurred. Now, who was "neighbor to him that fell among thieves?" The answer was, "he that had compassion on him. "Go thou and do likewise." "Who is my neighbor," then, according to Jesus Christ? The man who needs my aid, no matter whether he be black or white—whether he be a believer or an unbeliever. I ask have not the rich "a perfect rule?" so perfect that but few follow it! Strange, if these New Testament regulations are imperfect, that somebody has not improved them in this *age of progress.* I do not believe they are capable of being improved;

perhaps my worthy opponent can offer some amendments. "Love to God," and "love to all men" is the sum; but each in its proper manifestations. Such is the perfection of the boundless benevolence of the Christian religion.

On all these important subjects the means of amplification are most abundant, but in the present controversy we can select but a few items. To engross them all would require a volume.

Christianity in its whole, and in all its parts, is in perfect harmony with that angelic anthem which announced the nativity of its benignant author. Nor could it have been otherwise. A religion originating in infinite wisdom could not contain the elements of its own destruction—could not be the patron of war and strife. Designed, as it was, to unite men into one common brotherhood, it must therefore in itself be a bond of union to draw the contending nations together on terms of peace and everlasting amity. Its perfect adaptation to bring about this blissful consummation has been tested upon an extensive scale. Its influence was seen upon Jews and Gentiles in its original promulgation. Their hostilities were of long standing. They grew out of religious and political differences. But the Gospel made of the "twain one new man, and so made peace;" and such has always been its influence. I refer you to "Christianity Triumphant," pages 91, 92.

"This point is placed in its proper light by the amiable and intelligent Thomas Clarkson, in his life of William Penn. "There is no government," says he, "nor any code of law or jurisprudence in

Europe, though almost all Europe is called Christendom, which has been raised upon Christian principles as its foundation. The different governments of Europe had their beginning before Christianity appeared. Hence they were built upon Heathen notions of false honor and superstition. All we can say of the best of them is, that as the light of Christianity arose, certain barbarous customs and certain vicious principles of legislation were done away, and that others were substituted by degrees, which were more pure, and more benevolent, and more congenial with the religion which was outwardly professed: but there is no one of these at the present day, which was originally founded upon Christianity, or which, notwithstanding its improvements, has attained to a Christian model. There is a strange mixture of Jewish, Papal, and Heathen notions, in their respective codes." Vol. II, page 402. If, therefore, war has not been altogether abandoned by those countries called Christian, it is because of those lower and baser principles which are still mixed up with the laws and institutions of those countries. Wherever Christianity has been fairly and thoroughly wrought into the laws and institutions of a country, it has prevented war, as in the case of the government founded by William Penn; and in proportion as Christian principles have been allowed to influence the old and earthly governments of other nations, in such proportion war has lost its glory, and peace and goodwill have begun to prevail.

But the Gospel has been tried on a national scale in other places besides Pennsylvania; and in those places the results have been the entire cessation of war."

MR. HARTZEL'S EIGHTEENTH ADDRESS.

And such has always been the influence of Christianity. See "Christianity Triumphant," pages 92 to 94.

"We have some beautiful illustrations of the tendency of the Gospel in the accounts of its influence upon the inhabitants of the South Sea Islands. No people upon earth were more fierce and savage than they were previous to the introduction of the Gospel. They were almost perpetually at war, and their wars were of the most cruel and exterminating character. The following facts, from the work of John Williams, entitled Missionary Enterprise

in the South Seas, will tend to show the awful character and condition of those people, with respect to war, while in their unconverted state, and the happy change which was effected among them, by the influence of the Gospel of Christ.

"I visited Hervey's Island," says John Williams, "in 1823, intending to place a native teacher there, as I expected to find a considerable population there; but on learning that by their frequent and exterminating wars, they had reduced themselves to about SIXTY in number, I did not fulfil my intention. Some six or seven years after this I visited the same island again, and found that this miserable remnant of the former population had fought so frequently and desperately, that the only survivors were five men, three women, and a few children, and at that period there was a contention among them as to which should be king." "Mauke is a small low island, discovered by myself and Mr. Bourne, in 1823. It is about fifteen miles in circumference. By an invasion of a large fleet of canoes, laden with warriors from a neighboring island, about three years previous to our arrival, the population, previously considerable, was, by the dreadful massacre that ensued, reduced to about three hundred. Mitiaro is a still smaller island, of the same description. By famine and invasion this island has likewise been almost depopulated, there not being an hundred persons remaining." (Page 17.) In those islands, through the influence of Christianity, those desolating wars have now entirely ceased; the inhabitants neither slaughter one another, nor live in fear of murderous invasions from their neighboring islands.

Rurutu was an island of savages, but behold the change effected by the Gospel. "Some time after the introduction of Christianity into Rurutu, Captain Chase, who commanded an American whaler, and who was in the habit of touching frequently at Raiatea for refreshment, determined, on his last visit to us, to call at Rurutu, on his way to America, in order to procure a supply of yams, when, unfortunately, his vessel was wrecked upon the rocks. The natives, who would formerly have devoured the wrecked mariners and plundered the wreck, now, under the influence of those better principles which the Gospel had taught them, afforded the crew all the assistance in their power, from the moment the ship struck upon the rocks. When landing things from the ship, they were put into the hands of the natives, and carried up to the native mission house, a distance of half a mile, and not a single article of clothing was taken from any man belonging to the ship, though they had it in their power to have plundered them of every thing that was landed. While the captain and his crew remained on shore themselves, the natives treated them with the utmost kindness, and did their utmost to make them comfortable." This island was visited by D. Tyerman and G. Bennet, a deputation from the London Missionary Society, some time after the introduction of the Gospel. They saw in every direction the pleasing effects of the religion of Christ. The people were decently clothed and living in neat-looking white houses, and were blessed with plenty and peace. In the place of worship, the deputation were struck with the orderly behavior of the people, as well as with some signal trophies of the Word of God. "These were spears," as they observe, "not beaten into pruning-hooks it is true, but converted into staves to support the balustrade of the pulpit staircase; for the people here learn war no more, but all, submitting to the Prince of Peace, have cast away their instruments of cruelty and their idols together. So great a change effected in so short a time is almost beyond credibility; but we witnessed it with our own eyes." (45 50.)

Speaking of Aitutaki, another island, John Williams says, after he had witnessed the happy changes produced among the natives by the Gospel—"Little did I expect to see so much accomplished in so short a time. Eighteen months ago they were the wildest people I had ever witnessed; now they had become mild and docile, diligent and kind." Next day he preached to from fifteen hundred to two thousand people, just emerged from Heathenism. "Many of them," says he, "were dressed very neatly, and I could not help contrasting their appearance with that which they presented on our first visit. At that time they were constantly killing and even eating one another; but now they were all with one accord bending their knees together in the worship of the God of peace and love." Mr. Bourne visited this island some time after; he says, speaking of the natives, women as well as men,—"They are diligent in learning, and numbers can read. Family and private prayer are very general. Every thing has remained quiet since our last visit: neither war nor rumor of war has been seen or heard, although formerly it was their greatest delight, and the bodies of their slain enemies formed the horrible repast at the conclusion of every engagement." (61, 62, 101.)

These facts speak for themselves. There must be some wonder working power in Christianity—a power *unique and possessed by itself alone.* A brief inquiry into this will be the subject of the present argument.

Argument 5. 1st; Most, if not all, civil wars grow out of civil government directly or indirectly; but the "Prince of peace" said, and yet says: "My kingdom is not of this world; if my kingdom were of this world then would my servants fight:"

and, as I understand him, I would give them license to fight for me. Now, whence will the Christian get his commission to become a soldier? Not from Christ, if he is consistent with himself, and Mr. Barker says he is.

Mr Barker.—No!

Mr. Hartzel.—I refer you to the "Christian," by Joseph Barker, Vol. 1, page 20.

"Unbelievers cannot prove that ever Christ taught doctrines that were inconsistent with each other; they cannot prove that he ever either contradicted himself, or contradicted the truth."

And if a professing Christian goes to war as a politician, surely he does not go as a Christian, and Christianity is not responsible for his conduct.

Second. The example of Christ was that of an unresisting subject. His doctrine was, "Render to Cæsar the things that are Cæsar's." He handed over to the treasurer his "tax" when demanded. But when Cæsar required of him to tell a falsehood to save his life *he would not do it.* He told the truth and suffered the penalty. And all his teachings are in unison with these examples. But let me here observe that Jesus Christ did not legislate for the kingdoms of this world. God's moral government over his people, and his general providential government in the kingdoms of men are different things not to be confounded.

The first lesson Christ gave his Disciples was in these words, "And seeing the multitudes, he went up into a high mountain, and when he was set, his Disciples came unto him, and he opened his mouth and taught them saying, *I say unto you that ye resist not evil.*" The teachings of the Savior forbid the indulgence of all those passions and lusts which generate war either between individuals or nations. Feelings of resentment are among the most fruitful causes of strife. Evil for evil is the prompting of the natural heart. But Christ says to his followers, *not so.* "Love your enemies, bless them that curse you; do good to them that hate you, and pray for them that despitefully use you and persecute you." On one occasion three of his Disciples felt some Jewish resentment against a Samaritan family for not opening their doors for the hospitable reception of their Master. With a feeling of indignity they ask: "Shall we call down fire from Heaven and consume these as Elijah did?" "But he said unto them, ye know not what manner of spirit ye are of. The Son of Man has not come to destroy men's lives, but to save them." What a rebuke upon the *war* spirit. The love of fame—the love of wealth—the lust of power—the love of country—pride, anger, resentment; these, with all their kindred passions, all these war passions, are positively prohibited. And the opposite—universal love—forgiveness of injuries, etc., he enjoined upon his Disciples and encouraged these virtues by his own blessed example while with them. Before he left them, "He said unto them, all power is given unto me in Heaven and in Earth; Go ye, therefore, and teach all nations, baptizing them in the name of the Father, and of the Son, and of the Holy Ghost. Teaching them to observe all things, whatsoever I have commanded you, and lo! I am with you always, even unto the end of the world." The Disciples did as he commanded them, as may be seen from Romans 12; 17, 21.

Recompense to no man evil for evil. Provide things honest in the sight of all men. If it be possible, as much as lieth in you, live peaceably with all men. Dearly beloved, avenge not yourselves, but rather give place unto wrath: for it is written, vengence is mine: I will repay, saith the Lord. Therefore if thine enemy hunger, feed him, if he thirst give him drink; for in so doing thou shalt heap coals of fire on his head. Be not overcome of evil, but overcome evil with good." Follow peace with all men and holiness, without which no man shall see the Lord," are Christian qualifications and motives.

The great Teacher lays down two principles of action by which his kingdom is to be regulated, namely: love to God, and love to man." "Love worketh no ill to his neighbor," says the Apostle Paul. The Apostle James says, speaking on the government of the tongue, "Wherewith bless we God even the Father, and therewith curse we men, which are made after the similitude of God. These things ought not so to be."

A warring, fighting Christian is a contradiction, an inconsistency, an anomaly.

I shall now give some historical facts in defence of

my argument. I quote from "Infidelity refuted by Infidels," pages, 260, 261. Gibbon says:

"If we seriously consider the purity of the Christian religon, the sanctity of its moral precepts, and the innocent as well as austere lives of the greater number of those who, during the first ages, embraced the faith of the Gospel, we should naturally suppose that so benevolent a doctrine would have been received with due reverence, even by the unbelieving world; that the learned and the polite, however they might deride the miracles, would have esteemed the virtues of the new sect, and that the magistrates, instead of persecuting, would have protected, an order of men who yielded the most passive obedience to the law, though they declined the active cares of war and government."

Again: "Christianity Triumphant," pages, 60, 61, 62.

"The whole tenor of Gospel truths and Gospel precepts, and the whole spirit which the Gospel seeks to breathe through the hearts of men, are at perfect variance with the spirit and business of war; and men cannot experience the full regenerating influence of the Gospel, without being obliged to renounce all connexion with war in all its forms.

There is nothing in the example of Christ to favor war; in the whole of his conduct Christ was the very opposite of a warrior. "When he was reviled he reviled not again; when he suffered, he threatened not; but committed his cause to Him that judgeth righteously." He was unkindly and unjustly treated from first to last, but he never sought to avenge himself. And when they came to take him prisoner, he made no resistance. His disciples would have defended him, but he would not allow them; and when Peter drew his sword, and struck one of those who came out against him, he rebuked him, and said, "Put up thy sword into its place; for all they that take the sword, shall perish with the sword." And when they scourged him, and mocked him, and on the testimony of false witnesses condemned him to be crucified, he uttered not a single revengeful word. "He was led as a lamb to the slaughter, and as a sheep before her shearers is dumb, so he opened not his mouth." And when afflicted with the bitterest pains of death, so far was he from the spirit of revenge, that he prayed in behalf of his murderers. "Father, forgive them; they no not what they do." As he inculcated the principles of peace in his preaching, so did he exemplify them in his conduct, both in life and in death.

And the Apostles followed the Savior's example. They used no arms but the "armor of righteousness." "The weapons of our warfare," said they, "are not carnal, but mighty through God, to the pulling down the strongholds of the devil." Though their object was to conquer the whole world, and produce a radical and thorough change in the principles and practices of society in all lands, yet the only weapons of their warfare were truth and charity. Nor did the ancient Christians use any other weapons. No violence was allowed in any of the churches of Christ. If they provoked one another, it was to love and good works; and, if they conquered their enemies, it was by heaping benefits upon them.

The first Christians were never charged with acts of violence: the objections brought against them by their enemies were just of an opposite description. They were charged with REFUSING to fight; it was objected to them as a crime that they would not take the soldier's oath, nor enter the military profession. Celsus, who lived at the end of the second century, in a work which he wrote against the Christian religion, makes use of this as one of his objections. He charges the Christians with refusing, in his time, to bear arms for the Emperor, and that in a case of necessity, and when their services would have been accepted. And the charge was true; the Christians of those days did not attempt to deny it. When Origen wrote in answer to Celsus, he admits the fact, that the Christians would not bear arms, and he justifies them on the principle that war is unlawful. "We no longer take up the sword against any nation," said he, "nor do we learn to make war any more." "We have become, for the sake of Jesus, THE CHILDREN OF PEACE." "We pray for our king," says he, in another passage, "but we take no part in his wars, however he may urge us."

If the Christian religion was the production of nature, its dictates would be in harmony with it. In the old Heathen world, war was the business and glory of men; while the women and the slaves performed the domestic drudgery at home. It was one of the means of wealth to keep up their extravagance and pageantry. Civilization effected no change in this respect. The Romans, the most civilized, were no better in this respect than the rudest savages. That "might gives right," was the rule of action, and the moral sentiment of the age approved it. I refer you to "Christianity Triumphant," pages 50, 51.

Nay, so far did the Romans carry things, that they represented the murderous work of war as virtuous, and as the only way to glory. To lead forth armies, to waste the lands of strangers, to destroy cities, to overthrow towns, to murder free people or subject them to bondage, was, with them, the path to immortality. "If a man kill but one, he is held for a villian;" as one observed, "but those who murder infinite thousands — who moisten the fields and dye the rivers with blood — is promised a place with the immortal gods." "So deep root had this doctrine taken among the Romans," says Hakewell, "that he who shed most blood was deemed the best and worthiest man, most like the gods, and fittest for a place in their lofty habtiations."

What we see in the Greeks and Romans is no more than the natural workings of man's animal nature, whenever it is left unsubdued and uncontroled by the influence of true religion. War is natural to man in his unregenerate state. War still continues to be carried on as the principal and regular employment among unenlightened nations. Among the nations of the South Seas, previous to the introdnction of Christianity, wars were perpetual, and they were waged with unmingled and insatiable cruelty. Among the original natives of Africa and America, war still continues to be carried on in this ceaseless and cruel way. It still occupies the chief place among the business of life. Martial heroism and contempt of death, are the leading points of education in many parts of the globe, and, in every case, the dark places of the earth are full of the habitations of cruelty. And among all nations, in proportion as men continue to be governed by the inclinations and passions of unregenerate nature, war is still regarded with favor, and is followed as a lawful and an honorable calling, and as the path to earthly glory.

In view of these undeniable facts, may we not claim an argument in favor of our proposition; namely, that in the New Testament "man has a perfect rule of life."

MR. HARTZEL'S NINETEENTH ADDRESS.

Mr. Barker did not present the overture I submitted to him with reference to contradictions exactly as it was. It was this: If he would present in due form a few of the most palpable ones, such as could not be reconciled, and such contradictions as would invalidate the testimony of witnesses in a court of law, he should have the benefit of them, or he might strike them out as interpolations. I really do not see that such alleged contradictions, as he has produced, are entitled to any consideration in this discussion.

With regard to the alleged contradiction in the book of Genesis, I have only to say, that every reasonable person would in this examination take two things into the account. First, the brevity of the history; second, the fact that the second chapter of Genesis is, in part, a recapitulation of the first. I gave in the former part of this discussion, the names of a number of distinguished writers on Geology and other matters connected with the account of creation, as given in the Bible, who find no such contradictions there—writers are entitled to respect for their knowledge of physical science. I refer those who wish to examine the subject further to them. *

* To do justice to any writer we should inquire, first, who is he writing to? second, and what is he writing for? With these interrogatories before the mind, we will approach Moses and Geology. Moses wrote to the Jews. He wrote to them on religious and moral subjects. If his writings were best calculated to promote these ends, he must stand acquitted; if not, he must be condemned. The true basis of man's religious and moral

The next contradiction is found in the New Testament, in regard to Judas. There are two points in which the statements are supposed to differ. In the account as given by Matthew, it was the "high priests" who purchased the field; Judas having returned to them the "thirty pieces of silver." While in the account in Acts, it was Judas himself that purchased the "field." Again: the first account says that "Judas hung himself," while the other says that "he fell down—burst assunder in the midst, and his bowels gushed out."

With reference to the first point, I need only

---

obligation is the character of God as Creator and Moral Governor. These and other kindred convictions produce, in the human mind, religious affections, reverence, godly fear, etc. "Geology does not account for the origin of matter, nor aid us in forming a conception of its creation." Its use in religion must, therefore, be secondary. The history of creation, as given by Moses, is in harmony with man's OPTICAL view of the material world; and, therefore, adapted to the Jews, (for whose special benefit he wrote,) and equally adapted to the common intelligence of all the masses of mankind, under the same obligation to love and serve the Creator. The knowledge of physical science never was essential to inspire the soul with love to God and man. If geology must be understood—if the subterraneous formations of the earth must be understood—if astronomy must be understood—then the duties of religion could have no claim on the early portions of mankind, and now on but a favored few, if any; for the sciences still as MUTABLE as the morality for which Mr. Barker and other infidels plead. But Mr. Barker is witness for me, that philosophy was never favorable to Christianity, but Christianity to philosophy. Hear him. "Christianity Triumphant," page 367: "Go among the nations where Christianity is unknown, and you will find that philosophy has produced none of those great improvements there. Go back to those ages when Christianity was unknown in our own country, and philosophy did nothing for us then. How do you account for these things? How is it that philosophy does no good anywhere but where Christianity begins to prevail: and that the good that it does in any country, is in proportion to the regard which is paid to Christianity by its inhabitants? How is it that philosophy has done so much for the Quakers, the Methodists, the Moravians, and other religious people, who seldom or never mention the name of philosophy; while it does so little for other people, who make such great boast of philosophy? What do you say to these things?" What do you say to these historic facts now, Mr. Barker? And to this extract, from the same page, written with your own hand: "The men who first refused to fight, did not say we are philosophers, and therefore we cannot fight; they said, we ARE CHRISTIANS, and therefore cannot fight." These were philosophers of the right kind; they saw none of these frightful contradictions between Genesis and Geology. But they believed the words of Moses, that God in the "beginning made the heavens and the earth;" and in the words of David, "thou, Lord, in the beginning laidest the foundations of the earth, and the heavens are the works of thy hands;" and joined with Jesus in these words of praise, "I thank thee, oh Father, Lord of heaven and earth;" and with Paul, "through faith we understand that the worlds were framed by the word of God," who is now "upholding all things by the word of his power." Moses has, in an eminent degree accomplished the objects for which we wrote. For it is a fact as Mr. Barker says, to which all men are witness, that philosophy has done nothing where Christianity is not, and has done most where it prevails. These undeniable facts furnish the conclusion, that the religion of the Bible and philosophy are not ANTIPODES, else a system of moral and religious falsehoods has been most favorable to that growing intelligence, which has enabled man to discover scientific truth. To this CONCLUSION THE observe that we sometimes attribute to the instrument what properly belongs to the agent. Judas furnished the means. The "priests" were the contracting party. "This is the price of blood," unfit for sanctified purposes, let us give it to the "potter," etc.

Again: with regard to the second point—"His bowels gushed out." There are a thousand things in the Bible that depend upon testimony. We must have history to explain history; we adopt this method of investigation with respect to all historic matters. Cave, in his "Lives of the Apostles," (I think I am correct as to the work—I will not be positive—at

---

INFIDEL IS DRIVEN, UPON HIS OWN ADMISSION. While the Christian believes that all religions and scientific truths are harmonious. I say then, we are not afraid to meet all the difficulties (if any there be.) growing out of any well established GEOLOGICAL or any other SCIENTIFIC FACTS, ONLY we wish to meet them at the right time and place. Some of the Scripture statements might not be in harmony with the discoveries of physical science without affecting, in the least, the objects of these writings, and yet contain a "series of communications supernaturally revealed and miraculously attested," and furnish man "a perfect rule of life." But as the learned St. John says, in his Elements of Geology, page 288: "The science of geology has, through misapprehension of facts and opinion, been regarded with jealousy as favorable to infidelity, and even atheism, teaching the eternity of matter, itself guiding and renovating power, and dispensing with a deity in the creation and regulation of the world. On the contrary, those who with the competent knowledge of the science of geology, and the art of interpretation, have carefully examined this subject, confidently assert that no other science furnishes an equal number of striking illustrations of natural and revealed religion." Atheists, Deists and Christians, all lay claim to geology. This only proves what the same author says, page 287: "Although geology is by no means complete, since in no science are facts more rapidly accumulating, and theories and systems are but expositions of the present amount of knowledge on the subject," etc. It is not a subject for such a controversy as this, either in its verbal or book form; but. whenever Mr. Barker shall feel disposed to open upon the Bible from this point, I doubt not he can be furnished with an opponent.

But for the present let me say, that when infidels leave the entire field of history, prophecy, miracle, with all the different kinds of internal evidence, those bulwarks of truth, upon which revealed religion stands, and fly to geology, they give evidence of the exceeding barrenous of their soil. But we freely admit the secondary use of physical science in the business of religion. Thomas Dick, with many other Christian writers, (who are as competent to read and interpret nature as those found in the ranks of infidelity,) shew clearly the harmony between creation and the Old Testament scriptures, "adapted to the purposes of a limited dispensation addressed to one people only. When we bear this more distinctly in mind, many of those difficulties (admitting them for the sake of the argume t,) are removed. And this is surely the true view to be taken by the Gentile Christian to whom it is only a guide and instructor, SECOND and SUBORDINATE to the New Testament, a dead letter without it, but able to make us wise unto salvation "only through faith which is in Jesus Christ."

The cosmogony of Moses is in perfect harmony with the man's OPTICAL view of the physical world, and the objects to be accomplished by his writings; THEREFORE, all this infidel RANT about contradictions is without cause and equally without meaning. While the Christian religion has promoted that intelligence, which has enabled men to study the works of God intelligibly, and nature becomes a concurring witness. Hence it is, that Newton, Bacon, Lock, Gallileo, and all who have made the most important discoveries in science were believers in revealed religion.

any rate I give it as a matter of history,) that Judas, after he had thrown the money down before the "high priests," was standing in an upper chamber. In descending the stairs he fell headlong with his bowels upon some pickets below—rent the region of his bowels, and they "gushed out." So he "hung himself," and all his "bowels gushed out." However be that as it may; if the account cannot be perfectly reconciled, it would not follow that Matthew and Luke, one or both, are false witnesses. It is a principle in all legal investigations, that some discrepancy between witnesses does not affect their credibility. Mr. Barker must be aware that it is not so easy to make out contradictions between historians and witnesses, as some people imagine. It is easy to bring out discrepancies in the statement of witnesses, but these do not necessarily invalidate their testimony, but often give strength and credit.

As to my friend's third contradiction. I must be excused from investigating it, for I would have to spend one half hour in a classification of the matter. If it had been presented in an intelligible form, I would have attended to it. First he said "three contradictions," then he said "three or four"—no definite statement in his own mind.

Mr. Barker. I consider this as one contradiction.

Mr. Hartzel. I feel no solicitude about that vague matter, and will therefore pass it. *

* Infidels claim that the Bible is not entitled to rational belief, on account of the many contradictions found upon its pages. If Christians can claim equality with them in numbers, intelligence and integrity, the objection has no weight, for they find no such

In answer to his definition of a "perfect rule of life," I will say that the word "*perfect*" has a relative meaning. We do not mean by the word "*perfect*," in the proposition, divine perfection. We speak of human or Christian perfection. We only mean a "rule of life" perfectly adapted to man—perfectly suited to man's wants and duties as a social and moral being. There is *divine* perfection, *angelic* perfection, *Christian* perfection. The object of this "rule," however, is not to teach man his physiological duties. A "rule of life" relates to *ethical* subjects, not to physiological. The present discussion

---

contradictions, Let the youthful reader make due allowance for the prejudices of the one, and the prepossessions of the other, then, if the beligerents are equal as to candor and competency to examine questions of this kind, the objection is neutralized. But what is a contradiction? "An assertion of the contrary of what has been said or affirmed; denial, contrary declaration; contrary opposite; adverse as contrary winds.—*Webster*. Matthew and Luke speak of Judas for different purposes, Matthew, to make his suicide a historical fact. Luke records the words of Peter to one hundred and twenty disciples, on the necessity of appointing another apostle to fill the vacancy occasioned by the death of Judas. The supposed "contradiction" concerning the "purchase" of the "field" is disposed of. There may be a remaining doubt in regard to his "hanging himself," and falling headlong. After a more careful examination of this OLD INFIDEL HOBBY, I see more clearly the injustice done to this item of history. As Peter referred to Judas for a definite object, he would mention such incidents in his sad apostacy and death as would bear directly on that object; hence he called the attention of the audience to the prophecy of David: "His bishopric let another take." Again: "From which Judas by transgression fell." Matthew speaks of Judas as a traitor and a suicide, but Peter speaks of him as an apostate "Apostle," and an object of the divine displeasure. The difference in design accounts for the difference in narration. We may set aside what Cave has said, and then there is no difficulty in reconciling the statements. It is at least a supposable case, that a man who "hung" himself might "fall headlong," etc. It is not probable that there would have been much search or inquiry for the absent Judas. He may have selected a retired spot—he may have hung upon the gallows until he fell to the ground by his own weight—or, he may have been found "hanging" in a state of decomposition, and being cut down from the gallows, in either case he would fall "headlong;" and that he would "burst assunder," in the region of his bowels, is even more than probable. That such cases have occurred, no one will deny. This reconciles the supposed contradiction. If the conflicting testimony of two, otherwise credible witnesses, were as fairly reconciled, before a legal tribunal as the above, their testimony would be fully accredited.

It may be objected, perhaps, that the gratuitous supposition of some unmentioned fact, which, if mentioned, would harmonize the apparently counter-statements of the two historians cannot be admitted, and is in fact a surrender of the argument. But to say so, is ONLY to betray an utter ignorance of what the argument is. If an objection be founded on the alleged ABSOLUTE contradiction of the two statements, it is quite sufficient to show any MEDIUM of reconciling them, and the objection is, in all fairness, dissolved. And this would be felt by the honest logician, even if we did not know of any such instances in point of fact. These equitable rights are denied to none, but the sacred writers. The infidel takes it upon himself, in the plentitude of his wisdom, to say, that there is no fact omitted, which, if it had been mentioned, would explain the whole difficulty. This is assuming that sacred writers must omit nothing, however unimportant. If, for instance, Matthew and Luke agree in everything pertaining to the character of

was provoked by the discussions had in the convention. We did not then and there discuss man's physiological relations, but his *moral* relations and *moral* duties.

Mr. Barker says, the Disciples, many of them, are slaveholders. Mr. Barker does not understand the elements of church government, as set forth in the New Testament. We are only responsible for those who are members with us "in particular." I would say to Mr. Barker, that our Church is based upon the congregational principle of church independence.

Jesus Christ, all his teachings, all his miracles, all the incidents connected with his death, burial, resurrection and ascension — give the same moral and religious duties; but differ in one unimportant statement concerning a traitor, that with infidels has, power enough to neutralize their entire mass of evidence. A discrepancy in a minute point of historical detail, shakes the foundation of the whole edifice of revealed religion! There is yet another supposed contradiction between Matthew and Luke. Matthew says, "Jacob begat Joseph the husband of Mary" Luke says, "Joseph was the son of Heli." If Luke had said Heli begat Joseph, then we would have a contradiction — for these statements would be contraries, and admit of no reconciliation. Now, if we can show that a Jew could have two fathers, be the begotten son of one father and the legal son of another father, then the difficulty is fairly solved. I shall now show that there was such a regulation among the Jews. The law requiring a man to marry a deceased brother's wife had two specific objects; first, that "his brother's name be not put out of Israel." See Deut. 25: 6. Second, t at his inheritance should be continued in his name and tribe. The reader may consult the book of Ruth upon the subject. In the fourth chapter, Boaz proposed to the nearest kinsman of Elimelich to take the widow of their deceaaed brother, and "raise up the name of the dead upon his inheritance." He refused. Now it became the duty of Boaz, he being the next in relationship. He did so; and said to the "Elders and all the people, ye are witnesses this day," etc. "Moreover, Ruth the Moabitess, the wife of Mahlon, have I purchased to be my wife, to raise up the name of the dead upon his inheritance, that the name of the dead be not cut off from among his brethren, and the gate of his place; ye are witness this day." This was the law to perpetuate the name and inheritance of a deceased brother.

There was also another law that secured these ends when a man deceased leaving daughters only. And Zelophehad had no sons, but daughters. Numbers 26 33. "These said to Moses and all the people, 'Our father died in the wilderness.' 'and had no sons.' Why should the name of our father be done away from among his family, because he has no sons?" Numbers 27: 34. "The daughters of Zelophehad speak right. If a man die and have no son, then ye shall cause the inheritance to pass unto his daughters."—7, 8. The daughters of Zelophehad were married to their father's brother's sons, and their inheritance remained in the tribe of the family of their father.—Num. 36: 11, 12. Their husbands were now the sons of Zelophehad by law. His lands were transferred to his legal sons: as such they stood upon the public records to build up the "name," and the "inheritance" for the deceased Zelophehad.

Under these legal regulations, Joseph, the son of Jacob, might have married Mary, the daughter of Heli, and stood upon the records as the begotten son of Jacob, and the legal son of Heli. I am not obliged to prove that it was so, only that it might have been so, and according to all legal and historic investigation, the difficulty is fairly met. I have reconciled the two contradictions, which infidels have ever regarded as the most palpable and important to their cause. My space forbids any farther notice of what they are pleased to call contradictions. I hope the reader will pardon me for having bestowed upon them this much attention. Is it safe to reject the whole mass of evidence from such DATA? To the man that can do so let me say, "go in peace." If any man WILL BE AN INFIDEL, let him be an INFIDEL.

We have no authority over our brethren of other churches, more than to admonish them; after that, we are not responsible for their conduct. If my friend wants proof of this, he shall have it. The Methodist church is a confederacy. If I become a Methodist, I become responsible for all the official acts of their General Conference, etc. So of many other church organizations. We go upon the principle of local church independence in all our churches. We, as a congregation, have no fellowship with slaveholders. A brother's opinions do not come under our jurisdiction. We have to do with overt acts.

Mr. Barker. I am glad to hear it. Would you refuse to commune with Alexander Campbell?

Argument 6. We shall not inquire of the New Testament with respect to the most exciting and interesting question—the question of slavery. Before we open the Sacred volume, we shall read an item of history upon the subject. It will aid us in our understanding of the divine teachings, and in forming a higher appreciation of them. The passage I propose to read is in "Christianity Triumphant," pages 100, 104:

"The religion of Christ has proved itself the friend of liberty, and the enemy of slavery. Previous to the introduction of the Gospel, slavery prevailed throughout all the nations of the earth. It was least prevalent among the Jews, the religion of Moses having in a great measure effected its extirpation among them. Among the rest of the nations, it prevailed to an extent truly appalling. A great deal has been said about the free states of Greece, and about the liberty of the Romans, and yet slavery was a common thing both among the Greeks and Romans. 'In all the ancient republics,' as Bishop Porteus observes, 'by far the greatest part of the inhabitants were not freemen, but slaves. In the 110th Olympiad, there were at Athens only twenty-one thousand citizens, and forty thousand slaves. In the small island of Ægina, there were four hundred and seventy thousand slaves. It was common for a private citizen of Rome, in the times of Paganism, to have ten or twenty thousand slaves. In fact, every private family was a little despotic kingdom. The master was the tyrant, and the servants his wretched subjects, whom he bought and sold, whom he could punish and torture as he pleased, whom he could put to death with or without reason, and even for his own amusement. It is true, indeed, that the VERNŒ, or home-born slaves, were sometimes treated with lenity, and even with tenderness and indulgence; but these favorites of fortune bore a very small proportion indeed to that immense multitude who were made to feel the utmost rigor of their condition. In general, these wretched beings were continually exposed to every evil that the most wanton tyranny could inflict, They were compelled frequently to till the ground in chains or confined in subterreanean dungeons, and strained to labor beyond their strength by the severest treatment. They were obliged to suffer every insult, and every injury, without resistance and without redress. They had no protection afforded them, could have no justice done to them, nor any reparation made to them. They were subject to the cruelty, not only of their own masters, but of every one that met them. They had no place to flee unto, aud no man cared for their soul." The hurt that was done to them was estimated in the same manner as a hurt done to a beast; nothing was considered but the diminution of their value, and the loss sustained by their master. The injury or the pain endured by the slave himself, never came into consideration. Their evidence was scarcely ever taken but by torture; they were not supposed to be capable of being applied to in any other way. If their master happened to be found murdered in his house, all the slaves in the family, which sometimes amounted to several thousands, were frequently slain, even those that were confessedly innocent. A certain Roman being found murdered in his own house, all the slaves, to the number of four hundred, were instantly put to death, says Tacitus, and this was done, he adds, according to ancient custom.—Annals 14–43. Nay, they were sometimes made the sacrifice of a youthful frolic, and murdered in the streets and roads by thousands at a time, merely for amusement.—[Porteus on the Beneficial Effects of Christianity.

"It would be endless to produce all the instances which we meet with in history, of the incredible barbarity of the ancients towards their slaves. The few that here follow may serve as a specimen. Two thousand Lacedemonian slaves, who had been promised their freedom, and were led round the streets of Sparta in triumph, with garlands on their heads, soon afterwards disappeared, and were never heard of more: they were all secretly destroyed.—Thucyd. L. IV.

"The youth of Sparta, it is well known, frequently lay in ambush for these wretched slaves in the night, and sallying out upon them unexpectedly, with daggers in their hands, murdered in cold blood every Helot they met with. The Ephori also, the rulers of Lacedemon, as soon as they entered office, DECLARED WAR AGAINST THEM IN FORM, that there might be the appearance of destroying them legally.—Plut. in Lycur. At the time when L. Domitius was prætor in Sicily, a slave happened to kill a boar of uncommon size. The prætor, struck with the account he had received of the man's dexterity and intrepidity, desired to see him. The poor slave, overjoyed at this distinction, presented himself to the prætor, expecting, no doubt, applause and reward; but Domitius understanding that he had killed the boar with a hunting spear, the use of which (as well as all warlike arms) was forbidden to slaves, ordered him to be immediately crucified. And such horrible barbarities were looked upon as common things, and scarcely censured by their philosophical moralists. 'It was the custom of Vedius Pollio, when his slaves had committed a fault, sometimes a very trifling fault, to order them to be thrown into his fish-ponds, to feed his lampreys,' says Bishop Porteus. In Rome, the porters at the gates of the grandees were chained slaves. Masters used to put their aged, sick, and infirm slaves into an island in the Tiber, there to perish without pity or assistance.—Ryan.

"Such was the mournful condition of nine-tenths, or nineteen-twentieths of our fellowmen, under the most enlightened and civilized governments of the Pagan world. And this awful and deplorable system of slavery was connived at by the Pagan philosophers and moralists of those ages. It was a maxim of Plato, that no friendship could subsist between a master and a slave; and Aristotle had a maxim very similar. Masters were commanded not to use their slaves cruelly in times of war, it is true, but this was not out of respect to the feelings or interests of the slaves, but merely to prevent the slaves from taking advantage of the war to shake off their own chains. I do not recollect a single instance in which the philosophers and moralists of Greece and Rome undertook to plead the cause of the slave, or to recommend to mankind any plan for their improvement or emancipation. That noble principle of benevolence which prompts men to pity the oppressed and fallen, and inspires the wish to relieve, and elevate, and bless the outcast and neglected multitudes of mankind, had no place in the philosophy of heathenism. Cruel institutions and customs were left to grow unchecked, and were allowed to spread their deadly influence unrestrained; and the multitudes of afflicted and injured mortals who crowded the lower ranks of life, were left without relief and without consolation.

"Not so with the Gospel. The Gospel proclaimed deliverance to the captives from the first, and its object and its tendency throughout was to bring bondage of every description to a perpetual end, and to diffuse the blessings of freedom through all nations of the earth. One of the first occasions on which the Redeemer preached, he declared that the Lord had appointed him to preach glad tidings to the poor, to heal the broken-hearted, to preach deliverance to the captives, to restore sight to the blind, to set at liberty those who were oppressed, and to publish a general and an everlasting Jubilee. And the whole tenor of his doctrine was in accordance with this blessed design. He taught men that they were alike the offspring of one God, and that they ought to respect and love each other as brethren. He commanded men to love their neighbors as themselves, and to do to others as they would have others do to them."

This is a brief, but true account of the extent and enormity of human slavery at the commencement of the Christian religion. It existed among all nations, but was least prevalent among the Jews. The religion of Moses had, in a great measure, effected its extirpation among them. This is good testimony for the character and mission of Moses, that he should have effected more in this respect, than all the Abolitionists of America have accomplished. How long have they been laboring, both in and out of Congress, to abolish slavery in the District of Columbia? How many lectures have been delivered? How many pamphlets have been written? How many legislators have stood up and pleaded loud and long for the emancipation of the slaves in this ten miles square, under the jurisdiction of Congress? What has it all amounted to? It continues to be the hot-bed of slavery.

The laws of Moses must have differed widely from those of surrounding nations. But let us come to New Testament times. The existing government, under which Christianity began its career, was a wide-spreading, absolute monarchy; and more than half (my friend says nineteen-twentieths,) of this mighty mass of people were slaves! Political action was out of the question; nay, this crushing despotism was against the Christians and in favor of the slave-holders. The religion itself was sufficiently obnoxious, on account of its novelty and uncompromising opposition to idolatry, and to every form of corruption sanctioned by the government, which government, we should say, was as good as could be expected, and defended its citizens in many of their rights. We do not quarrel with civil governments—it is "hard to bring a *clean* thing out of an *unclean*."

Now, with all these fearful odds, and this bitter opposition against a few obscure Galileean fishermen, on human principles, what was to be done? Jesus Christ came to "preach deliverance to the captives," and to break down every form of oppression. But he must do it in a certain way, without strife, without clamor, or military parade. It was written of him, "He shall not strive nor cry, neither shall any man hear his voice in the streets. A bruised reed shall he not break, and smoking flax shall he not quench, till he send forth judgment unto victory."—Matthew 12: 19, 20.

Permit me here to read an extract from Mr. Barker. "Christianity Triumphant," pages 104, 105:

"It is true the religion of Christ did not forbid slavery in so many words, nor did it expressly command masters to liberate their slaves; but it did that which was much better—it breathed into the hearts of its disciples such a spirit of love, and enjoined upon them such a line of conduct towards all their fellow-creatures, as could not fail, among all its faithful disciples, to bring slavery to a perpetual end. Christian masters were not commanded to set their slaves at liberty, but they were commanded to look on them as brethren, to love them as they loved themselves; and it was im possible for them thus to esteem and love them as brethren, and yet hold them in cruel and degrading bondage. Christianity did not expressly command masters to liberate their slaves, but it commanded them to render to their slaves that which was JUST and EQUAL; it commanded them to do to their slaves as they would wish their slaves to do to them, and every one may see that by the time the masters did this, there would not be much difference between masters and their slaves. Christianity did, in this respect, as it did in many others, it accomplished great changes with little noise. It did not lift up a loud cry about reforms, but it silently effected them. It was like leaven which a woman took and hid in three measures of meal, until the whole was leavened. There are great numbers of men who make loud outcries against prevailing evils, and yet do nothing towards remedying them: they talk much and clamorously about improvements, but never bring their improvements to pass. Christianity took a different course. It talked little, but did a great deal of work; it was humble and modest in its pretensions, but vast and glorious in its performances. It did not make confusion by foolishly shaking the branches of the tree of evil, but it secretly struck at the root, and the trunk and the branches came down to the ground together."

MR. HARTZEL'S TWENTIETH ADDRESS.

Tell Mr. Pillsbury, who applauded in his letter to the "Bugle," the speeches of Mr. Barker in the Bible Convention, as superior to the Bible itself, that I would rather be the author of the extract just read from Mr. Barker, than of all he said in the Bible Convention. This extract sets forth the genius of the Gospel—the divine philosophy of Christianity. Well and truly might an Apostle say—"The weapons of our warfare are not carnal, but mighty, through God, to the pulling down of strong holds." Jesus Christ laid the foundation deep and broad for the uprooting of every system of oppression. In his early instructions to his Apostles, he gave all the moral principles by which they should govern themselves, in regulating the affairs of his "kingdom," promising them further aid when he should have left them. "I will give you a mouth and wisdom which all your adversaries shall not be able to gainsay, nor resist." In this was the secret of their success.

Now let me have your concentrated attention to the last precept in Christ's sermon on the Mount: "Therefore all things whatsoever ye would that men should do to you, do ye even so to them." Christ gave this law of moral right to his disciples—and, to the well instructed in the kingdom of God, it is an infallible rule. It never errs, when applied by those whose desires, tastes and affections have been purified and chastened; but to apply it to the ignorant slaveholder, drunkard and gambler, as his standard of moral obligation, is *most* preposterous. Is this law found in any slaveholding canon? Light and darkness cannot dwell together.

When Christ's Disciples indulged in feelings of rival greatness, he corrected them, and cast out the demon of worldly domination, as may be seen from Matthew, 20th chapter. The mother of Zebedee's children, desirous that her sons should occupy the most honorable positions in Christ's kingdom, besought the Lord in their behalf. When the ten heard it they were moved with indignation; "But Jesus called them unto him, and said, ye know that the Princes of the Gentiles exercise dominion over them, and they that are great exercise authority upon them. But it shall not be so among you, but whosoever will be great among you, let him be your minister; and whosoever will be chief among you, let him be your servant." All the world has been, and yet is mistaken upon the subject of true, genuine greatness. We see the workings of this error. It makes of one man a wholesale murderer; of another a despot; of another a slaveholder. What bitter fruit has grown upon that accursed tree! The great may exercise authority—the strong may oppress the weak—"But whosoever will be great among you, let him be your minister; and whosoever will be chief among you, let him be your servant," was a new revelation, and as offensive as it was novel.

I ask now, can a man be a *Christian*—I mean an *intelligent Christian*—and at the same time a slaveholder? These terms are not convertible. They are incompatible with each other. Genuine Christianity is a reversing of things. Among the Gentiles the great were served; among the Christians the great were to serve. In the parable of the good Samaritan, Jesus struck another blow at the root of this entire system of selfishness. He there taught his followers, that their benevolent regards were not to be confined to a sameness of country or religion. As Christ taught the Apostles, so the Apostles taught the churches. Under the influence of a more exalted benevolence than Judaism, Peter commands the members of the church to "honor all men." Slaveholders live in open violation of this command, and every kindred precept. What! honor a negro? Yes, "*honor all men.*" Let us next hear the Apostles, for we must go to their teachings, as the earliest ministers and instructors of those duties enjoined upon Christians. I will call your attention to 1st Corinthians, 7th chapter, beginning with the 21st verse:

"Art thou called being a servant? care not for it: but if thou mayest be made free, use it rather. For he that is called in the Lord, being a servant, is the Lord's freeman: likewise also he that is called, being free, is Christ's servant. Ye are bought with a price; be not ye servants of men. Brethren, let every man wherein he is called, therein abide within God." In all my interpretations of the Scriptures, my first question is, what gave rise to the subject? So now, what called this forth? We gather from the first verse of the chapter, which we have quoted, that the church had propounded some questions to the Apostle with reference to marriage, circumcision, and slavery. This understood, we proceed:

"And the woman which hath a husband that believeth not, and if he be pleased to dwell with her, let her not leave him. For the unbelieving husband is sanctified by (to) the wife, and the unbelieving wife is sanctified by (to) the husband." Religious differences did not effect the legality of the relation;

nor yet the legitimacy of their offspring. "But if the unbelieving depart, let him depart. A brother or sister is not under bondage in such cases: but God hath called us to peace."

Then in regard to circumcision. "Is any man called being circumcised? let him not become uncircumcised. Is any called in uncircumcision? let him not be circumcised." There was the literal circumcision, and the literal uncircumcision. Let not the Jew disclaim being a Jew according to the flesh, nor the Gentile being a Gentile according to the flesh. For now, "Circumcision is nothing, and uncircumcision is nothing, but the keeping of the commandments of God." Then the Apostles enjoins, "Let every man abide in the same calling wherein he was called."

Then comes the statute bearing upon slavery. What the precise form of the question was, we are not informed. Twenty-first verse: "Art thou called, being a servant? care not for it; but if thou mayest be made free, use it rather." Yours is a hard lot: "care not for it." Be patient; bear the injuries with becoming submission. We use the same form of expression to those in hard allotments. "But if thou mayest be made free, use it rather." The desire for freedom was a lawful aspiration; and no Christian master could refuse to grant his slave a justifiable desire and be guiltless, *if duties are reciprocal.* In Christ, the slave and the freeman stand upon equality. Christ does not disregard the one nor esteem the other on account of these political differences. This was to comfort. It was the best the nature of the case would admit. Again: 23d verse, the Apostle says: "Ye are bought with a price; be not ye the servants of men." Mr. Barker says, Paul never forbade slavery. Let me ask Mr. Barker the meaning of this last sentence, "*Be not ye the servants of men.*" Is it not used in a *prohibitory* sense, and in the *imperative* mood? Paul, then, did command free Christians not to surrender their freedom and become slaves, for the following reason: "Ye are bought with a price, be ye not the servants of men." For the same reason he says in the 6th chapter, "Flee fornication." "For ye are bought with a price; therefore glorify God in your body, and in your spirit, which are God's." This was forbidding it with a strength of feature worthy of himself, and worthy of the cause.

The next passage to which we invite attention will be found in 1st Timothy, chapter 6: 1, 2.

"Let as many servants as are under the yoke count their own masters worthy of all honor, that the name of God and his doctrine be not blasphemed. And they that have believing masters, let them not despise them, because they are brethren; but rather do them service, because they are faithful and beloved partakers of the benefit." There are evidently two orders of "masters" in this passage. One, in the first verse, and the other in the second. The first unbelieving, the second believing. The "servants" of these "masters" stood in these relations. The one was under the "yoke," the others were not under the "yoke." The first are required to give their "masters" "honor"—to *count* them worthy of "all honor." Now, on what ground does the Apostle claim "honor" for the masters in the first verse? He does not base it on the worthiness of the "master," but commands it, "that the name of God be not blasphemed." Surely a Christian master would not blaspheme the name of God, if his "servants" should fail to "honor" him; but it is presumable that a heathen "master" would "blaspheme" "the name of God," and quarrel with the religious profession of his slave. Christians are required to walk in wisdom towards them that are without—to pursue such a course towards unbelievers as to win them to Christ; as is further shown in the 1st Epistle of Peter, 3d chapter, 1st verse.

"Likewise, ye wives, be in subjection to your own husbands; that if any obey not the word, they also may without the word be won by the conversation of the wives."

Who does not know, that when a man becomes a Christian by profession that there is an enlargement of expectation with reference to his future behavior? Both saints and sinners have an indisputable right to claim something as the fruit of their profession. This, on the part of many, is an unintended compliment to Christianity. It would be in perfect harmony with the genius and spirit of Christianity for a slave to suffer for the sake of his "unbelieving master," and it would also be the most certain way of securing to himself better treatment, and perhaps freedom. Those who have "believing masters" are to do them "service, because they are faithful and beloved partakers of the benefit." Such motives to fidelity could never have been urged in case the old relation had continued; but the character of the "master" ("faithful and beloved,") and the motives to obedience presented to the "servant," imply that both "master" and "servant" were Christians. I have examined the word "*partaker*." It means, according to Webster, a participator, a reciprocator. It does not make the "servant," but the "master," a "partaker of the benefit." "*Partaker*" means nothing more nor less than a participator—one who has or takes a part in common with others. To talk of a Roman slave, as such, being a "partaker" with his "master" in the "benefit" of his toil would have been the superlative of nonsense, and could not have been urged as a motive to fidelity. Suppose you try it in the case of an American slave. Say to him, be "faithful;" you are a "partaker"—you expect to eat of the corn for which you toil. Yes, so will my master's mule. He and I have an equal interest. We shall eat of it through the winter, that we may be able to raise another crop for our "master." Can we suppose an Apostle would have been guilty of such a piece of mockery?

We will next invite your attention to Colossians,

4th chapter, 1st verse. "Masters, give unto your servants that which is just and equal; knowing that ye also have a master in Heaven."

If this language means anything, it goes to show that Christians could not hold their slaves as they had formerly held them—that the property relation was done away; and with that the profitableness to the "master." I wish particularly to call attention to the language of this statute. "*Masters give to your servants that which is just and equal.*" Here are two words utterly incompatible with the idea of slavery. There can be no such thing as justice and equality between a proprietor and his property. To command a man to give goods and chattels, that which is "just and equal," would indeed be a new and a strange kind of parlance. Had the language been, "render unto your slaves that which is *merciful*," that would have been in harmony with property relations; whereas, the other is at utter variance with every thing of the kind, and consequently here the property relation could not have existed. Did the Roman slave law require justice and equality from master to slave? This was more than food, raiment, and medicine. It would require righteous compensation for services according to the standards of apprecia-tion, and respectful treatment in all religious and social relations, as defined by Christianity. Can we demand such treatment of a man to his horse? To talk of equality between a man and his ox, is to talk without meaning. "*Partakers of the benefit.*" Slaveholders never were "partakers of the benefit," but *receivers of the "benefit."* There was nothing reciprocal between a Roman "master" and his slave. Let these specified duties be required of professing Christian slaveholders in these United States, and slavery will soon come to an end, at least so far as the church is concerned. That such was the tendency of Christian principle and practice, and would be again if these were allowed to control the parties, we can have no doubt. If proof of this is required it will be found in "Christianity Triumphant," by Joseph Barker, pages 110, 111:

"Throughout the whole of those benevolent efforts, which have ended in the abolition of this accursed system, we behold nothing but the influence of the religion of Jesus Christ. We find no society of unbelievers passing resolutions against the slave-trade and slavery, or sending forth their advices to their friends, backed by powerful reasons, to keep themselves clear from the gains of oppression, and to employ their influence in seeking the abolition of the evil. From first to last the glorious and god-like achievement is the work of the religion of Christ. They were Christians that first pleaded against it in their social circles; they were Christians that first resolved against it in their solemn meetings; they were Christians that first formed the anti-slavery society; they were Christian legislators that first lifted up their voices against the evil system in the high places of power; they were Christians that went across the seas, and endured the hardships of persecution, to teach the oppressed and injured slaves the religion of Jesus Christ; they were Christians which sent up from almost every town and village in the country their petitions for the liberty of the slaves to our Houses of Parliament; and it was the influence of Christian principle that at last prevailed to set the afflicted and injured multitudes free. Oh yes, Clarkson was a Christian, and Sharpe was a Christian, and Wilberforce was a Christian; and the men that are still watching over the interests of the liberated slaves are Christians; and those noble men and women also are Christians that are lifting up their voices against slavery in America. Christianity is the friend of liberty in all its lovely forms, nor will it cease to war with oppression and slavery, until their last remains shall perish from the face of the earth. The Gospel was sent to make a world free, nor will it cease its operations till the blessed work is done. The rod of oppression shall be broken; the lash which was used for the torture of humanity shall be cast away; the chains and manacles of the slave shall be dissolved, and there shall not be left a slave through all the dwellings of mankind. The Gospel shall continue its operations till liberty of soul, and liberty of limb, shall be the portion of every child of man."

I will now read a short extract from Gibbon. Surely he cannot be suspected of favoring the Christian religion; for he was an infidel, and sought by every opportunity to throw disgrace upon Christianity. The extract I read is from vol. 4, page 269:

"Whatever restraints of age, or forms, or numbers, had been formerly introduced to check the abuse of manumissions, and the too rapid increase of vile and indigent Romans, he (Justinian) finally abolished; and the spirit of his laws promoted the extinction of domestic servitude. Yet the eastern provinces were filled, in the time of Justinian, with multitudes of slaves, either born or purchased for the use of their masters; and the price, from ten to seventy pieces of gold, was determined by their age, their strength, and their education. But the hardships of this dependent state were continually diminished by the influence of government and religion; and the pride of a subject was no longer elated by his absolute dominion over the life and happiness of his bondsman."

By consulting Gibbon more extensively you will discover that the Romans had placed an injunction upon manumission. Christianity having begun its work the country was rapidly filling up with persons of servile birth, raised first to the distinction of freedmen, and finally to the honor of citizenship. And hence the restraints and checks imposed upon manumissions. These laws, intended to check manumission, Justinian abolished. He again opened the door to the Christian "master," to let the slave go "free." In this favorable opening for manumission, it had gone on so rapidly that it was done away in the western provinces, and through the combined influence of *government* and *religion*. The Christian was now the prevailing religion, that acted upon the government and the government upon slavery; and our historian says the "subject had no longer the absolute dominion over the life and happiness of his bondsman." This was A. D. 552. Justinian, a professed Christian, was at this time Emperor; a weak man we admit, in some respects, but a professing Christian. He did a good work in removing these *checks*, intended by the Roman Senate to prevent the too *rapid manumission* of slaves. Now in view of these positive facts, and of the extract last read from Mr. Barker, what shall we say of professing Christians who appeal to the New Testament, or of unbelievers who calumniate the Christian scriptures as a pro-slavery document, that they may make slavery the occasion of throwing discredit upon them? Is it true that a pro-slavery system made anti-slavery men and promoted the extinction of slavery?

Who have been the successful advocates of the abolition of slavery from the first to the present century? Did the heathen philosophers and moralists advocate the cause of the oppressed? Nay; in the ages when they flourished, slavery was universal, and more than half of mankind were slaves. While the world was in this deplorable condition we see a few Jews rising out of obscurity, and silently, and unobtrusively setting on foot a system that has made successful war upon this monster of wickedness for eighteen centuries. And who has carried on the war? Who *first* moved in the matter, and who are now doing the work of redeeming man from bondage? That much has been effected in our own and in other lands will not be questioned; and what has been effected, has been done by the same instrumentality. I ask again, through whose agency has this been accomplished? I answer in the words of Joseph Barker, "through Christian influence *first* and *last*." I ask, then, whether these facts do not clear Christianity from the pretensions of pro-slavery professors and of Anti-slavery infidels? I ask again, must Christianity be uprooted in order to do anything effectually against the system of American slavery in that portion of our country where it yet exists? Let the church practice the Christianity of the New Testament and she will soon throw off this disgrace; and until she does carry out Christianity both in principle and in practice, it is *wrong*, it is *unjust*, it is *wicked* to hold Christianity responsible. Would it be thought just or honorable to charge upon our civil code all the thefts and murders committed by pretended American citizens? He is only a true American, who is one inwardly as well as in outward pretension. I appeal to that *discriminating* test of the Great Teacher of our religion: "The tree is known by its fruits."

But one will ask, has not the anti-slavery cause been espoused by men called infidels for the last ten years? I answer *no*. That is the *nominal* cause, not the real one. Other questions have been raised—other questions have taken precedence in that portion of the Anti-slavery movement. The question with this portion is, the "church," the "Bible," the "Christian ministry," the "United States Constitution," etc. The effect of all this dragging in of irrelevant questions upon the anti-slavery society has been a separation in that society. The American anti-slavery society does not now occupy the position it once occupied. The separation will widen. Our friend and others have done as the French Atheists did. What was the cry of Robespierre and his confederates? Liberty! Liberty! Liberty! What *we do*, is in order to gain liberty. What deprives the people of their *liberty?* The "church." The "church" must be removed. The church is the "bulwark" of despotism. And the Bible is the bulwark of the church. Hence they go to work to remove the Bible. Let us cast the Bible away; it is the cause of all this mischief. The Bible was proscribed. And, my dear friends, what horrible depravity developed itself. The rage was against the Bible. The Bibles were gathered together, thrown into a pile, and burned by the public hangman in the city of Paris. And when all this was done, what was the result? Did France enjoy liberty? No. Instead of liberty, the most crushing despotism the world has ever witnessed! A most horrible system! So now. Our friends have espoused some of the great popular questions of the age, just as infidels have always done. I saw this ten years ago, when some eastern agents travelled through our state. I then had charge of a pulpit at Warren. They could get no house save the court-house in which to hold a meeting. Application was made for our meeting-house. We replied, go in—a privilege our folks always grant—we will attend and hear, with the liberty of reply if thought proper. But the meeting was a scene of confusion. We heard them in a series of addresses. We did not publicly say that they were infidels. But I declared, as my conviction was, to some of my personal friends that they were. These were prophetic words. Although they said many good things against slavery; but the precedence they gave to other questions made them *harbingers* of a movement for abolishing the "Bible"—the putting down of the "church" and "ministry." Yes, they were the forerunners of my friend Mr. Barker.

But we must not pass by Moses. He, too, is entitled to respect on this great question. I am not obliged to defend the morality of the law; but will say, you have seen the fruits of this, and of the Pagan morality, in contrast, and can judge for yourselves which is best. Jesus Christ did not refer his disciples to Moses to learn their moral relations and duties. He did, however, treat Moses with the greatest respect—with that respect due from one great legislator to another. He did acknowledge his authority as the Lawgiver of Israel.

Some of the precepts of Moses "were not good," as may be seen from the sermon on the mount. "It has been said by them of old time, an eye for an eye, and a tooth for a tooth, but I say unto you, that ye resist not evil," and in Ezekiel, it is said, "I gave them statutes which were not good." But imperfect as the Levitical law was, it was the best the most enlightened nation under Heaven was capable of receiving. The Jewish law, when compared with the laws of other nations, as a civil arrangement, was so far in advance of the age, that we are compelled to acknowledge its divine origin, or admit an effect without an adequate cause. Its provisions for the relief of the poor, and their guaranties against oppression show clearly to an unbiased mind, that God was its author. In it we find all the germs and seeds of that more perfect system communicated by Jesus Christ, the mediator of a new and better Covenant. As we cannot plant the seed, and the same day have the full grown stalk and mature grain in nature—so neither can we have it in grace. My opponent concurred with me in these views when a Methodist preacher, and I am sorry he does not do so now. "Christianity Triumphant," pages 428 and 430:

"In answer to the 148th infidel objection—that "if God was the author both of the Jewish religion and the Christian religion, and if the Christian religion be different from the Jewish—if God commanded something to the Jews, which he forbids to Christians. God must be changeable." He says, "The religion of Christ differs very considerably from the religion of the Jews, and yet God might be the author of both without being changeable. God is the author both of the sun and moon, and the sun and the moon differ widely from one another, and yet it does not follow that God is changeable. He made the sun and moon for different purposes; the sun to rule the day, and the moon to rule the night, and they are both well adapted to their purposes. So with the religion of the Jews, and the religion of Christ. The religion of the Jews was like the moon, or like the morning star, adapted exactly to its place and time; but not adapted for the whole world, or for all times. The religion of Christ is the sun intended to bring in the full light of day, and adapted to all ages, and to all climes."

"God is a parent, we are his children, and God is unchangeably attached to his children, and invariably seeks their highest happiness. What course shall we expect his unchanging wisdom and goodness to pursue? Will he treat mankind in one unvarying way from first to last? By no means. While the human race is in its infancy, he will exercise their feeble powers with childlike labors, giving them little tasks and easy ones, such as their childish state requires. Thus did God deal with the first generations of men; he laid few burdens on them, and those but light ones. The laws he gave to the Patriarchs were very few and far from strict, but they were as many and as strict as in those rude and infant ages could be of service to mankind. It was necessary that some laws should be given thus early, and it was necessary that those laws should not be many or severe, and the kindness and wisdom of our Father appointed it so. But after a number of generations had passed away, men became intellectually and morally stronger; they were capable of greater exercises and they needed them; and God, always the same affectionate Father, gave them more work. He gave the law by Moses, and accompanied the law with fuller revelations of his character and providence. Under this new dispensation the human family rose still higher, and gathered more inward strength, and became prepared for greater and better things; and it was then that God, in the same unchanged and unchangeable wisdom and benevolence, abolished former systems, and gave a full and perfect system of truth and duty by Jesus Christ. But in all these changes we see the same unchanging Father, pursuing the same grand end, the greatest happiness of the human race."

But before closing this argument let me give a brief summary of my New Testament gleanings.

First: Jesus Christ gave this in solemn charge to his apostles, "Whatsoever ye would that men should do unto you, do ye even so unto them." If we would that men should enslave us, then we may enslave them. This is the moral in the present case.

Second: He taught them that genuine greatness consisted not in the exercise of lordship, but in the most humble ministrations of kindness. "He that will be greatest among you, let him be your minister, and he that will be chief let him be your servant. Even as the Son of man came not to be ministered unto, but to minister and to give his life a ransom for many." The moral of this—the practical lesson, is at war with slavery.

Third: He told them that the love he required extended to all who stood in need of their aid, without regard to country or religion. Under the healthful exercise of this principle, slavery *never* could have been born. And any love that stops short of this, is the love of a patriot, which is the love of the world and never comes within the list of the Christian virtues as taught by Christ and his Apostles. Under such instructions the eleven sat for some three years, and these divine teachings were honored by their Master's daily example.

Fourth: The Apostles were appointed to preach the Gospel to all nations. They did so; Ethiopia not excepted. This brings us to their instructions imparted to the churches, as we have already seen. 1st, They commanded Christian slaves to accept their freedom when it could be had. This was a decided testimony against the lawfulness of the relation. No good man would say to minors or indentured apprentices, "care not for it, but if ye may be made free use it rather." We would rather have incendiaries in our midst than men seeking to break up necessary and lawful relations, and subvert the order of society. 2d, He said to the free, "you are bought with a price: be not ye the slaves of men." Do not surrender your freedom and become slaves. 3d, "Brethren, let every man wherein he was called therein abide with God," (with this exception, "If thou mayest be made free use it rather.") Let this evil be circumscribed in the church—let it extend no farther—let the "servant" desire freedom, and let the "free" neither become "servants" or "masters." This would have put an end to slavery in the church, within one generation. 4th, "Servants" who had "unbelieving masters," and were still "under the yoke," were to "honor" them for the sake of the Gospel. It is a law of Christianity, that we are to suffer wrong rather than to give occasion to the enemies of Christ, to speak reproachfully: that we are to suffer a present temporal wrong for the sake of a present spiritual and eternal good of others, is a principle everywhere inculcated in the Gospel.

Fifth: The "servants" who had "believing masters" were to be "faithful," because they were "*brethren beloved*," *reciprocators* of the benefit; and these "masters" were to give them that which was "just and equal." Many see slavery in the church from this point. No passage has been more tortured than this. Suffice it to say, that wherever there is a slave population there are manumissions more or less, and that such manumitted slaves generally continue with their "masters," and serve them as before in new relations, and from considerations, as per agreement. It is, at least, highly probable that the Gospel found some in this condition, and others soon passed into it, upon Mr. Barker's own showing. Manumitted slaves are always dependent upon others for employment and the means for subsistence. Roman slavery was peculiarly favorable in this respect; in many of its features wholly unlike our negro slavery. As soon as the slave was manumitted, he was a citizen. There being now no occasion for a separation, the "master" continues to be the "master." He still directs his own business and his men. There was no reason to designate the parties by new titles. They were still "master" and "servant." The terms were as apposite to the new relations as to the old. There are "masters" and "servants," and the titles are applicable where slavery never existed. To assume that the titles "*master* and "*servant*" necessarily imply slavery, is to say that there are no terms to designate the ordinary relation, between the employer and the employed, in the New Testament. If, then, we show that new duties were required—duties that could not exist under the old slavish relation, the candid will be satisfied that my position is the true one.

Sixth: We say, then, that the requisition, "Master give to your servants that which is just and equal," is not in harmony with the former relation.

If Paul had said, "masters" give that which is *merciful* to your "servants," this would have suited the condition of slaves. But as there can be no such thing as justice and equality between the proprietor and his property, I am forced to this conclusion — and were it against my creed, I am confident the conviction would be the same — *that the "believing masters," addressed by the Apostles, were not slaveholders, nor their "servants" slaves.*

Seventh: Honor all men, is another Christian duty enforced both by Christ and his Apostles. It is impossible to obey this injunction, whilst we are holding in bondage any portion of the human family. It follows, therefore, that there is no fellowship between slavery and Christianity, and *and that no man can be an intelligent Christian, and an American slaveholder at the same time.*

Finally: The great point has always been overlooked, by those who appeal to the Bible: namely, who shall be the slave? The law of Moses was specific upon this point. "The brother that has waxen poor, and the heathen that are around about you shall be your servants." But with Christ and the Apostles before me, I ask, who shall be the slave? Suppose I see that it is quite convenient to have slaves, and I resolve on having one or more; I ask then, whom shall I enslave for my benefit? Will they tell me? Why, Moses told the Hebrews of whom they might make servants. The Jew could act intelligently — act under instruction — and cannot the Christian do the same? When our slaveholders get the New Testament to answer intelligently these two questions, then they may act as the Jews did. First, May get I me a slave? Second, Whom shall I get? Having these answered, go ahead; but be sure you understand your orders. If the heathen round about you, then you must go to the American Indians. If the African heathen, so be it. Be sure that you obey orders. You profess to be a Christian; you acknowledge the authority of Christ, do you? Yes, I do. Be sure then, that you get the "yoke" upon the right neck, for you must take care that you commit no blunder in this affair. If you get the "yoke" upon the wrong ox, when you yourself were the one intended, it would be rather a serious matter; and Jesus Christ may ask you, some day, who has required this at your hand? "O! the depth, both of the wisdom and goodness," of Jesus Christ our Lord, to adapt a scheme of love and mercy to a sin-ruined world, so as to give his Gospel free access to all; to deprive none of its benefits and blessings, neither the "master," nor the "slave," on account of previously existing relations, however wrong and oppressive; and yet not to justify the wrong, but to correct the evil—to lay the foundation for its future destruction, and promote the good, present and eternal, of such as had stood in wrong relations to each other. The greatest display of wisdom, human or divine, consists in the best selection of means, and their judicious adaptation to bring about contemplated ends.

We must then say, that Christianity has accomplished what the wisdom of the worldly-wise could never effect. Under the old system the evil was fostered, and it grew; under the latter it was reproved, and it died. Such is the testimony of its enemies. Surely, their rule of human right is not our rule of right—our enemies, themselves, being judges.

The heathen world was full of organic evil—legalized evil. But Christianity in her youthful, in her virgin days, made war upon them all. Christianity is a unit—there are not many Christianities. Where the same consequences do not follow, Christianity is not. It may be a modification or a corruption of it, but it is not that identical thing. Upon the principle of causation it cannot be.

But to close my argument on the perfection of the New Testament ethics, I will read a few passages as a specimen of the whole.

Galatians 5: 19: "Now the works of the flesh are manifest, which are these: adultery, fornication, uncleanness, lasciviousness, (20,) idolatry, witchcraft, hatred, variance, emulations, wrath, strife, seditions, heresies, (21,) envyings, murders, drunkenness, revellings, and such like; of the which I tell you before, as I have also told you in time past, that they which do such things shall not inherit the kingdom of God." (See Galatians 5: 22–26;) (Ephesians 4: 17 to end of the chapter;) (1 Thess. 5: 22.) Our friend was positively right when he said, that "the Religion of the Bible is the enemy of all vice."

Argument 7: I have something to offer upon New Testament history. The New Testament writers have given such demonstrations of integrity, that the charge of imposture, savors either of ignorance or invidiousness. They have incorporated such an amount of the civil and religious history of their times with their writings, as to place them beyond the reach of honorable suspicion. They have committed themselves in a way that impostors never do. They say that Herod was "Governor of Judea" when Christ was born; that he died soon after, and "Archelaus, his son, reigned in his stead." That when "Joseph returned from Egypt," he was afraid to take up his residence in Judea, but passed into Gallilee, as a matter of safety. Augustus Cæsar was at that time Emperor, and "Cyrenius was Governor of Syria." That Tiberius was Emperor at the time John the Baptist entered upon his ministry. Pilate was Governor of Judea; Herod Tetrarch of Galilee; his brother Philip of Iturea; and Lysanias Tetrarch of Abilene; and Annas and Caiaphas were the High Priests; that Herod of Galilee imprisoned the Baptist, and cut off his head; that when Christ was crucified, Tiberius Cæsar was still Emperor—"Pontius Pilate Governor, and Caiaphas High Priest."

In the book of Acts, the Cæsars still held the Empire, and many other officials are named, both civil and military: such as Gallio, Festus, Agrippa, Felix, Lysias the Chief Captain, and Cornelius the Centurion. The places where the Apostles preached, wrought miracles, were persecuted and whipped, are named, together with Paul's shipwreck, and many other minute incidents and details, all of which belonged to, and are recorded in the histories of those times, which histories are still extant—open to the investigation of friend and foe.

This was throwing out the banter to all coming generations. "Gentlemen, will you examine our claims?" They have been examined by the wise and good; and what has been the result? See "Christianity Trinmphant," pages 295, 296:

"The wisest men that the world has known, and the greatest patrons and friends of knowledge for many ages past, are to be found in the ranks of Christianity. The founders of Christianity themselves were the first who entirely threw down the prison walls of knowledge, and sent it forth to run at large among all ranks, and to wander through all lands. Foolish as the world accounted the first heralds of the Gospel, they were the wisest that had ever appeared in the form of men, and they did infinitely more towards the spread of knowledge through the earth, than the pretended wise ones among the Gentiles had ever thought of doing. The first Christian converts showed the same spirit as their teachers, and went everywhere disseminating the truth. And so it has been in succeeding generations. And the greatest lights of the world which have appeared in later ages, are all to be found in the ranks of Christianity. Wickliffe, and Luther, and Melancthon, and Bacon, and Malebranche, and Newton, and Locke, and Boyle, and Clarke, and Taylor, and Barrow, and Tillotson, and Wilkins, and Hale, and Baxter, and Milton, and Penn, and Watts, and Wesley, and Raiks, and Williams, and Morrison, and thousands upon thousands more in all the different branches of literature and science are all to be found among the disciples of Christ. Our best poets, and historians, and philosophers have been Christians. Unbelievers have occasionally distinguished themselves as writers, but in consequence of their want of fidelity to the interests of truth and virtue, their works have hastily sunk into disrepute and forgetfulness. None but Christians can afford to be faithful to truth without betraying their cause, and the works of Christians are the only works which bear about them those marks of candor and fidelity, which are necessary to secure to works a high and permanent place among the illuminators and guides of the human race. The works of genuine Christians are gathering fresh glories around them, and year after year exerting a still mightier influence; while the productions of pollution and unbelief are sinking deeper and deeper among the shades of death."

If the New Testament writers were men of truth and integrity, then the extraordinary and miraculous things recorded by them are as true as things ordinary or common; for they are so blended that they cannot be separated. Indeed, it is the supernatural that gives authority to all the rest of the system, whether of precept or promise. If Jesus Christ was no more than the son of carpenter Joseph; if he did not perform the miracles the Evangelists say he did; if he did not rise from the dead; if he did not ascend to the skies: then is Christianity a tissue of the most prodigious falsehoods ever uttered. But these are not lies. The Apostles were men of truth and integrity. We refer to the "Christian," by Joseph Barker, page 19:

"Unbelievers cannot prove that the men who wrote the Gospels, the Acts, and the Epistles, were not good men—men of truth and integrity—men of purity and charity."

Mr. Barker says, "they were good men," and good men will not lie; and Christianity, as we have it in the inspired record, is worthy of rational belief—*God's inspired truth.*

But if my opponent is right, as soon as a man declares himself a believer in Christianity according to the record, he forfeits all claim to common sense—the best sense in the world. Nor can the best men, and wisest men that have ever lived, clear themselves of the charge of ignorance and superstition? Bacon, Locke, Newton, and a thousand others, have reason to blush for having believed and professed such a superstition.

Argument 8: A few words as to Bible biography. A simple statement of facts in the most unadorned and artless style, is peculiar to this part of sacred composition. The writers from Moses to John maintain this singularity. They had frequent opportunities for embellishment. They record many touching incidents where a lively imagination would have found ample scope for display in the exercise of genius, as well as to add some grace to the sketch. But no attempt of this kind is made. Some thirty or forty, during a period of nearly two thousand years, writing at different times, and under different circumstances, each maintaining his own individuality; and yet a sameness among themselves; and yet differing from all others. Orators and poets draw upon their compositions to enrich their pages. Byron laid the subject of his best poetical effusions in Bible history. I allude to his poems on the destruction of Senacherib, Joseph and his brethren — the best efforts of this master-spirit in poetry.

The Bible writers never favor their friends, or those of their own party. Moses records the perfections and imperfections of Abraham, the father of his nation, without praise and without blame, as John the Apostle does the weaknesses of Peter, a fellow Apostle. In the same manner do they treat their enemies. They mention Herod, and speak of his wicked acts; but do not so much as say, that he did wickedly. This is a characteristic peculiarity of these writers. How will we account for it on human principles, without supposing a superintending Providence, by which the writers were directed and inspired?

But when they were not writing history, they would occasionally indulge in a word of praise or blame. There is not a single eulogy on the doings of Jesus Christ, in either Matthew, Mark, Luke or John. This is strange enough on infidel principles, but no marvel to the Christian. When Peter was preaching Christ to the Gentiles, he said that "Jesus Christ went about doing good." This much by way of encomium is not found in the four biographies of our Lord. Who, that speaks or writes of the Jesus of the New Testament, free from any restraint, will not be lavish of his praise, even extravagant, and yet not enthusiastic.

Paul, in his Epistle to the Galatians, says "that he withstood Peter to the face, for he was to be blamed." But that was not in regard to doctrine — it was a mere act of dissimulation on the part of Peter, occasioned by the presence of some Jewish brethren. Of all men under Heaven, those engaged in a conspiracy must be most careful of their conduct toward each other. Suppose these men had been impostors, would not Paul have said to himself, if I provoke Peter to anger he will turn state's evidence, expose the imposture, and the whole matter will be out; and then, alas! alas! Honest men only can use such freedom.

As biographers, the Bible writers possess this characteristic difference. We can all see why it should be so. If they had indulged in praise and blame, as other writers and historians do, they would have corrupted the text with their own comments. They give the facts as all impartial biographers and historians should, and let the reader make his own comments upon the moral qualities of the man, and leave it to God to say what is right and what is wrong. In this consists their peculiarity, namely: that they record simple facts, in regard to miraculous or other occurrences, and leave them with the reader to draw his own conlusions. Here lies a historian before me, (Gibbon;) and, so far as I know as a chronicler of simple facts, he is reliable. I never heard his integrity questioned, so far as a statement of mere facts is concerned. But in recording facts pertaining to the Christian religion, against which he had strong prejudices, he would slur them over in some way, to favor his own prepossessions in respect to infidelity. There is William Wirt, who wrote the life of Patrick Henry, when recording something rather to the discredit of his *beau-ideal*, he always apologizes for it. He speaks, for instance, of his indolence and disregard to his father's wishes. Henry's father sends him to school, and supposes his son is at his studies, but Patrick is by some stream fishing. But his biographer makes him full compensation when he says, he then laid his plans for all his "future greatness." But the sacred historians record without comment, both the vices and virtues of those whose doings they have written out. Perhaps, indeed, if our characters were written by Moses', Matthews', or Johns', we would not look upon ourselves with as much complacency as we do.

MR. HARTZEL'S TWENTY-FIRST ADDRESS.

Mr. McNeely will read a passage from the Declaration of the late Joseph John Gurney; page 6:

"Also in the words of the General Epistle of the yearly meeting of London, for the year 1836. It has ever been, and still is, the belief of the Society of Friends, that the Holy Scriptures of the Old and New Testament, were given by inspiration of God; and, therefore, the declarations contained in them rest on the authority of God himself; and there can be no appeal from them, to any other authority whatsoever; that they are able to make us wise unto salvation, through faith which is in Christ Jesus, being the appointed means of making known to us the blessed truths of Christianity; that they are the only divinely authorized record of the doctrines which we are bound, as Christians, to believe, and of the moral principles which are to regulate our actions; that no doctrine which is not contained in them can be required of any one to be believed, as an article of faith; that whatsoever any man says or does, which is contrary to the Scriptures, though under profession of the immediate guidance of the Spirit, must be reckoned and ACCOUNTED A MERE DELUSION."

Surely this testimony frees the *Quakers from the charge of infidelity*. I wish to make some remarks bearing upon the words, believers and unbelievers. When I spoke of unbelievers, not moving forward in the great work of human emancipation, I had no reference to such believers *only who were church members.* I find thousands who believe the Gospel—who have the fullest confidence in its truth, and yet have no connection with any of the different Protestant organizations. So far as I know, those who have denied the truth of the Gospel of Jesus Christ, have not been the active movers of any *scheme of benevolence.* I have listened with fixed attention to Mr. Barker's replies to my arguments, that in the New Testament we have a perfect rule of life. I proceed, then, with the fullest assurance, that there is nothing to be offered on the negative.

He has given us some quotations from Christ's sermon on the mount, and raised a quarrel with the blessedness Christ pronounced upon those of certain dispositions and traits of character. These beatifications are not precepts. If Mr. Barker could have shown that the duties enjoined upon "husbands" and "wives," "parents" and "children," the "rich" towards the "poor," the "strong" towards the "weak," were not in harmony with these relations, and calculated to promote universal benevolence and good will among men, he would have done so. The fact that he has not done this is evident that he could not. If Mr. Barker had read the first verse of the fifth chapter of Matthew, in order to show to whom this beautiful discourse was addressed, his course would have been better calculated to enlighten us upon the subject than all his biting remarks.

"And seeing the multitudes, he went up into a mountain: and when he was set, his *disciples* came unto him: And he opened his mouth, and taught them saying: Blessed are the poor in spirit: for theirs is the kingdom of Heaven. Blessed are they that mourn: for they shall be comforted. Blessed are the meek: for they shall inherit the earth. Blessed are they which do hunger and thirst after righteousness: for they shall be filled. Blessed are the merciful: for they shall obtain mercy. Blessed are the pure in heart: for they shall see God. Blessed are the peacemakers: for they shall be called the children of God. Blessed are they which are persecuted for righteousness' sake: for theirs is the kingdom of Heaven. Blessed are ye, when men shall revile you, and persecute you, and shall say all manner of evil against you falsely, for my sake."

I admit that this discourse would not be adapted to the world in its unenlightened condition. These blessings the world cannot enjoy; for these pure and holy, these self-denying precepts, the unconverted will not, nay, they cannot obey. Therefore, Jesus Christ withdrew from the multitude, that he might give this lesson to his Disciples, who were prepared to receive it. I declare before Heaven, this lesson of our Lord did never appear, to me, so beautiful and lovely, as while I listened to Mr Barker's attempt to ridicule it. I am sure every intelligent Disciple will regard this attack as an eulogy; but lest it might have been regarded by some in the light of an objection, we have bestowed upon it this passing notice.

Argument 9th. I now proceed to an argument upon miracles. I have selected for my present purpose, on this subject, a miracle recorded in Acts, 3d chapter. When Peter and John were about to go into the temple, a certain man, lame from his birth, was carried and laid at the gate. "And Peter fastening his eyes upon him with John, said, Look on us. And he gave heed unto them, expecting to receive something of them. Then Peter said, silver and gold have I none; but such as I have give I thee: In the name of Jesus Christ of Nazareth rise up and walk. And he took him by the right hand, and lifted him up: and immediately his feet and ankle bones received strength. And he leaping up stood, and walked, and entered with them into the temple, walking, and leaping, and praising God." The opposing Jews called this "a notable miracle," and well they might, for so it was. There was every thing connected with it that could give notoriety to any event. 1st: It was performed in a great city. 2d: It was performed at the beautiful gate of the temple, the most frequented place. 3d: The subject of it was over "forty years of age"—"lame from his birth," and supported by the charitable contributions of those who visited the temple either from motives of curiosity, or for the purpose of worship. The history goes on to say, that when Peter pronounced upon this cripple the word of healing, that immediately "his feet and ankle bones received strength," that he "leaped up, stood, walked into the temple, leaping, and praising God." This is a minute description, and if it had been a falsehood, it was of the easiest exposure. But the writer makes it still more liable to the severest investigation, by both friend and foe, by giving the time of its occurrence. He does not say *anno domini*, but that which is equal; he says, "Annas and Caiaphas were high priests." In regard to this item of history we must take one of two positions; either it is true, or it is not true. If true, then this was a real miracle—an intelligible miracle, bearing directly upon the resurrection of Christ and the inspiration of the Apostles. This is our position; and infidels must say it is a forgery. Has any negative testimony been given? Our friend certainly ought to have some. He might have, and we have a right to demand it. We shall show that this demand is reasonable. Suppose that after this treatise became public property, some one should have undertaken to ferret out this item of history. Say, in fifty years or more after the event, some unbeliever had determined to examine into this matter. He would have gone into Jerusalem and accosted some aged person, sixty or seventy years old. Sir, are you a resident of this city? Yes. Did you live here at the time that "Annas was High Priest?" Yes. Did your father live in this city at that time? Yes. This would have brought it within the time specified. These men were in the city, and would doubtless have heard of such an occurrence had it taken place. The inquiry proceeds: did you know a man, some forty years old, who was "lame" and helpless from his "birth"—was constantly about the city, and was supported by public charity? No; I did not. Did you ever hear of such a miracle being performed? No; never. I will put it even a hundred years after the occurrence, and suppose this investigation to have been made, with the above result. This published to the world would have been a complete refutation, and would have stamped the cause with eternal infamy and disgrace; and the same, or at least similar facilities for detection, cluster around nearly all the miracles in the New Testament history. Why were the early enemies of Christianity so impolitic? Why did they put the pretended miracle workers to death, and thus lend their aid in building up a cause they were so solicitous to destroy, rather than to investigate those extraordinary tales in the Gospels and Acts, and publish the result of such examination to the world? On any principle of human policy, the absence of such documentary evidence is unaccountable; or, will my friend say that such denial, upon such investigation, might have been published and the work have perished. Well, he does say "infidel books must perish;" but in that case it would not have been an infidel book, but would have been a *faithful* book, and preserved by the faithful; for the unbelievers, in that case, would have been the faithful, and such refutation would have been preserved as the most invaluable treasure. Well, then, we have positive testimony, and *no* negative. I suppose we shall believe the record, and give the opposition another occasion to *laugh* at our *credulity* and *superstition*.

In relation to the miracles of the New Testament, one of two positions must be taken by the infidel. Either they were "masterly frauds, or fictions." If frauds, they must have been committed at the time, and by the persons to whom they are awarded. If fictions, they were fabricated after Christianity had already gained a tolerably fair footing. It would seem, in that case, that the impostors considered them as all-important to keep up the credit of the scheme. In regard to the first of these hypothesis, if frauds on men's senses, they did "succeed beyond anything in the history of fraud or fiction since the world began." The infidel must believe that a vast number of apparent miracles, involving the most astonishing phenomena, such as the instant restoration of the sick to *health*—the blind to sight—the deaf to hearing—the lame to soundness—the dead to *life*—the feeding of hungry *multitudes*, under circumstances where an adequate previous existing amount of food was *out of the question*. That these things were performed in open day, in the midst of multitudes of the most discriminating enemies, imposed alike on those who received and rejected them; "they differing only in this, whether they came from Heaven or Hell—not a very trifling difference either."

Yes, this was the point on which the beholders split. "No man can do the work which thou doest, except God be with him." "When the Messiah cometh, will he do more miracles than this man doeth?" "He casts out devils by Beelzebub, the prince of the devils." Some could hardly decide with either, and with a tone of authority asked, "by what name or power have ye done this?" This demand was made to Peter and John, when they healed the cripple. The infidel must believe, too, that these conspirators against men's senses and common sense, were Galileean fishermen—"the scum of the nation," which was itself regarded as the most ignorant of all nations; and the infidel must farther believe, that these individuals had conceived the no easy task of abrogating the religion of their fathers. The whole nation, for fifteen hundred years, believing that they had received it from God, were greatly attached to it on account of its antiquity, and held it in the greatest veneration as the religion of Heaven; and other nations were scarcely less attached to their systems of superstition, commended by the moralists, sanctioned by the state, possessing all the lure of pageantry, splendid temples, gilded altars, costly victims, and priests clad in the robes of beauty and of glory.

These operators required all these nations, both Jews and Gentiles, forthwith, to abandon their own religions and receive theirs; and that, too, upon such evidence as they offered for their consideration. To the Jews they said, your covenant has waxed old and "is ready to vanish away;" and to the Gentiles they said, "the God whom ye ignorantly worship declare we unto you." No impostors have ever undertaken to subvert the established religion of the country, but to incorporate the new with the old as an improvement. The Mormons did not attempt to do this—the Mahometans did not. And when we consider the character of this new religion—this substitute—who but fools could have promised themselves success? A religion without temples, altars, priests, or victims; without any of the trappings, so essential to catch the attention of the gross and the vulgar. Look at our modern synagogues and chapels, their splendid domes, their lofty spires, their external pomp: are not these for effect? But primitive Christianity had nothing of this kind to beguile the people into a false estimate. The founder, a crucified Jew, abrogating the "Jewish ritual"—improving the morality of Moses, giving it an application to the heart—discriminating the motives of the soul; and to the Gentiles, Oh! *how offensive*, emanating from such a source, correcting all their false morality, and setting on foot a new system of ethical duties. This one precept was enough to repulse the heathen world, viz: "Except a man deny himself he cannot be my disciple." The opposite of every system of Paganism, which is but another name for self-indulgence. I have no earthly doubt that this element (deny thyself,) has proved more offensive to the world than any thing else in the entire system.

Nothing can be more offensive to an unregenerated heart, than this precept—*deny thyself.* The infidel says, true; and yet the adventurers had every probable hope of success. We all agree that they did succeed, to an enormous extent, in the face of all opposition; and in three centuries left the heathen temples tenantless, or nearly so, and their priests without employment.

But the infidel must farther believe, that the original actors in these unparalelled "frauds," acted not only without motive, but against any assignable motive. That they maintained an uniform consistency in unprofitable falsehood, and this they did not only collectively, but individually and separately, in different countries, before different tribunals, under every kind of examination and cross-examination, in defiance of every menace, with the axe, the cross, the stake, and kindled fire before their eyes. They persisted in their "fraud," and induced thousands to join them who were equally obstinate in their belief in these "cunningly devised" tricks. The infidel must believe that Christ and the Apostles befooled the people, or that they "befooled" themselves into the belief of miracles. "These are hard alternatives of a wayward hypothesis;" but the hardest is to come yet, namely: that these men, in a rude and ignorant age, *without learning*, without science, had originality enough to invent the most pure, the most sublime system of morality ever offered to the world. And, with all their conscious *villainy*, had the *daring effrontery* to *preach it;* and yet, more extraordinary, had the *strange inconsistency to practice it.* And now, in the language of another, let me say to him who can receive all these paradoxes, (and they form but a small part of what might be mentioned,) "O, unbeliever, great is thy faith!"

The same incongruities arise from the denial of prophecy. If not the same, they are no less perplexing. Indeed, there is not a position, that infidelity ever has assumed, or can assume, but that is infinitely more encumbered with difficulty, than the belief of all the different branches of evidence upon which the Bible rests for its defense, and claims our unfaltering faith and confidence.

We may then say, without feeling in the least abashed, "That the Jewish and Christian Scriptures contain a series of communications, supernaturally revealed and miraculously attested—from the latter man may acquire a perfect rule of life." I feel that I have fully redeemed my pledge in the amount and variety of testimony adduced. But we shall offer the testimony of some of the first infidel objectors, as concurring witnesses, to meet the cavils of the captious. "Infidelity Refuted by Infidels," from page 271 to 276:

"Indeed if Josephus, Tacitus, Governor Pliny, the Emperors Trajan, Adrian, and Antonius the Pious, Celsus, Porphyry, and Julian the Apostate, be faithfully and candidly examined, to say nothing of the Mishna, the Talmud, Philo, and those of humbler fame, we shall find that—

"1. The Jews' religion—

"2. The immediate antecedents of the Christian institution—

"3. The existence of Jesus Christ, and his extraordinary character and wonderful works—

"4. The call and mission of the Galileean fishermen as Apostles—

"5. The genuineness of the writings collected in the New Testament—

"6. The rapid and marvellous progress of the cause—and,

"7. The excellent character of the Christians, illustrative of the tendencies of the religion—

"Are clearly and amply tested in the very light in which they are set before us in the Christian books.

"The following facts contain almost all the New Testament history; and I need not again repeat that they are unequivocally quoted, or alluded to, as a part of the Christian religion by the unbelieviug witness above named, who wrote—

"1 That the Jews' religion preceeded the Christian, is of the highest antiquity, and distinguished by peculiarities the most extraordinary, from every other ancient or modern religion.

"2. That John the Baptist appeared in Judea; in the reign of Herod the Great, a reformer and a preacher of singular pretensions —of great sanctity of life, and was well received by the people; but was cruelly and unjustly murdered in prison by Herod the Tetrarch.

"3. That Jesus, who was called the Messiah, was born in Judea, in the reign of Augustus Cesar, of a very humble and obsure woman, and amidst a variety of extraordinary circumstances.

"4. That he was, while an infant, on account of persecution, carried into Egypt; but was brought back again into the country of his nativity.

"5. That there were certain prophetic writings of high antiquity, from which it had been inferred that a very extraordinary personage was to arise in Judea, or in East, and from thence to carry his conquests over the whole earth.

"6. That this person was generally expected all over the East about the time in which the gospel began to be preached.

"7. That Jesus, who is called Christ, taught a new and strange doctrine.

"8. That by some means he performed certain wonderful and supernatural actions in confirmation of his new doctrine.

"9. That he collected disciples in Judea, who, though of humble birth and very low circumstances, became famous through various parts of the Roman Empire, in consequence of the progress of the Christian doctrine.

"10. That Jesus Christ was the founder of a new religion, now called the Christian religion.

"11. That while Pontius Pilate was governor of Judea, and Tiberius emperor at Rome, he was publicly executed as a criminal.

"12. That this new religion was then checked for a while.

"13. That by some strange occurrence, not mentioned, it broke out again and progressed with the most astonishing rapidity.

"14. That in the days of Tacitus there was in the city of Rome an immense number of Christians.

"15. That some Christians were, during the reign of Nero, or about thirty years after the death of Christ, persecuted to death by that emperor.

"16. That constancy (called obstinacy by some Pagan governors) in maintaining the heavenly and exclusively divine origin of their religion, is the only crime proved against the Christians, as appear from all the records of their enemies, on account of which they suffered death.

"17. That in the year 70, or before those who had seen Jesus Christ had all died, Jerusalem and the Temple were destroyed by the Romans, and all the tremendous calamities foretold of that time by Moses and Christ, were fully visited upon the disobedient and gainsaying people.

"18. That the Christians made a confession of their faith, and were baptized, and met at stated times to worship the Lord.

"19. That in their stated meetings they bound themselves, by the solemnities of their religion, to abstain from moral evil, and to practice all moral good.

"20. That the communities which they established were well organized, and were under the superintendence of bishops and deacons.

"21. That Jews, Gentiles, Barbarians, of all castes, and persons of every rank and condition in life, at the risk and sacrifice of the friendship of the world, of property, and of life, embraced this religion and conformed to all its moral and religious requisitions.

"These specifications, independent of all that is quoted by Celsus, Porphyry, and Julian, from Old or New Testament, in their proper import and connexions, do fully contain all the peculiar elements of the Christian religion as displayed and enforced on the pages of the New Institution. These constitute the skeleton of the New Testament. Were we to clothe these bones with the summaries which we have given out of Celsus, Porphyry, and Julian, to which we here again refer the reader, we should have the whole frame of the Christian institution, differing only in color from that found in the Book. The color of these facts and documents consists in the interpretation of them. Of course the twelve Apostles of the Messiah interpret them differently from those witnesses whose testimony we have just now heard. The difference of the interpretation, however, all men of sense will admit, affects not the proposition before us, viz: that *the testimony of our Apostles is fully sustained by all the leading facts, by all the ancients of the first and second centuries who have all spoken of, or alluded to, the Christian religion.*"

MR. HARTZEL'S TWENTY-SECOND ADDRESS.

Lord Herbert styles it the best religion. Tindal confesses that "Christianity, stripped of all additions which policy, mistake, and the circumstances of time have made to it, is a most holy religion." Lord Bolingbroke says, "No religion ever appeared in the world whose natural tendency was so much directed to promote the happiness of mankind." Chub admits, that Christianity "If it could be separated from everything that has been blended with it, affords a much clearer light to mankind, than any other traditionary religion, as being better adapted to improve and perfect human nature." Rousseau says, "the majesty of the scriptures strike me with admiration, and the purity of the Gospel hath its influence upon my heart." And yet, he says, "I cannot believe the Gospel." That a man of such a character could not believe the Gospel is no marvel, but highly complimentary to Christianity. Paine made similar concessions to the aforesaid; but he could not believe the Gospel, I suppose for similar reasons. To these we shall append a few concessions from learned friend. "Review of the Bible," page 89:

"The Bible is the friend of all truth and virtue, and the enemy of all error and vice."

This is a brief but true statement of concessions by some of the leading infidels, ancient and modern.

They concede too much to justify their opposition. One thing is manifest from their writings, they had most incorrect views of the Christianity of the New Testament. They were waring, and yet are with the false exhibitions of it rather than the thing itself; for upon their own admissions, it is an exotic, a plant of an unearthly growth. Can they say of any other what they say of this? "It is the best;" "it is most holy;" "it promotes the happiness of mankind," etc. Take Joseph Barker's *fifteen* principles upon which he based the concession, "that the Bible is the friend of all truth and virtue, and the enemy of all error and vice." Can they concede this much to any system of infidelity? Let them select the best from Celsus to Joseph Barker. Let them revise it and correct it, and then sit in judgment upon its merits. Will they concede to their own what they have to the Bible? I am willing to refer the decision to themselves. Or if they are not pleased with this test, I will propose to them another. Let them take any other, claiming a human or divine origin—any of the Pagan *myths*, and when by consent of the whole infidel fraternity, or a majority if they cannot agree, or friend Barker himself, and now having made the selection, he or they may throw it into their little "allembec" and *distil* it until they have nothing left but the *essence*, and then they shall have the privilege of another purifying process; they may put it through their best crucible once and again, until they are satisfied they have expurgated all the dross—then we will submit the book to a competent committee for examination, and if said committee shall decide that it is the "best," the most "holy" religion—"best calculated to promote the "happiness of mankind"—that it is the "friend of all truth and virtue and the enemy of all error and vice." I again pledge my honor as a man and as a Christian, that I will be forthcoming in the sum of $1000 for such book upon the delivery of it, or I will give them yet another chance. Joseph Barker may write out a religion himself, and have the benefit of the copyright and as soon as he can get the aforesaid decision in its favor, I will be forthcoming to him in the specified sum. This I submit as a standing proposition. Until this is done, or something of the kind, I must say that your eulogies upon the Bible are most uncandid, if not invidious, and your thrusts at it uncalled for. Suppose Christians would eulogize infidel books and then speak of them as you do about the bible, you would say hypocrites—and justly too. But somehow, *infidels escape the charge of hypocrisy.* There is a reason for this; though they would do with the Bible as one of old did with his fellow—give him one hand in token of friendship, and with the other thrust a dagger through his heart. When such admissions in favor of the Bible as the foregoing, (and they are but a few of the many that might be cited,) and infidel opposition to the Bible are before my mind, and their zeal in carrying it forward—a zeal worthy of a better cause. I can come to no other conclusion, (despite all my charity—and the allowance I am ever disposed to make for weak humanity,) than, that infidelity is a disease of the heart, not of the head.

We will read a few extracts from the "Christian," By Joseph Barker, from page 145 to 155:

"Infidelity is not born with us. We not only are not born infidels, but we are not even born with an inclination—a predisposition to infidelity. On the contrary, we are born with a strong inclination or predisposition to believe. We are born, in fact, with a strong inclination to believe everything that is told us by those who are older than ourselves." "If, therefore, men become unbelievers, it is in spite of their nature. To become infidels, men must do violence to nature. Nature must be shocked and perverted before it can disbelieve; before it can reject the great principles of religion. Nor does infidelity arise from a want of evidence of the truth of Christianity, or from any defect in the character of that evidence. The evidences of the truth of the Christian religion, appear to me to be as complete and decisive as can well be imagined. The doctrines themselves bear every mark of truth that doctrines can bear." And I ask, what is there more wonderful, in what Christianity tells us with respect to the future life of man, than there is in that which the earth itself tells us, with respect to the origin of the earth, of the vegetable and animal tribes which still remain to grace it, or which have perished in its past revolutions, or of the human race itself? The more I look at nature, the more am I astonished that men should find a difficulty in believing the teachings of Christianity with respect to the future destiny of man. A great portion of Christianity is proved to be true by every good man in his own experience; and there are many portions of the history of Christ which are sufficiently proved to be true, by the experience of every religious reformer. "At the same time, the historical evidences of Christianity are quite sufficient to satisfy an unprejudiced man who is acquainted with them, that the historical facts of the New Testament are true, or that the records of them contained in the Gospels and Acts of Apostles are substantially correct." "And if infidelity does not arise from any want of evidence of the truth of Christianity, much less does it arise from any defect in the character of Christianity. No one that understands Christianity, can say that it is a defective, a foolish, or a mischievous system. No one that understands Christianity as taught and exemplified by Christ can help regarding it as a system of freedom, of purity, of benevolence, and of peace. "Again, infidelity does not originate in greatness of soul.

It is not an unusual largeness of intellect, or a peculiar elevation of moral principle, or extraordinary benevolence and conscientiousness that leads men into unbelief. Unbelievers generally have not been distinguished for peculiar greatness of intellect, or for great superiority with regard to benevolence and conscientiousness. On the contrary, those who have deserved to be called infidels, have, in general, been remarkable for widely different qualities." "Who are the men that have distinguished themselves above their cotemporaries in later times, either for largeness of intellect or vigor of mind, or purity of character, or fulness of benevolence, or disinterested and unwearied efforts in the cause of human freedom and human happiness ? You will at once refer to such men as Newton, the fame of whose intellectual greatness has run through the world; and Milton, whose labors in the cause of liberty, and whose superiority as a poet, have raised him to a lofty and eternal eminence. And Locke, whose depth of thought, and power of elucidation, have secured to his writings universal respect; and Penn, whose learning and intelligence were both of them great—whose purity and temperance, whose courage and benevolence were still greater, and whose labors in the cause of truth and righteousness, of universal freedom and improvement have scarce had a parallel in the history of our nation. All these were Christians. And the best and greatest of our own days are Christians. The best and greatest men in England, the greatest and best men in Europe, and the greatest and best men in America, are Christians; and even some among the greatest and best men in Asia have been Christians." "Again, infidelity does not originate in greatness of knowledge. It does not spring from a large acquaintance with science. A belief in Christianity is in no way dependent on ignorance for its strength. And doubts and disbelief of Christianity are in no way indebted to knowledge for their existence. The greatest scholars, the most devoted investigators of nature, most ardent lovers of science, the greatest admirers of the wondrous works of creation; the men that have gained the largest acquaintance with literature and art, are to be found amongst the believers in Christianity." "We observe again, that infidelity does not originate in superiority of moral character. As we have already intimated, those who are really infidels are not, in general, superior characters. There is reason to believe, that in a great many cases the infidelity of people has originated in moral depravity. There is no reason to believe that it has in any case originated in moral purity, or virtuous excellence." "Then again, some become unbelievers through the influence of vice. They are unwilling to give up their bad practices, and therefore reject and at length disbelieve the religion that condemns their bad practices. They are unwilling to live in accordance with the requirements of religion, and therefore deny and at length disbelieve the religion whose requirements annoy them. It is unpleasant to believe a religion which condemns us. It is unpleasant to believe a religion which forbids us to do what we are anxious to do, and which requires us to do that which we are unwilling to do. It is an old saying, that "men love darkness better than light, because their deeds are evil." It is an old custom for men to reject a message from Heaven, because it clashes with their inclinations and pursuits. "How can ye believe," says Jesus, "who receive honor one of another?" "How can ye believe," he says again in effect, "who refuse to act in accordance with the light which you already possess? Act righteously and you shall soon know of the doctrine which I teach, whether it be of God, or whether I speak of myself."

Again, when I think of the wicked and profligate lives of some leading infidels, I am yet more confirmed in this conviction. I know that infidels are disposed to repel this charge—they do this by comparison, but their comparisons are unfair. They compare their best infidels with the most delinquent professors; perhaps such as are not esteemed by the church. Suppose Christians would compare their most worthy professors with the most base and unprincipled men professing infidelity, and then shout *victory!* A just comparison will be between the founders of Christianity and of infidelity and their adherents. That will bring Christ and the Apostles, Volney, Carlyle, Voltaire, Paine, with others into the comparison. I cannot commit such an outrage upon your feelings as to carry the comparison farther than to name the parties. I will, however, select one of the greatest infidel boast, namely Monsieur Voltaire, with a few kindred spirits, and read a few sketches from the pen of Joseph Barker, and let him speak for himself of these infidel worthies. I shall do this partly from a sense of duty to an absent friend. I allude to Mrs. Wilson. To make myself understood, let me say that Mrs. Wilson, in her correspondence with Joseph Barker, referred to the wicked lives of Voltaire and Paine, as I have just done. Mr. Barker called into question the integrity of my religious sister, as you will see.—Liberator April 22, 1853:

"Mrs. Wilson's tales about Voltaire and Paine require no answer. He would be a simpleton, indeed, that could place any reliance on the tales of church and bible men respecting the lives or deaths of heretics and unbelievers. I know what priests and bigots are, when provoked by heresy or unbelief. They are the most unconscionable liars, and the most infernal haters, on God's earth. I have had experience of their cruelty and lies. And I have read church history, and no little of priestly controversy. I cannot conceive a more awful perversion of humanity—a more inhuman or infernal monster—a more unutterable or unbounded hater; a being more reckless of truth, or more ravenous for innocent blood, than the priest or bigot. Talk of tigers; they are spirits of gentleness and love compared with the priest or bigot, when excited by the presence of the man who sets at naught his authority or speaks to him of reform. But Mrs. Wilson refers us to the genuine letters between the Rev. Father Capuchin and the Archbishop of Anneci. I know what genuine letters mean. Letters between two chief priests respecting an unbeliever.

"But she refers us to a General Biographical Dictionary. Does she suppose we do not know how General Biographical Dictionaries are made? But she says, Voltaire cried out, "I shall go to hell." Then why do you say he was an infidel—infidels do not believe in hell. Again she says Voltaire's creed was the essence of Popery."

You shall now hear Mr. Barker in defense both of Mrs. Wilson and myself. "Christianity Triumphant," pages 413 to 417: In answer to the 130th infidel objection, that—

"When the Catholics and Protestants were persecuting and utterly destroying each other, in the kingdom of France, Voltaire, out of his own purse, built a colony to keep them from each other. Point to a Christian that has done as much. It is to Voltaire and those like him that we owe the freedom that we now enjoy."

Ans. There is nothing in the history of Voltaire to warrant those commendations: what our opponents say in his favor is quite a misrepresentation. The idea of Voltaire building a colony, and thereby separating the Protestants and Catholics of France from one another, is altogether monstrous. But if Voltaire had done so, yet for our opponents to suppose that no Christian had ever done as much, shows them to be strangely ignorant of Christian history. What did Penn do? What did Richard Reynolds do? What did Professor Franks and Oberlin do? What did Wesley do? What did John Williams do? What did the men and women do whose deeds of benevolence are noticed in preceding pages of this work? To think of comparing Voltaire with Christian worthies, is out of all character. As Voltaire appears to be the best man that unbelievers have to boast, I will here give a brief outline of his history:—

He was educated by the Jesuits at the school of Louis le Grand, and very early showed a leaning to licentiousness and infidelity. When he left the Jesuits, his father sent him to the schools of law; but he formed a connection with a number of leading infidels, and all his father's efforts to induce him to devote himself to some regular employment were in vain. He soon became a proficient in lewdness and infidelity. To break him off from his associates, his father sent him into Holland; but there he seduced a young lady, and conducted himself in other respects so badly, that he was sent back to France in disgrace.

He now pursued clandestine authorship, and meeting both with protection and persecution, he rose to some eminence as a wit. He went on in feasting and wantonness, and writing anonymous pamphlets. He formed an acquaintance with Rousseau, and quarrelled with him, and they were never friends more. He is next found throwing his "Henriade," a poem he had composed, into the fire in a rage, because some friends, whom he had called together to hear it read before its publication, suggested some improvements. He next quarrels with the Chevalier de Rohan, and learns fencing that he may challenge him to a duel, and is sent to the Bastile six months for his pains.

He next came to England—associated with some English infidels, and got a large subscription made for him, which laid the foundation of his fortune. He then returned to France, and by lottery gambling, and some successful speculations in African wheat and Spanish commerce, greatly increased his stock of money. By army contracts he gained eight hundred thousand francs. He now pursued his work of authorship briskly, but wrote such works for obscenity and blasphemy, that he concealed himself and his name.

He now retired to Cirey, with a lewd woman of the name of Chatelet, with whom he lived on terms of infamous intimacy. Here he feasted, and wrote, and revelled in uncleanness, and quarreled with his harlot, corresponded with the infidel King of Prussia, was very miserable, and had the mortification to see his harlot run off with M. de S. Lambert.

He returned to Paris, visited the King of Prussia, got distinctions, a good salary, gay suppers, but showing himself over greedy, he disgusted the king, quarreled with him, abused the king's literary friends, composed a libel called 'The Private Life of Frederick II.,' together with other libels, returned to Paris, but never forgave his infidel brother king Frederick.

He now, at the age of sixty, took up his residence at Ferney, where he lived for the last twenty years of his life. Here he educated a daughter of Corneille the dramatist, and got her married; and assisted the family of Calas, and of Sirven. Two young officers, one of them, De Barre, were accused of blasphemy and obscenity in their orgies, and with having destroyed a cross at Abbeville. These young men were condemned to death, and De Barre actually suffered. One of Voltaire's works was found in the young man's possession, and had served to corrupt him. When Voltaire cried out against the sentence, it was justly answered, that the guilt also attached to him, for having corrupted the young men's imaginations by his filthy and impious writings.

His chief occupation at Ferney was a bitter and ceaseless war against the religion of Christ. Sometimes it was a large book, sometimes a penny pamphlet; now a treatise on divinity, and then a tale or a song; but hostilities never ceased Let it be remarked that it was after he was sixty years of age that his infidelity became most shameless, his ribaldry most insolent, and his obscenity most offensive. Yet with all his zeal for pollution and impiety, such was his timidity, or his consciousness that he was wrong, that all his attacks on Christianity came out with false names, and when they were attributed to him, he would deny them even with an oath. "Vanity and personal feeling," says my author, "mixed with all his doctrines, and colored his best works. A disposition to make light of every thing spoils all. He is also ever wanting in impartiality; the promotion of infidelity is ever kept in view, and truth and history are made to bend to this. 'I am tired,' said this poor creature, 'of hearing it said, that twelve men were sufficient to establish the Christian religion; I am anxious to show that it requires but one to destroy it!'" Poor man!

His opposition to Christianity, as one of his biographers observes, did not arise from a love to truth or to mankind, but from the spirit of misanthrophy and sensuality. His whole conduct was unworthy of one who pretended to be a reformer. "Not only was the moral conduct of Voltaire censurable," says one of his biographers, "and his conversation licentious, but his writings were replete with gross indecency and insulting outrage to all that is modest and uncorrupted. Nor was it merely by the indulgence of sensuality that he was unfit to serve as a model: he was subject to anger, and envy, and hatred, and was full of malice, falsehood and hypocrisy. Sometimes he would be seen tearing with his teeth a stupid pamphlet, written to depreciate his genius; at another time we find him writing anonymous libels against men whom in public he flattered. And as to his pretensions to benevolence, what was he ready to sacrifice, or even to risk, for the welfare of mankind? By the course he took he gained more power, riches, and fame, than he could possibly have acquired in any other way. As for any serious danger to his life or liberty, there was none; but when the smallest danger appeared, even of his having to encounter the ecclesiastics, what was his conduct? He fled from the danger, made the most hypocritical submissions, feigned what he did not believe, and professed himself a disciple of that religion which he daily insulted. In writing to Mr. and Msle. d'Argental, he says—'My angels, if I had a hundred thousand men, I know what I would do; but as I have them not, I shall take the Sacrament at Easter, and you may call me hypocrite as long as you please. No, my dear marquis, no! the modern Socrates will not drink hemlock.'" In the same sense he wrote that, "if he lived at Abbeville, he would take the sacrament every fortnight." (Correspondence.) Is this the man that is to be compared with Him who laid down his life for mankind, and freely sealed the truth with his blood? Is this the man who is exalted above those martyrs to the interests of truth and human happiness, of which the history of Christianity is full?

That Voltaire did some good I do not pretend to deny: the most malignant and selfish and debauched characters in the universe will sometimes do a kind turn. Nero himself was kind on occasions, and murderers and thieves are kind and honest when it suits their interests, and it will sometimes happen that men are placed in such circumstances, that they are obliged to do some seeming act of kindness, or fall into disgrace. This was the case with Voltaire; and hence, in the midst of a long life of pollution, and deceit, and rage, and malignity, there appear some particles of better seeming things, like here and there a spark amidst the smoky clouds of a troubled volcano. But none that had any regard to truth and decency, would ever think of comparing the conduct of such a character with the peaceful, the pure, the chaste, the benevolent and godlike lives of such men as Howard, and Boyle, and Penn, and Wesley, and thousands more, who have made it their business, and felt it their happiness, to toil and plan and suffer for the welfare of their fellow-men."

Again, "Christianity Triumphant," pages 339 and and 340:

"Rousseau held the doctrine of irresponsibility, and he surely could not imagine that new-born infancy could have any voluntary faith; and yet he exposed his own five little ones in the street, and left them to perish. William Beadle held the doctrine of irresponsibility; he believed that man had no power either over his belief or conduct; and yet he murdered in one night his wife and all his children, and then destroyed himself. Diderot, one of the principal leaders among the believers in irresponsibility in France, who professed to believe that men were no more to be blamed for their unbelief or crimes, than the winds which blew down the trees, still contended that evil-doers should be put to death, to furnish powerful motives or circumstances to prevent others from doing evil. D'Alembert, another leader of the same school, used his influence with the Censor of the Press in France, to induce him to suppress the writings of such as wrote against himself; and when the Censor of the Press sent him a letter mildly declining to do so, he cursed and swore, and in his fury tore the letter to pieces. When the believers in irresponsibility in France got hold of political power, their deeds of blood and death were revolting and diabolical beyond all parallel. The ministers of religion were hung to the lamp-posts without a trial: the guillotine was kept going night and day: terror seized on all hearts, and a cruel death presented itself to every eye. The history of the dreadful deeds perpetrated by the disciples of irresponsibility in France, is about the darkest, the most appalling, and the most heart-rending tale in the whole history of crime."

Also page 418 of the same book, answering the 131st infidel objection, viz:

"What half century has produced more wars than the last?"

Ans. And in what half century have infidel philosophers and statesmen had so much to do with the affairs of nations? The horrors of the last century should teach us what we are to expect when power falls into the hands of unbelievers. Compare the history of Europe when power was in the hands of such men as the infidel Frederick, and the infidel philosophers of France, with the history of Philadelphia for seventy years, while under the government of Christians, and you may then find the secret of the world's troubles, and you may see that the only hope of mankind is in the spread of the principles of the Gospel."

As I have yet a few moments, let me say, if the Gospel is not true, if Christ did not rise from the dead, all that man can calculate upon is the present life. If this is all, my main objections to slavery are removed. It has long been a settled sentiment of my mind, that if this life is not preparatory to another, the elevation and refinement of man is unfriendly to his happiness. In that view I would say with the heathen, "Let us eat and drink, for to-morrow we die." What may suit a man's inclinations are his chief good. If this be so, I must say with Mr. Barker, the Christian religion is not best calculated to promote human happiness, (we should say gratification,) as it forbids jesting, laughing, etc., it is said that slaves usually enjoy the "jest," the "laugh," the "ludicrous tale," the "merry dance" quite as well as their masters do—perhaps as well as Mr. Barker. Mr. Barker, if there is no immortality for man, let the slaves alone, for the more ignorant and brutish, the less they will feel when they come to die. All the ox suffers in his exit is the pain of dying, while the infidel philosopher suffers infinitely more from the gloomy prospect of being as though he never had been—

> "Go mock majesty! go, man!
> And bow to thy superior of the stall;
> Through every scene of sense, superior far;
> They graze the turf untill'd; they drink the stream
> Unbrew'd, and ever full, and unimbittered
> With doubts, fears, fruitless hopes, regrets, despairs;
> When the worst comes, it comes unfeared—one stroke
> Begins and ends their woe; they die but once;
> Bless'd incommunicable privilege; for which,
> Proud man who rules the globe and reads the stars,
> Philosopher or hero, sighs in vain.

Then the moral offense of slavery is taken away. From that point I have brought my best arguments against slavery; so have the most efficient pleaders of the cause of the oppressed. William L. Garrison's best appeals have been from the Bible in behalf of the moral condition of the slave, as his writings clearly show.

MR. HARTZEL'S CLOSING ADDRESS.

It is very common with disputants of a certain class, to speak vauntingly in their closing addresses, of what they have done, and what their opponents have not done. It never was so with me. It is not so now. If my work is not done now, it will have to go undone. It would have seemed more proper for Mr. Barker, instead of telling what he had done, to let somebody else decide what he had proved and disproved. I will trust to the good sense of the audience. I know the course pursued by declaimers in discussion is to parade what they have done with great assurance. He has repeatedly said, that we wandered out of our course in this discussion; perhaps so, the report will decide that question.

Mr. Barker has brought forward this again—"Jacob have I loved, Esau have I hated." We have already stated, that the word "*hate*," in the Bible, often means "to love less," or "to give preference to another," (so defined by Webster.) "And I hated Esau, and laid his mountains and his heritage waste for the dragons of the wilderness."—Malachi 1: 3. Never has anything been more literally fulfilled than the predictions concerning Esau. I cannot offer many proofs now. The prophetic denunciations against Esau and his descendants are numerous. The prophets declare, expressly, that his heritage shall be laid waste, etc. "There shall not be any remaining of the house of Esau: for the Lord hath spoken it."—Obadiah 18. Of Jacob, Esau's brother, Jeremiah says: "Israel shall not cease to be a nation before me forever."

About the beginning of the Christian era, the land of Edom was destroyed. Petra, the capital of Edom, has long been in ruins; and not so much as a representative has Esau—even his name is blotted out from under Heaven. Jacob, the twin brother of Esau, has yet more than four million of representatives. God had a reason for prefering Jacob as an honored progenitor of the Messiah, and rejecting Esau, for making them the subjects of prophecy, and the fulfilment of prophecy. *Their present condition is a clear proof of the truth of God; all the world is witness.* All the predictions of the Old Testament have a direct bearing upon the Gospel, its times and circumstances. The Gospel is so interwoven with the history of those days, that it forms an essential part of the history of the Roman Empire during its decline and fall. The prophecies have been one of the most knotty questions that infidels have had to deal with, because of their direct bearings upon the propagation of Christianity. Gibbon has attempted to account for the early prevalence of Christianity, by leaving prophecy out of the number of his secondary causes. "Infidelity Refuted by Infidels," pages 258, 259, Gibbon says:

"We may still be permitted, though with becoming submission, to ask, not indeed what were the first, but what are the secondary causes of the rapid growth of the Christian church? It will, perhaps, appear that it was most effectually favored and assisted by the five following causes:

"1. The inflexible, and if we may use the expression, the intolerant zeal of the Christians, derived, it is true, from the Jewish religion, but purified from the narrow and unsocial spirit, which, instead of inviting, had deterred the Gentiles from embracing the law of Moses.

"2. The doctrine of a future life, improved by every additional circumstance which could give weight and efficacy to that important truth.

"The miraculous power which was ascribed to the primitive churches.

"4. The pure and austere morals of the Christians.

"5. The union and discipline of the Christian republic, which gradually formed an independent and increasing state in the heart of the Roman Empire."

Candor would have required him to inquire into the primary causes first, but then he would soon have found himself entangled with the evidence of prophecy. If we had time, we would amplify here. We must, however, refer to these secondary causes—"*the miraculous powers that were ascribed to the primitive church.*" He did not say, the "miraculous power" *possessed* by the primitive Christians—that would not have answered his purpose. That would have accounted for the origin of Christianity. Who then did ascribe "miraculous powers" to the primitive churches? Miraculous powers are among the means of extending the Gospel, *and must have been awarded to the primitive churches by the unconverted, otherwise miraculous powers could not have been a cause of multiplying converts to Christianity.**

*Nothing has been more perplexing to infidels than to account for the o igin of Christianity upon their own principles. Therefore Gibbon, this master SOPHIST, steps ov r all the primary, the originating causes, and seeks to accou.t for its rapid growth by secondary causes. This only aggravates the difficulty, he says: "The virtues, energy, and zeal of the early church was a main instrument of the succe s of Christianity, wheras it is the very origination of the early church, with all these EFFICACIOUS and ENDOW-

Our friend has called in question the credibility of Celsus.

Mr. Barker. Did I call in question the credibility of Celsus? Nothing of the kind. I claimed that Celsus was not a witness in the case. I do not deny but that he was an excellent man.

Mr. Hartzel. It was not then the credibility of Celsus he called in question. We will simply read an extract, for which we are indebted to Joseph Barker. See "Christianity Triumphant," page 26:

> "Celsus was another enemy of the Christians, and wrote against them 140 years after Christ's ascension; but his charges, when properly understood, are so many commendations."

Celsus must, then, have seen enough of the Christian religion to know something about it, and we receive him as a concurring witness.

Mr. Barker has again called in question some matters connected with the affairs in France, at the time

---

MENTS that we want to account for. It is as though he had told me that we might account for the success of Christianity, from the fact that it had succeeded to such an extent as to render its further success very probable." As for these secondary causes, when examined in the light of candid reason and fact, they were so many hinderances. Is it at all probable that the "early" Christians by their intolerant zeal "could have TEASED both Jews and Gentiles into the belief and practical acceptance of a religion the opposite of theirs, and at war with all their habits of life? Or, that the doctrine of a future life" to be enjoyed ONLY upon the condition of "denying all ungodliness and wordly lusts, and living soberly, righteously, and godly, in the present world," would have given to Christianity such powerful attractions, when viewed with the eye of an ACCOMMODATING JOVIAL HEATHENISM," it would have been "about as inviting to the soul of a heathen as the promise of an eternal lent to an EPICURE." Again, the miraculous power ascribed to the primitive churches, but not possessed on infidel principles, was one of the auxiliary causes of the "rapid growth" of Christianity. There is a latent insinuation in this, which betrays a want of candor on the part of the historian.

The history of the New Testament declares that the miracles were exhibited, not to such ONLY as were in favor with the new religion, (as are the pretended miracles of Papists, and Mormons, to confirm those who are already initiated,) but in the presence of multitudes of the most astute eagle-eyed enemies. These New Testament facts are confirmed by the profane history of those times. Why not assail these historic facts? Why not attack Christianity in the FRONT rather than the REAR? Ah! that would have brought him in contact with its origin. The supernatural causes which called it into existence; nothing but these mighty agencies, and its aggressive character can solve the PROBLEM of its "rapid growth." Gibbon's failure is apparent to all; for his five reasons fail to account for the early triumphants of the Gospel. Still, his testimony is invaluable, as it bears upon the "pure" and holy lives of the first Christians.

infidelity was in the ascendant. "Christianity Triumphant," page 340:

"When the believers in irresponsibility in France got hold of political power, their deeds of blood and death were revolting and diabolical beyond all parallel. The ministers of religion were hung to the lamp-posts without a trial; the guillotine was kept going night and day; terror seized on all hearts, and a cruel death presented itself to every eye. The history of the dreadful deeds perpetrated by the disciples of irresponsibility in France, is about the darkest, the most appalling, and the most heartrending tale in the whole history of crime."

Mr. Barker has contradicted himself in his denial of what I said concering French Atheism, and is my witness against himself. I have not called in question the character of unbelievers, during this discussion, until my last speech, and then I did it from a sense of duty, in the language of Mr. Barker, as found in his own writings. With regard to Mr. Barker's universal salvation, I have certainly no objection. I only fear the doctrine is not true. But I do certainly hope, that these "murderers of fathers" and "murderers of mothers," he expects to take with him to the realms of bliss, will be "Pharisee" enough to "wash" their "hands" before they step into the presence of the Eternal.

We will now attempt a brief recapitulation. Our first argument was on the "authenticity of the Old Testament Scriptures." We claimed that the Old Testament Scriptures existed for fifteen hundred years before the coming of Jesus Christ. That the religion of the "Jews had certain public observances and institutions."

1. These imply, that there was a "cause," a

"reason," to which they owed their "origin," and that *God, himself, was the author of them.*

2. "That there was a time when that religion began." That time was the period of the Egyptian *Pharaohs.*

3. "That there was a place where these religious institutions began to be observed." That place where they began to be observed was *Egypt*; but more fully revealed to the Israelites during their sojourn in the *wilderness.*

4. "That there was a person through whose instrumentality, mainly, this religion had its origin;" and it was the concurrent testimony of many writers, that Moses was the man commissioned of God to conduct the Israelites into the land of promise. That Moses had given proof that the Lord had commissioned him to engage in the great work of their deliverance from bondage, and was God's *oracle* and *lawgiver* to the nation.

5. That all the Old Testament writers—all the New Testament writers—Josephus—a number of German and Portuguese Jews, together with Volney, attest the authenticity of the Pentateuch. We offered Volney, a learned and virulent infidel, as a witness of the historic credibility of the law of Moses; but Mr. Barker says he has nothing to do with Volney. I will read from Volney again, page 33:

"This stream of water without an issue is the river Jordan, and those naked rocks were once the theatre of events which have resounded through the world. Behold that desert of Horeb, and that Mount Sinai, where by means unknown to the vulgar, a profound and adventurous leader created institutions, whose influence extended to the whole human race."

This is a most important testimony, bearing directly upon the "authenticity of the Old Testament Scriptures." But Mr. Barker, in his *strait*, sets aside the testimony of *infidels* as well as that of *Christians*.

Again: in the Old Testament we have a series of predictions, with reference to many cities of antiquity, such as Nineveh, Babylon, Tyre, Jerusalem, etc. I offered Volney as a witness, that these prophecies have been fulfilled; that these cities have all been *destroyed*, and these *countries* made *desolate*. He says, that in "traveling three days, he passed over the ruins of a hundred large cities in the land of Syria." After having viewed this fearful desolation, so minutely foretold by the prophets, and their predictions literally fulfilled, he fully justifies the predictions by this exclamation, so full of descriptive emotion: "Great God! whence proceed such fatal revolutions? What causes have so altered the fortunes of these countries? Why are so many cities destroyed? Why has not this ancient population been reproduced and perpetuated?" So Volney gives just as many good *testimonies* as there are cities in ruins, or countries depopulated. And having given his testimony to the fulfilment of these predictions, we give the testimony of more than a hundred witnesses: Every city in ruin, and country in desolation, is a *witness for the truth* of *God*.

6. Again: we showed that God fulfilled his promises to Abraham: that the Jews were still "a great nation;" that Abraham had still "a great name;" and, that his seed had been "a blessing to all families (nations) of the earth."

7. That the prophecies in regard to the destruction and preservation of the Jewish nation had been literally and *miraculouslg* fulfilled.

8. That a series of predictions had been fulfilled with respect to the time of Christ's coming, and the beginning of his earthly reign.

9. That another class of prophecies had been accomplished in regard to the death and resurrection of Jesus Christ.

10. That Jesus *himself* had rested his pretensions to the Messiahship upon a series of predictions, the most complex imaginable. That he would be put to death in a certain way, and by certain hands; that he would "rise again the third day," and "ascend to Heaven;" that the Apostles should witness these things. *They did.*

11. That such demonstrations were essential to the future propagation of his religion, and the extension of his kingdom in the world. All these things, with such details as we were able to make, we brought to bear directly upon the first feature of the proposition, namely: "that the Jewish and Christian Scriptures contain a series of communications supernaturally revealed and miraculously attested—in the latter, man has a perfect rule of life." We did not say all

men, but we said *man* has a "perfect rule of life." We opened our defense of this by showing, that nothing short of infinite wisdom and goodness could give such "a rule of life." Specific arguments were offered in defense of this affirmation.

1. The duties of "husbands" and "wives." These we showed were perfectly philosophical, because in harmony with the differing peculiarities of man and woman.

2. That the parental obligations, as taught in the New Testament, are no less in harmony with these relations, and the promotion of the highest degrees of domestic happiness.

3. So of filial obligation. The regulations given in the New Testament in this respect, are, as in the other case, in the highest degree calculated to promote filial respect, with the faithful discharge of corresponding obligations.

4. That the Gospel was especially favorable "to the poor" in providing for their wants; requiring the "strong to bear the infirmities of the weak."

5. That the Gospel both in principle and in practice was opposed to "war," and that the words, *warrior* and *Christian* were a contradiction in terms when viewed in the light of the Gospel.

6. That the Christian religion was not favorable to the relation of "master" and "slave;" that the instructions Christ gave to his Apostles and they to the churches, did encourage manumission—destroyed

the property feature in the relation *and forbade its extension.*

7. That the biographical writers of the Old and New Testaments, possessed a peculiarity of character, such as is nowhere to be found among uninspired biographers. They never "praised"—they never "blamed," but contented themselves with a plain statement of facts. If you believe Mr. Barker, they never censured, though they did record many things disgraceful to the beloved subjects of their memoirs, without flattering their virtues, or animadverting upon their weaknesses.

Now be it distinctly understood, that any opinion of theirs on moral good or evil, interspersed with their biographical sketches, would have been most fatal to the whole of tho divine revelation, as that would have corrupted the text and a false standard of virtue would have been introduced.

8. We offered an argument on miracles, claiming that the miracles of the New Testament were either masterly frauds or fictions, if they were not facts.

What did Mr. Barker say to that argument? He said they were fictions; but he offered no argument to prove that they were not real miracles. We proved that the miracles are so blended with the whole history of the Christian religion, that it is impossible to separate them from either the promissory or preceptive parts, or to read the history of those times without coming in contact with records referring to the miracles of the New Testament, as one of the means by which the Christian religion was propagated.

9. The Christian religion did not aim at puting down moral evil by prohibitory laws. Prohibitory laws cannot put down any system of evil. Prohibitory laws, unless the people are in favor of them, and public sentiment will sustain them, are vain and foolish, and can accomplish no good. How long have we been laboring to put a stop to the sale of ardent spirits as a beverage by prohibitory laws? It is according to our experience and observation, that prohibitory laws, when the public bias is against them, are of no avail.

Mr. Barker. The Maine law has proved efficient in doing away intemperance.

Mr. Hartzel. Where sir?

Mr. Barker. If Mr. Hartzel introduces new matter, I must reply to him.

Mr. Hartzel. I had spoken before in relation to prohibitory laws. I am only repeating what I have before said—that the condemnation of social legalized wrongs, can accomplish nothing in building up a new system. Every such attempt in the beginning of the Gospel would have resulted in defeat.

Mr. Barker will not, nay he cannot, raise an objection here, for he has most clearly proved by his former writings, that the Gospel affected slavery with all other organic evils by moral principle and not by political action. The Gospel therefore did not begin in this way. It went forward upon principles perfectly unique and original. Nothing short of an infinite mind could have devised a scheme so efficient to the removal of evils of such general prevalence, sanctioned by law, consecrated by age, and so congenial to the depraved heart as slavery, polygamy, war, etc.

Paganism, by the power of positive laws, could never have abolished them; and Judaism could only show their enormities, "for by the law is the knowledge of sin," and restrain them to some extent. But a system of moral principles established by God, were the means by which it was effected. The Gospel exercised an influence where it was believed and obeyed, that brought about this revolution. Its principles are designed to promote all these happy results.

10. The facts of history show—Mr. Barker's own writings show, that the Christian religion contains a system of ethical duties that are adapted to every state of society—based upon man's relations and in perfect harmony with them.

Thus I feel I have sustained my proposition. It is not for me to boast of what I have done (as Mr. Barker did) or say what my opponent has not done, but will leave the matter with the audience and the public for their consideration and candid decision.

I regret that I have not been able to make a better defense of a cause so good, and means so ample. I do not say I feel satisfied. I ought rather to regret that I have not been more successful in arranging and classifying my proofs so as to bear more directly upon the question. I have, however, done the best I could. All my circumstances have been unfavorable. The state of my health and other circumstances which I might name, have operated against me.

Now I am willing that the report of this discussion shall be published in proper form, and let it go to the world. We will send it out upon a mission, and let it accomplish all the good it can. I did not desire the publication of my speeches when I left home. I knew not that Mr. Barker desired a report, or that he had made arrangements to that effect. It was with the utmost reluctance that I consented to it.

I feel myself under great obligations to the friends and citizens of Salem for their respectful attention and orderly behavior during the several sessions of this discussion. I feel thankful for the liberality with which they opened to me their houses, and treated both myself and several members of my family with the utmost Christian kindness and hospitality. I also feel much obliged to the moderators of this discussion. They have presided impartially. And lastly I wish to say that I have no unkind feelings towards my friend Mr. Barker. I hope always to meet him on terms of friendship; as his views now are, of course we cannot agree in sentiment. Perhaps we shall agree better hereafter, if not, no matter, that concerns another. If I regard him in great error, as I surely do, I hope ever to give him the kindliest treatment, and feel the most affectionate regard for the welfare of Joseph Barker, with whom I have discussed great principles for five days successively. Farewell.

We certify that the foregoing report of Mr. Hartzel's part in the discussion between himself and Mr. Barker, is correct.

JAMES BARNABY,
CAROLINE STANTON, } *Reporters.*

RESPECTFULLY SUBMITTED TO THE READER.

Perhaps you are especially interested in the propagation of the Gospel. By this I mean the multiplication of converts to Christ. Then, give attention to the following argument: Since infidels are so straitened to account for the early propagation of Christianity, why have they not undertaken to show that the Augustan age was especially favorable to the introduction of a religious *fraud?* Surely there is an argument to be drawn from that source, favorable or unfavorable! If it had been a time of great political agitation; if the empire had, at that time, been convulsed with civil dissentions, or by foreign aggression; if the public mind had been occupied with the exciting interests of war, how eagerly would they call to their aid such facts, to show that Christianity had chosen a favorable time—a time when the wise were otherwise employed, and could not investigate the claims of the new religion, and that Christianity had, in a stealthy way, taken possession, and then by the aid of pretended miraculous powers, managed to hold its footing: but infinite wisdom cut off every plea of that kind, and sent the Gospel into the world at a time the most favorable, to put all its pretensions to the severest test—a time of universal peace—a time when learning and philosophy prevailed; when the "Greeks were seeking after wisdom," and the wise had both time and inclination to examine every new thing; when the world was full of religion, and scepticism; when some worshiped all the gods, and others derided them all. The Augustan age would have been the most unsuitable for a religious adventure, and nothing but the most convincing evidence could have gained for the Gospel a reception.

*

In the history of Christianity, as recorded by the New Testament writers, we have the only rational account of its origin. Every attempt to account for its existence upon other principles have proved a failure. Neither can its propagation be accounted for on other principles than its proselyting character imprinted upon every page of the Gospel by the hand of its benignant author. "I came to seek and to save the lost." But for this you would never have seen a Bible, or yet have been troubled with reading this defense of it. Let not the unsustained assertion, that the Christian religion is like any other religion, promote a feeling of indifference to its claims. Let me ask you, "Is it like the *other* religious products of human nature, in daring to aspire to universal dominion, and that too founded on *moral* power alone? Never, till Christianity appeared, had such an imagination ever entered the mind of man! Other religions were national affairs; their gods never dreamed of such an enterprise as that of subduing all nations. They were naturally contented with the country that gave them birth, and the homage of the race that worshipped them. They were, when not themselves assailed, very tolerant, and did the civil thing by all other gods of all other nations, and were even contented to expire with great propriety (they usually did so) with the political extinction of the race of their votaries! Christianity alone adopts a different tone,—"Go ye, and preach the Gospel to *all* nations,"—and declares, not only that it *will* reign, but none other *shall*. It will not endure a rival; it will not consent to have a statue with the mob of the Pantheon. Whether this ambition—call it pride and folly, if you will, as you well may if the thing be merely human—was *likely* to suggest itself to man, considering the local and national character of other religions, and the apparent hopelessness of any such enterprise, I have my doubts. Arrogance it may be; but it is not such arrogance as is very natural to man.

"These, I said, were amongst a few of the things in which I must say I thought the theory of Christianity very unlike that of any religion human nature was likely to invent.

"If, I continued, I examine the past history and present position of Christianity, with an impartial eye, I see that it presents, in several most important respects, a contrast with other religions in point of *fact*. I shall content myself with enumerating a few. Look, then, at the perpetual spirit of aggression which characterizes this religion; its undeniable power (in whatever it consists, and from whatever it springs) to prompt those who hold it to render it *victorious*,—a spirit which has more or less characterized its whole history; which still lives, even in its most corrupt forms, and which has not been least active in our own time. I do not see any thing like it in other religions. Till I see Mollahs from Ispahan, Brahmins from Benares, Bonzes from China, preaching *their* systems of religion in London, Paris, and Berlin, supported year after year by an enormous expediture on the part of their zealous compatriots, and the nations who support them taking the liveliest interest in their success or failure; till I see this (call it fanatical if you will, the money thus expended wasted, the men who give it fools,) I shall not be able to pronounce Christianity simply on a par with other religions.

"Till the sacred books of *other* religions can boast of at least a hundredth part of the same efforts to translate and diffuse them as have been concentrated on the Bible; till we find them at least in half as many languages; till they can render those who possess them at least a tenth part as willing to make costly efforts to insure to them a circulation co-extensive with the family of man; till they occupy an equal space in the literature of the world, and are equally bound up with the philosophy, history, poetry, of the community of civilized nations; till they have given an equal number of human communities a written language, and may thus boast of having imparted to large sections of the human family the germ of *all* art, science, and civilization; till they can cite an equal amount of testimonies to their beauty and sublimity *from those who reject their divine original*—I shall scarcely think Christianity can be put simply on a par with other religions.

"Till it can be said that the sacred books of other religions are equally unique in relation to all the literature in which they are imbedded; similar neither to what precedes nor what comes after them,—their enemies themselves being judges; till they can be shown to be as superior to all that is found in contemporaneous authors as the New Testament is to the writings of Christian Fathers or the Jewish Rabbis,—I cannot say that Christianity is just like any other religion.

"Till we can find a religion that has stood as many different assaults from infidelity in the midst of it,—educated infidelity, infidelity aided by learning, genius, philosophy, freely employing all the power of argument and all the power of ridicule to disabuse its votaries; till we can find a religion which can point to an equal array of educated men, philosophic in spirit, in learning, and genius, deeply skilled in the investigation of evidence, deliberately declaring that its claims are well sustained,—we cannot say that Christianity is just like any other religion.

"Till it can be shown that another religion, to an equal extent, has propagated itself without force amongst totally different races, and in the most distant countries, and has survived equal revolutions of thought and opinion, manners and laws, amongst those who have embraced it, it cannot be said that Christianity is like any other religion.

"Till it can be shown that the sacred books of other religions have contained predictions as definite and as unlikely to be fulfilled as the success of early Christianity against all the opposition of prejudice and persecution, — its voluntary reception amongst different races contrary to all the analogies of religious history, — and the continued preservation of the Jews among all nations without forming a part of any, — I cannot think that Christianity is precisely in the condition of any other religion."

Again, it is unlike any other religion in its all-subduing influence of men's lusts and passions. When its precepts are obeyed, and its divine spirit is enjoyed, the "Lion has become a Lamb." It subdued the fierce spirit of a Saul of Tarsus, and thousands have been, and now are the living monuments of its regenerating power. Mr. Barker, too, gives the most decided testimony to this point. Christianity Triumphant, page 324, he says: "I was once as violent and revengeful as a youth could — easly be: a provocation would have thrown me into a fury, and an injury would have been almost sure to be followed with revenge. But that is not the case with me now; the religion of Christ has produced a happy change. Nor has Christianity produced any mischevous effects upon any of my kindred or acquaintances. My parents have been believers in the religion of Christ, and have lived under the influence of its principles for forty years; but it never made them either vicious or miserable." Finally, it is not a choice between many things; but a few important alternatives we submit to the reader.

It is to receive the testimony of Prophets and Apostles concerning Jesus Christ. The testimony of many early infidels and enemies as concurring witnesses. The testimony of universal history to the beneficial influence of the Gospel, in rescuing our sin-ruined world from ignorance, idolatry, and crime; or it is to receive the unsustained assertions consisting of, ridicule, misrepresentation, detraction and calumny, dogmatically affirmed and maintained against Christ; for whatever is uttered against Christianity, is said against Jesus Christ. What think you of Christ? is a question of momentous importance, for weal or for woe.

It is not a choice of religions, but will you have the Christian religion! or no religion? Will you enjoy its present blessings of peace and pardon, and the hope with which it inspires, the bosom of its possessor, of eternal blessedness. Upon what will you build your hopes for the future? If not upon the Gospel, what then; upon what form of infidelity? You know that many systems of infidelity are now abandoned. All who have trusted to these have been *cheated.* Is it not probable that the current infidelity will, also, be abandoned. Joseph Barker says, this is "probable." Infidelity is a negation, a denial of something that is. I admire its prudence, as it has nothing to give; it offers nothing. What are its promises for the present, or its pleasures for the future? It impudently asks you to give something for nothing. Would you think it honest to take even a toy, or a picture from a child, or a bone from a dog, without satisfactory equivalent? yet infidels would take from you the most exalted system of divinity, the purest system of morality, and that *only* which can inspire your soul with the hope of "*eternal* life." They would cut every cord that binds you to the throne of God. I know not what infidels can propose as the object of their toils, but to *detach* man from his Maker, and let the wreck float upon the ocean of doubt and uncertainty.

"Come unto me, all ye that labor and are heavy laden, and I will give you rest. Take my yoke upon you, and learn of me: for I am meek and lowly in heart, and you shall find rest unto your souls. For my yoke is easy, and my burden is light."

ERRATA.

Page 28, 40th line, instead "George Lent," read "George Tait."
Page 34, 1st line, for "some have exodiums," read "sermons have exordiums."
Page 36, 6th line, for "me," read "it."
Page 39, 15th line, for "this," read "then."
Page 49, 5th line, for "opposite," read "apposite."
Page 55, 18th line, for "quantity," read "quality."
Page 75, 14th line, for "translated," read "transmitted."
Page 84, 7th line, for "with," read "of."
Page 86, 19th line, for "presentation," read "preservation."
Page 125, 5th line from bottom, for "even," read "ever."
Page 128, 13th line, for "eyes," read "ears."
Page 172, 9th line from bottom, for "not," read "now."
Page 174, 9th line from bottom, for "civil," read "rival."
Page 192, 10th and 11th lines, for "Christians," read "Christianity."
Page 193, 1st line, for "expelled," read "excepted."
Page 253, 15th line, for "not," read "next."

NOTE.—Will the reader turn to page 29, and read the following sentence: "I became satisfied that he either did not comprehend a business obligation, or that he was unwilling to do what was right." Mr. Heaton, in a letter now before me, desires me to say, that this remark had a special reference to Mr. Barker's "asking one hundred copies of the book for writing his appendix." See page 30.

AUTHOR.

www.ingramcontent.com/pod-product-compliance
Lightning Source LLC
LaVergne TN
LVHW020216110826
845151LV00003B/742

* 9 7 8 1 4 2 5 5 3 2 9 7 0 *